In 1959, at the age of 11, Steve Strevens emi͟g
with his parents. After a rather unsuccessful ̲ ̲ ̲ ̲ ̲ ̲ ̲, he
joined the navy two weeks after his sixteenth birthday. He stayed
for 10 years, serving in Vietnam, Malaysia and Borneo and after
leaving the navy he worked at several jobs, including as a freelance
writer. He was a regular contributor to *The Age* for many years
and has been published in many major newspapers and magazines
both here and overseas. He is a multi-award-winning journal-
ist and has edited two regional newspapers. This is Steve's eighth
book. His books include *Slow River: A Journey Down the Murray*
and *Bob Rose: A Dignified Life*, the critically acclaimed biography
of Collingwood AFL legend Bob Rose. He lives on the Far South
Coast of New South Wales with his partner and their two ageing,
lovable but quite mad dogs.

THE JUNGLE DARK

STEVE STREVENS

MACMILLAN
Pan Macmillan Australia

First published 2015 in Macmillan by Pan Macmillan Australia Pty Ltd
1 Market Street, Sydney, New South Wales, Australia, 2000

Cataloguing-in-Publication entry is available
from the National Library of Australia
http://catalogue.nla.gov.au

'I Was Only 19'
Words and music by John Schumann1983
Universal Music Publishing Pty Ltd.
Administered by Universal Music Publishing Group. All rights reserved.
International copyright secured. Reprinted with permission.

Typeset in Bembo 11/16 pt by Midland Typesetters, Australia
Printed by McPherson's Printing Group

MIX
Paper from
responsible sources
FSC® C001695

*For Frank: Mallee boy, brave soldier, devoted family man,
community contributor and my mate.*

*And for Tibs, who was there at the beginning, who is there
at the end and who has endured a long, bumpy journey.*

CONTENTS

ACRONYMS

AATTV	Australian Army Training Team Vietnam
AO	Area of Operation
APC	Armoured Personnel Carrier
ARN	Army of the Republic of Vietnam
BEC	Battle Efficiency Course
CES	Commonwealth Employment Service
CHQ	Company Headquarters
DLNS	Department of Labour and National Service
DVA	Department of Veterans Affairs
FSB	Fire Support Base
LCM	Landing Craft Mechanised
LZ	Landing Zone
NVA	North Vietnamese Army
PHQ	Platoon Headquarters
PTSD	Post Traumatic Stress Disorder
R&C	Rest in Country leave
RAAF	Royal Australian Air Force
RAN	Royal Australian Navy
RPG	Rocket Propelled Grenade
RSM	Regimental Sergeant Major
SEATO	South East Asia Treaty Organization
TAOR	Tactical Area of Responsibility
TPI	Totally and Permanently Incapacitated
VC	Viet Cong
VMC	Vietnam Moratorium Campaign
VVAA	Vietnam Veterans Association of Australia

In war, there are no unwounded soldiers.

José Narosky

'I WAS ONLY 19:
A Walk in the Light Green'

Words and music by John Schumann

*Mum and Dad and Denny saw the passing-out parade at
    Puckapunyal,
It was a long march from cadets.
The sixth battalion was the next to tour, and it was me who
    drew the card.
We did Canungra, Shoalwater before we left . . .*

*And Townsville lined the footpath as we marched down to the quay;
This clipping from the paper shows us young and strong and clean;
And there's me in my slouch hat with my SLR and greens . . .
God help me, I was only nineteen.*

*From Vung Tau riding Chinooks to the dust at Nui Dat . . .
I'd been in and out of choppers now for months.
But we made our tents a home, VB and pinups on the lockers
And an Asian orange sunset through the scrub.*

*And can you tell me, doctor, why I still can't get to sleep?
And night-time's just a jungle dark and a barking M16?
And what's this rash that comes and goes, can you tell me what
    it means?
God help me, I was only nineteen.*

A four week operation, when each step could mean your last one
    on two legs:
It was a war within yourself.
But you wouldn't let your mates down 'til they had you dusted off.
So you closed your eyes and thought about something else.

Then someone yelled out 'Contact!' and the bloke behind
    me swore,
We hooked in there for hours, then a God-almighty roar;
Frankie kicked a mine the day that mankind kicked the moon:
God help me, he was going home in June.

I can still see Frankie, drinking tinnies in the Grand Hotel
On a thirty-six hour rec leave in Vung Tau:
And I can still hear Frankie, lying screaming in the jungle
Til the morphine came and killed the bloody row.

And the Anzac legends didn't mention mud and blood and tears.
And the stories that my father told me never seemed quite real.
I caught some pieces in my back that I didn't even feel . . .
God help me, I was only nineteen.

And can you tell me, doctor, why I still can't get to sleep?
And why the Channel Seven chopper chills me to my feet?
And what's this rash that comes and goes, can you tell me what
    it means?
God help me, I was only nineteen.

AUTHOR'S NOTE

This is the story of Frank Hunt – 'Frankie' – who 'kicked a mine' just as Neil Armstrong was 'kicking the moon' that fateful day in 1969.

It is also a glimpse into the Vietnam War, how young men became involved, how it affected them, and how their lives changed forever. And it is a story of how a song came to symbolise that war and become an anthem for all Vietnam veterans. 'I Was Only 19', written by John Schumann based on the stories told to him by his brother-in-law Mick Storen, has resonated with Australians since 1983, meaning so much to so many.

Frank Hunt grew up in the dry, farming Mallee country of Victoria. As he and his family battled through the tough times of drought and failed crops, he could never have imagined how his life would merge with other young men in the way it did in such dramatic fashion after he volunteered for the army out of desperation. How, after a year of training, he was sent to the Asian conflict from where he would return mentally damaged and physically wounded.

And what wounds they were. Frank spent almost two years in hospital recuperating from his injuries, having the Last Rites said over him five times, undergoing 25 operations and having 30-odd pieces of shrapnel and bone fragments left to float around in his body forever. While his physical being was slowly mended to a limited extent, his other wounds weren't so obvious; those of the mind never are.

'Frankie' was to become synonymous with the battles that the vast majority of those who served in a conflict against a totally misunderstood and underestimated enemy would fight long after the sounds of war fell silent.

This book is about the journey of Frank Hunt and the other soldiers of 3 Platoon, A Company, 6 Battalion, Royal Australian Regiment. It is their memories, their reflections, their pain and their years since. It is not, nor does it pretend to be, a historical record. Historians can quibble over facts, not over memories. Memories are mischievous. They can vary from person to person and from time to time – especially if you have suffered as these men suffered. Incidents are remembered in diverse ways, seen by different people from different angles and given different interpretations.

It's a tale of how history can be both universal and specific; how lives are changed in the eyes of the world and in the eyes of an individual, both at the same time.

These men went where not many have gone – and only those who have will completely understand. The story tells of the brutality of the Vietnam War that caused young men to grow up quickly, earlier than their time – innocent, carefree young men, sent to a place from which they would not return. At least not in the same way they left.

During its 12 months tour of duty, 3 Platoon saw six men killed and more than 40 wounded, yet theirs is not the worst nor is it the easiest of stories from the Vietnam War. It is just one that many will relate to, one that is in some way typical and one that left an indelible mark on history.

Prologue:
KICKING MINES AND THE MOON

Somewhere in the scrubby landscape about five kilometres east of Vietnam's imposing Long Hai Mountains, the buzz of the radio handpiece on Private Frank Hunt's left shoulder alerted him to an incoming message.

'Alpha 6 to 3 Alpha,' the voice on the radio crackled. 'The moon landing has taken place. Man has walked on the moon.'

It was about 9.30 on the morning of 21 July 1969. 3 Platoon, A Company, 6 Battalion, Royal Australian Regiment (6 RAR), was taking a 'walk in the Light Green'. This was the way soldiers described patrols through the areas shaded differently on the army maps. The Light Green designated a section that was lighter on jungle than normal while the Long Green was much heavier on jungle. It was far easier to lay mines in the sandy soil of the Light Green and that was where the biggest danger from mines lay.

Platoon Commander Lieutenant Peter Hines, five foot eight, fit and muscular, had worked his way through the lower ranks to officer status. That morning he had been leading his men on patrol for about an hour and a half, walking steadily and alertly through dense, short, almost mallee-like scrub that bashed their legs and made the going tough as they forced their way along. The platoon's three sections were moving silently through what was considered enemy territory. Their language consisted mostly of hand signals with a click of the fingers to attract attention.

Even though it was still early, the men were hot, sweaty and tired. Insects were biting, the humidity was sapping their energy and what was happening in outer space, even though historic, was not that important.

Frank, a short, skinny 19 year old, standing a couple of metres from Hines, said softly, 'Skip, the Yanks have landed on the moon.'

'Stuff the Yanks,' came the swift reply, the lieutenant, called Skip or Skipper by his men, concerned with more pressing matters.

The patrol was part of Operation Mundingburra and the men had been 'out' from their Nui Dat base for a week. Earlier they'd come across enemy signs stuck in the ground to indicate a minefield: a freehand drawn skull and crossbones with '*nguy niem*' painted on it – 'dangerous'. When Frank had radioed the news, Company Headquarters (CHQ) had ordered Hines to take his men in a reverse direction and go to another area.

After a few days during which there was a 'contact' with two enemy killed and a Viet Cong (VC) bunker destroyed, the platoon spent the best part of a day lying in ambush. Then, with no enemy arriving, Hines received more orders to patrol back towards a deserted village which had no real structures but was in the same direction they had been patrolling on the first day. However, they were not on the same track as the first few days. In fact they had gone in a loop and were approaching the same mined area from a different direction.

After 'stand-to' that morning, in an unusual move, 3 Platoon, 8 Section's two forward scouts, Privates Mick Storen and Tony Muir, had been called in for the morning orders briefing. They were to lead off. Normally the section commanders would attend the briefing and relay any relevant information to their sections. The men wondered what their attendance meant but they didn't ask and they weren't told. When they heard the orders, Mick and his mate Muir were concerned. They were told they were to go cross-country, not on a track, towards this village. Mick knew they were going back into the mined area but not on the enemy signposted track. He was apprehensive. They were heading in almost at right angles to the track and there would be no warning, no signs at all. Mick spoke up about his concerns but was told not to worry about it and to be particularly watchful.

The patrol moved off, each section strung out behind Mick and Muir, struggling with the heat, the weight of their packs and the lightly treed but tight saltbushy type scrub. An hour or so later, with the rumble of American B-52 planes bombing the Long Hais as background noise, they came across a thin track just wide enough for feet and worn down in the centre from the passage of, they assumed, Viet Cong.

Mick stepped carefully across the track and, using hand signals, beckoned Hines to come forward from his position about six metres behind. Everything appeared to be safe, so Hines ordered the platoon of about 25 men to stop, develop a 'harbour' and have a break.

A harbour consisted of soldiers strung out in an elongated oval shape on either side of the track. A machine gun post was set up at each end and as they arrived men either stood, squatted or lay down in a fighting position hidden in the scrub, ready for an attack from any direction or an enemy approach. Claymore mines were laid out at various intervals ready to be let off by the 'clackers' close to the soldiers on piquet – or sentry – position. 8 Section took one side of the track and 9 Section the other as they waited for 7 Section to bring up the rear so as to properly form the harbour. In the middle was Platoon Headquarters (PHQ): the sergeant, the lieutenant, the medic and the signaller.

A couple of the soldiers were ready to prepare a brew of tea and coffee when it was safe. With relief, as they arrived at the designated harbour, the men dropped their 45 kilogram packs on the ground. Nearly all the men smoked and they grabbed waterproof packaging from their pockets and began to roll their own. They were relaxed but still alert as Hines, who had packed the pipe he always smoked and put a match to it, walked a few metres up and down the track quietly telling his men about the moon landing and signalling to others further away. Unless you were very close, silence was imperative until the all-clear was given.

Mick was at the side of the harbour, some 20 metres away from Hines who, back with PHQ, was considering his next move. Private Alfie Lamb was standing about six metres away as his section had taken up a separate position in the harbour. Hines asked Lamb to spread the word among the men. Lamb did as he was asked. Hines then made his way a few metres further towards the other end of the harbour, conveying the news Frank had given him to those close enough. A few metres back to PHQ and Hines spoke to Platoon Medic Graeme 'Doc' Davis, asking him to check the back of his neck as he could feel something uncomfortable. Davis pulled whatever it was from his skin, Hines thanked him, looked around, took a step over a couple of packs and, out of nowhere, the world exploded. The noise was deafening and the scrubby floor surged into the air in a cloud of black smoke and dirt. Hearts leapt and pulses raced while shrapnel tore into nearly all the men.

Skip had stepped on an M16 Jumping Jack mine and their lives were changed forever.

PART ONE

Chapter 1
HISTORY AND DOMINOES

L anding on the moon was a monumental achievement. With an estimated television audience of more than 600 million watching pictures sent from the radio telescope at Parkes in New South Wales, the event had the world transfixed. America had succeeded in its ambitious space project. The years America had spent trying to stop what they considered was the Communist threat to the world were not as successful. Nor, by July 1969, was the war it had created in Vietnam as popular with the public as it had been in earlier years, either in America or in Australia.

In the late sixties there was some confusion in sections of the Australian community. Many didn't understand how their country had come to be involved in Vietnam. They didn't know much if anything about Vietnam's history or, in some cases, that the country even existed. Many didn't care much about politics, simply trusting their leaders to do what was right. They came to understand the way politics worked but, as for the history, they needed to go back quite a few years.

At the outbreak of World War II, Indochina was a French colony. During the war Japan took over Indochina and then after the war, when Japan was defeated by the Allies, France tried to reassert its territorial claims on its former territory. To do that they had to fight the Viet Nam Doc Lap Dong Minh Hoi, the League for the Independence of Vietnam, more commonly known as the Viet Minh. The Communist nationalists were led by Ho Chi Minh, who proclaimed an independent Vietnam in 1945. France refused to accept the declaration and eight years of war ensued. It ended with the French defeat at Dien Bien Phu in 1954. The peace settlement, known as the Geneva Accords, split the country in two at the seventeenth parallel; the North under Ho Chi Minh, and the South under the American-backed President Ngo Dinh Diem, who had deposed the former Emperor, the French appointee Bao Dai. Diem proclaimed the Republic of Vietnam in October 1955.

Included in the Accords was that a Vietnam-wide election, aimed at reunifying the divided country, be held in 1956. However, Diem claimed that the people of the North could not vote freely and, with the backing of America, he refused to participate. An agreement was reached that any Viet Minh soldiers in the South would go to the North while anyone who had fought for the French would head South. After the break-up, civilians could go where they chose. It was estimated that about one million people moved around the country.

Animosity between the North and South increased to such levels that in 1960 the North, aiming to overthrow Diem and reunite the country under Communist rule, created the National Front for the Liberation of South Vietnam. These soldiers were known as the Viet Cong (Vietnamese Communists). With the aim of creating an uprising against the Diem rule in the South and inspired by Ho Chi Minh, they embarked on a guerilla campaign. The South Vietnamese Army could not do much to counter the insurgents' tactics and the United States, alarmed at the prospect of communism spreading throughout South-East Asia, began to significantly increase its help to the South.

The Korean War finished in 1953 and afterwards the Communist Soviet Union helped the forces of Ho Chi Minh. Meanwhile, America was able to help Diem, as it could see that Diem was not going to be able to stop the Communist advance by himself.

Diem had instigated the building of what were known as strategic hamlets, fortified villages in the south where it was thought locals would be safe from the insurgent Viet Cong. However, the VC successfully infiltrated these so-called safe havens. In fact, the VC were everywhere, virtually controlling the countryside.

Led since 1961 by influential and charismatic President John F Kennedy, America heard constantly about 'Reds Under the Bed' and 'Better Dead than Red'. They also believed in what was known as 'the Domino Theory', a term first used by President Dwight Eisenhower in the 1950s to encapsulate the notion that when one country fell to Communism, so other countries would fall like dominoes and much of the world would suffer. That was something Kennedy, encouraged by history and the military, needed to stop.

The Americans had sent thousands of what were euphemistically called 'military advisors' to South Vietnam during the late 1950s and over the years that number had increased substantially. The situation at that time had more complications, twists and turns than could possibly be seen clearly, especially by the Americans, who were completely sure in their belief they could stop the Communist threat if they poured enough men and money into South Vietnam.

By the early 1960s Australia was closely watching everything America did. If it was American, it must be good, especially when it came to defending the country. Australia by and large believed what America believed when it came to Communism. After all, the US had saved the country during World War II, or so people were led to understand. Politicians and the media were worried about a perceived Communist threat from the north and welcomed America attempting to stop it. Australian Prime Minister Robert Menzies spoke passionately and eloquently about halting the threat before it reached Australia's shores. 'Forward defence' was the term used – fight everywhere but on our own land.

Australia had signed the ANZUS treaty after World War II thinking that America would protect it in war. However, the treaty was a commitment on the part of the US only to consult on defence concerns, not necessarily to defend Australia. Menzies wanted more than that. To that end, he made plans to garner American support by helping in its quest against Communism. The best way was to help out in Vietnam.

Military chiefs and international experts considered that Australia's first line of defence was in Malaya, where a confrontation was already being waged against Communist insurgents, and to which Australian troops and ships were committed. Menzies thought the defensive line should be South Vietnam, so that was that.

Menzies and his government were extremely popular at the time. Generally, people believed whatever politicians and the papers said was true. They trusted them. If there was a Communist threat to the country, then it needed to be stopped. The Australian way of life must be protected and if that meant supporting America in a war in a land that many hadn't even heard of, then so be it.

America asked for Australia's help and although Australia could not do much, in 1962 it entered the conflict by sending 30 men of the Australian Army Training Team Vietnam (AATTV) to help train soldiers of the South Vietnamese Army. It was a token gesture but a contribution nonetheless. Politicians debated sending the navy and air force as well as the army but defence department heads decided against it. Later the Minister for Defence said that Australia was asked by the South Vietnamese government to become involved. That was not true; it was the Americans who had asked and anyway, apart from that invitation, Australia had offered its services.

It wasn't to be the last half-truth, obfuscation or outright lie to be told in the ensuing years by politicians of all persuasions and from all the countries involved. This was the beginning of what was to be more than a decade of turmoil, protest, wrongful accusations and a split in Australian society, and the cause of much angst and difficulty for many of the men caught up in a war in which they would eventually see they had no reason to be involved.

There were a few protests in the capital cities about Australia's involvement but nothing that caused much of a stir. It wasn't younger people who protested but a few older, politically active, peace-loving types. They were apparently out of touch with what the vast majority of Australians thought, yet saw it as their duty to do something, at least.

The task of the AATTV was onerous and nothing the Australians would encounter in Vietnam had any sort of precedent. The two world wars had shown how the Australian Army could be relied upon in all manner of battles. From Gallipoli to the Somme and from Tobruk to New Guinea, Australians had covered themselves in glory. But fighting in the South-East Asian jungles was

totally different. Not only were the terrain and conditions difficult, the culture caused problems. The Viet Cong could not be
distinguished from ordinary non-Communist villagers as they
all dressed in the same 'black pyjamas'. For all those reasons and
more, the job of fighting them was difficult in the extreme
and never really became any easier for any of the Australian
troops over the years.

Chapter 2
IT ALL BEGINS

By 1965 Australia was changing faster than ever before. For women, mini-skirts were all the rage. Men loved bell-bottom trousers and paisley shirts. Australia had its own pop stars: Johnny O'Keefe, Billy Thorpe and the Aztecs, Ray Brown and the Whispers, as well as Jackie DeShannon and Judy Stone. A shift had taken place from the music of Roy Orbison, Elvis Presley and the like to the sounds of The Beatles, who were changing the world of music. Those of a more rebellious nature were attracted to The Rolling Stones, far from glamorous and with more attitude than most. Peter, Paul and Mary went from folk music to protest songs, and the social activism messages of Joan Baez and her contemporaries were being heard. Bob Dylan was telling us the times were indeed changing and in his song 'The Ballad of a Thin Man' he said that something was happening and we didn't know what it was. He was right.

A distinct divide between generations was becoming obvious. Hair was longer, clothes were full of colour, music was louder, and sex, with the advent of the contraceptive pill, was on the minds and menus of both men and women. Many young people didn't want to live the sort of life their parents lived and to conform to the older generation's wishes and beliefs. Some did but for others questions were being asked on all manner of subjects. A minority of younger people were beginning to query what was happening in Vietnam. Their concerns were not so much about Australia's involvement but because of what they had seen and heard about America and its approach to what was being described as a police action but was in reality a war.

However, none of the questions deterred Prime Minister Menzies. Lyndon Johnson, who had replaced Kennedy after he was assassinated, asked Australia to commit troops. It was not clear and it was never revealed whether it was South Vietnam that had asked or if Menzies had 'asked to be asked'. Some reports suggest Johnson had requested more advisors, an increase in the AATTV, but possibly he asked for more soldiers. No one from either Government was saying much, but the result was that late in April, Menzies told Parliament that Australia would send a battalion. Menzies brooked no argument from the public, there was little or no government debate and no questioning – nothing. Australia was going to help save the world – particularly itself – from Communism.

The papers were largely supportive, as was the community. Polls at that time showed that around 70 percent of Australians supported the war and just as many thought that Communist China was a direct threat to Australia. *The Age* said it was an 'inescapable obligation' to help out due to our geographical position and that we had a treaty with the US. Rupert Murdoch's newish broadsheet *The Australian* was the lone dissenting voice. It editorialised against the decision by the Menzies government, saying that it was 'reckless' to send Australian troops to 'a savage and revolutionary war' in which America was heavily involved. The editorial asked what Australia could possibly add to the conflict. Presciently, it said that in the future historians might 'recall this day with tears'.

The leader of the Labor Party, Arthur Calwell, opposed the decision and spoke to Parliament, saying that in future years his party's opposition would be vindicated: 'generations to come will record with gratitude that when a reckless government wilfully endangered the security of this country, the voice of the Labor Party was heard, strong and clear'.

Calwell had a bit each way, though. As well as his objection he said that he supported America's presence in Vietnam and that for them to withdraw might be humiliating. Calwell's deputy, Gough Whitlam, later to be the voice of strong opposition to the war, was somewhat unclear as well, saying he supported the American alliance and that its role in South Vietnam was 'above dispute'. However, Whitlam thought Australia's troops would be better off in Malaya or Indonesia.

None of this made an impression on Menzies, who thundered against Calwell and the Labor Party, saying Australia had no alternative but to help out. And so it came to be. At 1.30 am on 27 May 1965, with no protests or any crowds waving farewell as in previous wars, 338 men of the 1st Battalion Royal Australian Regiment (1 RAR) slipped quietly out of Sydney Harbour aboard HMAS *Sydney*, the former British aircraft carrier that had been converted to a fast troop transport. The *Sydney* was escorted by the flagship of the Royal Australian Navy (RAN), the aircraft carrier HMAS *Melbourne*, HMAS *Parramatta*, a frigate, and the destroyer HMAS *Vampire*. A second destroyer, HMAS *Duchess*, would later join the escort duties in a break from her role in the SEATO (South East Asia Treaty Organization) action in Malaysia and Indonesia. The only tangible dissent was a large banner strung out along one of the cliffs at the Heads that read: 'You Go To An Unjust War'.

That lack of protest soon changed when, shortly afterwards, the government decided that conscripts could serve overseas, something that was not in the plans when conscription, or national service as it was known, was introduced about six months earlier. Conscription had always been source of much debate in Australia. During World War I, two referenda were held to decide whether those who were called up for compulsory military service should serve overseas rather than just being used for home defence and both referenda were defeated. Then in World War II those called up were restricted to serving in Australia and its territories such as Papua New Guinea.

For the war in Vietnam, there was to be no referendum. In November 1964, all 20-year-old men were required to register with the Department of Labour and National Service (DLNS). The public was told the scheme was to help with numbers in the army, depleted by regulars serving in the Indonesian confrontation with Malaysia. The majority of the community had no objection to the scheme and many, the RSL in particular, embraced it as a way of pulling what were seen as troubled youth into line. But a smaller section of Australian society, the more cynical section, thought otherwise and when the government later said the national servicemen – or 'Nashos' as they were known – could be sent to Vietnam, that part of the community wasn't all that surprised.

Many more young men were available to register for conscription than was needed, so selection was determined by picking wooden marbles inscribed with birth dates at random from an old Tattersalls lottery barrel. The process had a few different names – the Lottery, the Birthday Ballot, even the Lottery of Death. The first few of these draws were televised, as if to show everything was fair and above board, then the rest were done behind the scenes. If a marble with your birth date was selected, then within a month a big brown envelope arrived in your letter box informing you of what was required. It would give a time, date and place where you had to turn up to become a soldier.

Once the news that conscripts would be sent to Vietnam became public, community disquiet increased dramatically. Protests started to become more regular and not just from the left-wing radicals who had already been protesting. Mothers, wives and girlfriends, some of whom had not been political previously, all made their voices heard. They joined university students and those whose number might come up in the future. This was different from just having a simple call-up. The young men being forced into service were not eligible to vote in elections for or against their fate. But they were considered old enough to use machine guns or hand grenades or be behind artillery that sent huge shells into villages or to plant landmines that had the potential to wound and maim when stood on by innocent feet.

Conscription was extremely strict. If you thought that you didn't have to register and simply didn't bother, then you could be prosecuted, and possibly convicted, with a jail term as long as the regular period of national service. Other ways that could land someone in jail included making false and misleading statements or attempting to trick the medical board examiners that they were unfit to fight. Young men attending university could avoid conscription, or at least defer, but if they failed a subject their application for deferment could be reviewed and in some cases they would be forced into the army. Other ways of avoiding the call-up included being married, having a criminal record, being mentally ill or being a minister of religion. You could also join the Citizen Military Forces, Citizen Air Force or Citizen Naval Force.

The most difficult way to avoid the call-up was to become a conscientious objector, saying that war was against your beliefs and morals. While there were some conscientious objectors, not surprisingly there were few ministers and even fewer married men of that age. Later, it was a joke among the Nashos that some of those who were mentally ill or had a criminal record made it into the army. It was always a disparate mob that met on the day they joined up.

Nashos were not the only story. While public debate continued on their role and whether or not they should be sent to Vietnam, other young men joined up freely. Their reasons were many and varied. Some joined for financial security, others for adventure. Many signed up because they wanted something to do, while others needed to escape. Whatever the reason, volunteers were never in short supply. One of them, Frank Hunt, would find his life intertwining with others in a way he could never have imagined.

Chapter 3

HARSH, HOT AND DRY

The temperature was '106 in the water bag' according to Frank Hunt's mother Eileen, the day she gave birth to twins.

In January 1950, the hospital in the small Victorian town of Wycheproof had little air conditioning to counter the fierce Mallee heat. A fan here or there, an open window in the evening, but not during the day as the north wind howled through the flywire that only partially did its job. On those days, when the windows were ajar, dust blew in and floated gently onto the beds, the wardrobes and the bedside tables like light reddish-brown snow.

Eileen was uncomfortable but happy. In what was typical of the time, her husband Maurie was not at the hospital. He was off playing tennis. With a local midwife in attendance, Eileen had produced her firstborn a little earlier and now, some 24 minutes later, her second child arrived in the world. The twins, Bryan and Frank, were the first of Eileen and Maurie's family, two more in a genealogical line that could be traced back to County Carlow in

Ireland and that would extend to four girls and two more boys — eight children in 10 years.

*

Since white settlement, the Mallee had been a hard place to farm, with money difficult to come by. In the early part of the twentieth century, crops failed in many if not most years. Drought followed drought and severe dust storms swept in, wave after wave, like the biggest ocean swells, all of it dirt from dry paddocks. One farmer's topsoil would be blown onto their neighbour's paddock which in turn had been blown somewhere else. The sun would be blocked out even at its height, dropping the world into darkness as though somewhere a light had been switched off. In those barren years, the blistering hot north winds piled the red dirt in drifts that almost covered the fences marking the barren paddocks. Dams dried up and tanks scattered around the wooden and tin houses to capture the rain when the heavens occasionally opened were left empty and rusting. Stock died and anything that did manage to grow was eaten by rabbits, kangaroos, emus or other creatures trying to survive.

There were the mice plagues when, literally, millions of the small rodents seemed to come from nowhere to create a stinking mass of vermin that appeared to make the ground move. Homes were inundated, food could not be protected and sheds had mice around the walls piled upon each other a metre high and a metre wide. On one night close by the Hunts' farm, more than 150,000 were killed with the stack of carcasses over a metre high, about three metres around the base and weighing about two tons.

In the most desperate cases, nothing much was gained from working on the farms and besides, with no rain and with no money for maintenance, there wasn't much farming work to do.

Some men tried to find work with other farmers in other districts but most of those farmers had problems of their own so work for anyone else was scarce. A lucky few received unemployment relief when working on government programs such as channel cleaning, but such work was difficult to come by. Many families were so dispirited they either sold their blocks for a pittance or simply walked away.

This was the life Frank's grandfather William lived after returning from World War I to the farm he had worked with his family as a young man. When the war broke out William had volunteered for the army and was accepted. His brothers were all regarded as working in essential services and were not required to join up. Rather, they needed to stay, farm and supply the needs of the forces.

After training, William was posted to the 3rd Pioneer Battalion – a force that supported other fighting forces preparing trenches, roads, bridges, communications and such like. The battalion was sent to Egypt and the Middle East before moving to fight in France and Belgium on the Western Front.

William's battalion took part in the Battle of the Somme, the bloody conflict that resulted in 60,000 casualties on the first day – where men charged from trenches towards machine guns and fell like so many khaki dominoes dropping in a line one after the other. Eventually a shell found its way to William, causing him to be sent to England to be treated and to heal. Six weeks later, he was back in the trenches.

In his time on the front line William was gassed twice and had pneumonia five times. Each time he made the short trip to England to recuperate. He was sent back to the front each time – back to what he once described to Frank as 'going into the torture chamber again'.

For years after he was discharged, William was the local RSL representative, working diligently for farmers and ex-servicemen in any way he could. But his war experiences had damaged him. For many years he and his wife Catherine slept in separate beds. William suffered badly with night sweats and nightmares. He'd kick and turn and cry out, returning in his dreams to the hell that was as real as it had ever been. He had shrapnel in his throat still when he died of cancer in 1965, aged 75.

When World War II broke out, Maurie had tried to enlist but, as he was working on his father's farm, he was told he was essential services and was rejected. However, he was called up to the militia, which gave men a basic level of training so they would be prepared if they were needed. After completing that training, Maurie decided to volunteer again. This time he was accepted and posted to the 20th Mounted Rifles, which later became the 20th Australian Pioneer Regiment. Maurie was to do the same things his father had done in the war that was supposed to have ended all wars.

Maurie's regiment went to New Guinea and the islands in the region to set up before the rest of the battalion arrived, as well as to fight the Japanese advance through the Pacific towards Australia. Stationed at Marque, a small island in the Netherlands East Indies, the regiment included a signal platoon, a mortar platoon, a machine gunners platoon and more. Maurie was wounded on more than one occasion but each time was taken behind the lines until he had recovered. The worst injury happened when a mortar shell exploded as the canister left the barrel, killing a couple of his mates. The incident haunted Maurie for years. Flashbacks and nightmares persisted and he later turned to drink as the only way to keep the ghosts at bay.

Maurie served in the islands until March 1945, when he returned to Australia. He was discharged in October 1946 and made his way back to the Mallee, to his family, and to Eileen. Three years later, in February 1949, they were married.

On his return, Maurie was granted a soldier settlement block, receiving 1280 acres at Reedy Dam, midway between Beulah and Birchip, which, if farmed and managed carefully, was enough to survive on – just.

*

Life never changed much in the Mallee, except around the edges. While winters could be freezing cold, the summers were always hot and dry. The north winds still blew in the dust and drought, and bad years came more often than good ones. Money was always short. Yet, as Eileen constantly told her children when they gathered in the kitchen or in front of the fire in the winter or under the shade of the huge peppercorn trees in the summer: 'We mightn't have much but there'll always be plenty of love.'

Eileen was always one to tell the children that: 'We won't be hungry. Dad will kill two sheep a week and we'll eat everything but the eyeballs.'

The kids loved that, pretending to be squeamish at the thought of eating some of the entrails.

The children never wanted for much as they knew no different. Many if not most of their friends were in the same position; each family had their own problems which they solved or tolerated in their own way. In the Hunt household, seldom were there any cross words or anger. Even when Maurie's drinking became worse as the kids grew into their teenage years, Eileen was the loyal wife and mother, tending to her flock.

The children attended the Immaculate Heart of Mary Catholic Primary School in Birchip until 1965, at which point Maurie agreed to send his three eldest children to the local higher elementary school, which needed to enrol more students in order to become a proper high school. More students meant more classes, more teachers and more funding. Maurie believed in education and, despite his Catholic beliefs, he was willing to help out. Not all those in the Catholic school agreed with him but he stood his ground. He was concerned with social aspects of the community over and above his religious beliefs.

When Frank asked him about his decision to change schools, Maurie told him: 'Son, you can have all the religious lessons all your life and you can read the Bible a hundred times over, but if you just treat others like you treat yourself, you'll be a good Christian person.'

Frank wasn't sad to see the back of the Catholic system. He mostly loved his school days and had a mentor and inspiration in Sister Frances. But the Mother Superior, Mother Brendan, was, to many of the students including Frank, sadistic and cruel. She would beat the students on a mere whim and children would tremble each time she walked into the room. She cracked Frank's hand with a broom handle one day, breaking two bones. When he left school, Frank had learnt two lessons: the first from Sister Frances about kindness and gentleness and love; the second from Mother Brendan about how not to treat others. Frank swore to remember them both.

School held a few problems for Frank but generally, life as a youngster was good. Even though they didn't have much, they enjoyed cricket and tennis matches in the summer and footy in the winter. All played in the yard or the paddock or the shed or wherever else they found space. Frank and Kieran were on one side while Michael and Bryan were the opposition. Fights were common but the boys were still very close, especially Frank and Kieran, who shared a special bond. Frank and Bryan had a connection by being twins and Michael was as tough as could be and looked after them all if trouble arose.

Frank and Kieran would spend time in the small sandhills trapping rabbits, always with the dogs – kelpie 'bitzers' Towzer and Brownie – in tow. After keeping a few for Eileen, the boys would sell the rest wherever they could for about 25 cents a pair, or keep the skins for sale to the Birchip skin merchant. Besides rabbits, Frank made a bit of money from 'dead wool', which was skin that could still be used from any poor sheep that had died. That and collecting empty bottles – both beer and soft drink – and returning them to the local shop for the deposit helped Frank's small bank account grow. Most of the beer bottles came from a place known locally as Comedy Corner, where a group of farmers would drop their children off at the bus stop in the morning and could frequently be found still there when the bus returned in the afternoon. Thankfully, Frank thought, his dad was not one of them. After school, barely able to see over the dash, Frank would illegally drive the family ute to Comedy Corner and pick up the pile of empty beer bottles left behind.

While television was almost non-existent in the Mallee in the early 1960s, the Hunts did have a radio that broadcast music of all sorts through the house. Maurie didn't sing but he loved bush poetry, and Eileen would sing Irish songs whenever she could. She passed that talent to her twin sons.

Frank and Bryan loved singing and their performances were in demand from the age of six. From church pageants to school concerts to footy club fundraisers to local charity balls, wherever there was to be a lineup of performers, Frank and Bryan would be there. They'd start with rock 'n' roll songs of the day followed by a few standards and then a couple of sad songs to make the older women in the audience think how lovely these little boys were.

Afterwards, men would applaud and pat them on the shoulder while the older ladies would hug them to their ample bosoms and tell them how wonderful their performances were.

Dancing was another of Frank's loves. He learnt ballroom dancing and whenever he finished singing, or even when he wasn't part of the entertainment, he'd whirl around the wooden floors of local halls with whichever of the women present would accompany him. Light on his feet, he was a popular partner for ladies both young and old.

Each year went by in much the same way. Frank's best mate was Digger Russell. Digger lived in town, so if Frank missed the school bus home, he would stay at his mate's house. Some of those missed buses were accidents, others more deliberate. And there were plenty of planned visits. Impromptu football matches were arranged on sheep sale days when local farmers were all in town. Kids would wait to go home with their parents, so the 'townies' played the 'farmies', with all the games ending in a fight.

Apart from one time when Frank and a couple of his mates tied a stray dog to the Anglican Church bell causing the bell to ring every time the dog moved, the kids didn't cause much trouble. One hiding was handed out when Frank and Bryan lit a fire under the header and were caught laughing at their idea of fun by Maurie, but mostly there was no maliciousness in anything that was done. The local cops were always on the prowl in town, but most of the time the farm kids went home on the school bus. There, they had jobs to do – feeding the pigs, filling all the water containers from the tank, checking on the chooks and ducks, cutting the firewood– and those jobs had to be completed, otherwise there would be trouble of a different sort.

Maurie drove the children the three kilometres across the paddocks to the bus stop in the morning, where they'd wait until the bus had picked up other kids from farms further away before climbing on board and enduring the 45 minute trip. After school the journey was reversed but the three kilometres back to the house had to be walked – no matter the weather – as Maurie would be working more often than not. The walk could take a long time or be as quick as possible, depending on the weather. There were muddy, stinking, yabby-filled dams to swim in during the heat of summer, and if by some chance the rains came in winter, occasionally Maurie made the effort to pick them up. Eileen never drove or even held a driver's licence.

Life was simple and ordinary; tough yet wonderful.

Chapter 4
A MAN'S JOB

In the early months of 1964, Eileen asked Frank, who had just turned 14, if he could do some more work around the farm. Maurie had been going away to sheep sales or clearing sales and drinking quite heavily, so the crop was not being sown. 'Francis,' she said, 'your dad really needs some help with the tractor work, so I'm relying on you.'

That year, driving the old Case tractor, Frank helped Maurie sow the crop. Even though he was not big enough or strong enough to lump a bag of seed or superphosphate, Frank managed by using a bucket to half empty the bags into the seed box of the combine. The following year, at 15, he sowed most of the crop by himself, using much the same method. This time it was under duress.

By his own admission Frank was 'useless at footy' but he did love chasing around the opposition players and antagonising them, urging them to fight and then running away to be near the umpire. Frank couldn't fight either so each of his plans was considerably flawed. One Saturday a big ruckman caught up with him and belted most of his top teeth out. Frank went to the dentist on Monday to be fitted for false teeth. Earlier that morning Frank had been filling the combine with super-phosphate and had managed to get some in his mouth which, together with the temporary patch-up dental work, caused his face to swell terribly. Despite that, he had to work. He was out of the dentist's at 9 am and on the tractor at noon.

Both crops turned out well and that year, 1965, he also share-farmed 70 acres with a neighbour which, after harvest, produced his first farming cheque of $787. Frank had worked with the farmer and was allocated a small parcel of the crop as his own. Frank had gambled on the crop being worth more than any meagre wage he may have received and it had paid off. From the money he banked, Frank paid his parents' long overdue fuel bill.

In 1966, at 16 years of age, Frank left school and worked full-time on the farm. The tractor had been upgraded to a second-hand International but Frank still had difficulty manoeuvring bags of superphosphate and wheat seed. But, with Maurie, the two managed to do what they needed to before they put the crop in the hands of the weather gods.

By now, Maurie was drinking heavily but wouldn't share his problems with Eileen, Frank or anyone else. He was alone in a cold world that no one else could understand or inhabit. Frank could see his mother become more worried about Maurie but even though there were a few arguments, nonetheless the Hunts had a very loving family home. Despite his problems, Maurie was a hard worker who did whatever he could for his family. He was totally despondent in bad years – of which there were many – because he felt he had let his family down.

One year the rains came at the right time and the crops were the best they had been for some years. But when a hail storm swept through the district, Maurie became quite mournful. He had underinsured the crop to save money and now with the crop wiped out he had no income. The bills mounted up relentlessly. One evening shortly after the storm, the kids all piled into the big old Hudson family car to take Frank and Bryan to a concert. They were driving down the road when Maurie burst into tears, devastated at what the future held for his wife and family. He was enduring a difficult year, perhaps the most difficult. Many a night the local policeman would knock on the door and hand over a summons demanding payment for goods received.

Frank was having a difficult time too. He had concerns about his father's drinking but he never wanted to paint the wrong picture of Maurie because Frank thought deep down he was the most wonderful, caring man. He knew his dad would do anything for anyone but Frank was always worried about another summons arriving or the work not being done or about the state Maurie might come home in that night. Would he be drunk? Would there be tears? How would the younger children react?

The Hunts were a God-fearing, church-going family, a typical Catholic family of the time. Each Sunday they all jumped into the car and headed off to Mass. Frank's faith was important and a local priest, Father 'Rip' Kirby, made a real impression on him. One year when Frank was sowing the crop and Maurie was sick, Father Kirby came out and drove the tractor for the day, giving Frank a welcome break.

At that time Frank harboured thoughts of becoming a priest, not necessarily because of religion but because of Father Kirby. He had spent time as an altar-boy and wanted to show the Father that he, too, could follow their God and be kind, compassionate and forgiving. But those thoughts eventually disappeared, along with all the other idealistic views of a deep-thinking 16-year-old Mallee boy.

*

While 1966 was a very difficult year, 1967 was full of promise. Or at least that is what the farmers of the Mallee thought. Then again, farmers thought that way each year. You just shut off the bad years and focused on what was coming up. You couldn't do anything else. You had to believe it would be a good season otherwise there'd be no point in going on. You just knew the rains would come and the crop could be planted at the right time. Other rains would follow and harvest would be smooth around November or December.

That was the plan, anyway. Not surprisingly, things often did not turn out the way they should have and 1967 was no exception. Frank had done all the summer fallowing in February and March, and all was ready for the first rain of the year to fall so the crop could be sown in April or May. But no rain came. Frank had bought sheep the previous year which had all lambed prolifically, with many sets of twins, but with little feed or water the lambs were sold as soon as was practical. Drought gripped the area. Dams were dry, dust storms stripped topsoil from the paddocks and deposited it on nearby farms. The little bits of grass and weed that did manage to poke their heads through the harsh, crusty surface soon died off.

Frank's ewes stayed on the farm. He tried to sell them but there were no takers. The sheep died in the paddocks, just skin and bone. Nothing else could be done as it would cost much more to take them off the property than to leave them to die in the barren paddocks. It was cruel. Frank would drive around the channels and the dams each day dragging dying sheep out of the mud and either slit their throats or shoot them. Slitting throats was the best option as bullets cost money.

Dead wool was the only thing to be gained, but even then, there was so much of it on other farms that the price dropped alarmingly. Frank saw all the meat going to waste so he wrote to the Catholic Diocese of Melbourne asking if they could arrange to take the sheep to the city, slaughter them there and give the meat to the needy. He never received a reply.

Without rain, only the farmers who liked to gamble sowed crops. Or those that could afford to waste seed. Frank was not one of them so that year, he and Maurie didn't put in a crop. In August, Maurie said to Frank: 'Son, you'd better start looking for a job, I reckon, I just can't pay you. You've worked here for two years or so for nearly nothing and I owe you so much, but I just don't know what else to do.'

Frank wouldn't get anything from his share-farming, so he tried around the district for labouring jobs, but to no avail. He asked for work at the wool stores and stock and station agents. He went to Melbourne to find work in a factory, but jobs in the city were scarce too.

Back home, he was reading the farming newspaper, the *Weekly Times*, one day and saw a recruiting advertisement for the army. He talked to Maurie about joining up. The pair thought the army was a good idea.

'It's a secure job and it's a family tradition, and you could do a lot worse,' Maurie said.

Frank wrote away for the information and Maurie signed the forms giving permission for his son to leave home.

Frank had hardly heard of Vietnam when he volunteered for the army. There may have been some vague mention of it somewhere on the farm at Birchip, but it wasn't a big issue for anyone there. Most were concerned with the drought and how it was wrecking their lives, rather than a weird sort of conflict in a far-off land in Asia. Eileen, though, wanted none of it. She didn't want Frank to go anywhere and tried to talk him out of it, but he had his mind set. She had heard a bit about the war in Vietnam and had discussed it with Maurie. But Frank didn't really read newspapers – there were not many around anyway – and he rarely heard the radio news. While he might have heard something, none of it registered with him. He was oblivious to everything. He was young and he was bullet-proof, or so he thought. Being killed or killing didn't enter his mind. This was all about money and the lack of it both for him and for his family.

At 17 years of age, Frank Hunt passed the physical, medical and psychological tests and on 27 November 1967, he was in the Australian Army.

Chapter 5
COMING TO KAPOOKA

Frank Hunt kept his decision to join up basically to himself. No one else apart from his family needed to know, he thought. Besides, the main reason for going was to ease the financial pressure on his family and he didn't want anyone in the district to know that. Before he left, he used some of his savings to pay two fuel bills and the outstanding grocery bill, so there would be no family debt. He also left his cheque book with about $3000 available that he made from selling his sheep and two years of share farming. He pleaded with Eileen not to tell Maurie about the money, worrying that he might use it for drinking. Frank urged her to use it only for herself or for urgent matters. Reluctantly, Eileen agreed.

He caught the train at Birchip in the early morning and after a four-hour trip, it pulled in at Spencer Street station in Melbourne. As instructed, Frank made his way to the army recruiting centre in the city, where a group of other recruits had gathered. From there a bus took them to Watsonia Barracks and, after an overnight stay waiting for others to arrive, it was another bus and train journey to the army basic training centre at Kapooka – 'a place of wind' in the local Aboriginal language – some 10 kilometres from Wagga Wagga. Originally established in 1951, the site was chosen because it was close to the birthplace of Field Marshal Sir Thomas Blamey, who served as a general in both world wars and was the only Australian ever to become a field marshal.

There were about 40 recruits in Frank's intake, a diverse selection of the nation's finest – a mixture of size, educational background, cultural heritage and religious beliefs. Frank was one of the smallest, fair-headed but brown-skinned from the Mallee sun, standing at just over five foot six and weighing about 50 kilos, if that. He had managed to squeeze in a letter home during his stay at Watsonia Barracks. He was young and impressionable, his words those of an innocent abroad in a totally new world:

> Dear Mum
> Just a few lines to let you know how I'm going ... we had our photos taken and dog tag number given to us and then we had dinner and boy was it good ... we had to polish floors and the toilets in the officers quarters ... our barracks are beautiful and there is not a thing we haven't got ... now I'm off to play table tennis and billiards so I'll say good bye for now ...

At Kapooka, waiting for the recruits as they filed out of the bus and stood around in an indeterminate mob, were two soldiers who somewhat politely showed them how to line up – or 'fall in'. The soldiers then stood back while a very intimidating, very large soldier – a sergeant with a loud, guttural voice – poured forth barely distinguishable words.

For a hundred years or more, the armed services believed that the louder NCOs yelled, and the more expletives they used, the more likely they were to train better men. It has never been proved and whether or not it works is debatable, but it has not made any difference. That was what happened and most senior NCOs thought it should continue. This sergeant was no exception.

'Letz git a few things right from the word go,' he bellowed. 'I am a sergeant, I am a soljer, I am a REAL soljer, you NEVER call me sir, you call me sergeant. Do NOT insult me by calling me sir!'

The sergeant showed the thunderstruck recruits how to fall in properly – the army's way of lining up, single file. The sergeant's subordinates hadn't done it to his satisfaction. Then he told the bemused recruits, rather quietly for him, how to number along the line. 'I will say "From the right, number" and you will call out your number in RAPID succession. The first man on the right hand end will be number one and the second number two and so on!'

'Frooom the right . . . number!'

The first few blokes managed to remember the number of the recruit standing next to him but by the time it reached double figures, things were different. The count was slow, there were distinctive gaps between the voices while the next man in line figured out what his number was, and the sergeant held his head in his hands.

'Bloody hell! Let's do it again.'

Frank shuffled about in his place in the line wondering what was going on. He thought it was a reasonably simple instruction.

Some 10 minutes later the line was numbered almost to the sergeant's satisfaction – at least, he let it pass, more in resignation than happiness – and the group was brought to attention and told to form three ranks.

'Line up in three rows!' roared the Sergeant sarcastically as if the recruits didn't understand what 'three ranks' meant. After showing that they did understand, the recruits were given the order to 'Ri–ight turn!', a manoeuvre that brought condemnation from the sergeant.

'Yor morons!' he yelled as a few of the recruits turned left instead of right. 'Yor other right!'

Eventually everyone was facing the same way and the sergeant gave them the order to pick up their small bags holding their personal belongings and then to 'Qui–ick march', something that was done very badly as far as he was concerned.

'Jee–zuz Christ, what have I got here?!'

Some were in step while others were not quite sure how to manage it. Some of them were marching square, whereby the arms are swung forward with the leg on the same side rather than with the opposite leg. Arms and legs went at all different angles and heights, much to the amusement and the chagrin of the sergeant.

'I don't know whether to laugh or cry,' he yelled. A corporal, a much more sympathetic man, it appeared, stood nearby, occasionally stepping forward to offer encouragement.

Soon they halted at the front of a two-storey brick building. Each man was handed a card with a room number and bed number on it, told to go inside where four of them were allocated to a room, drop their bags and fall in again. A time limit was imposed by the sergeant. 'You will do it in one minute.'

A few minutes later, and much to the exasperation of the sergeant, the last of the stragglers emerged from the barracks. The group fell in and marched in their distinctive style to the Quartermaster's Store, where they were to be given uniforms.

At the Q store, the sergeant, marching stiffly beside them and clip-clopping in his hobnailed, spit-polished boots, bellowed,

'Platoon ... halt!', at which directive five or six men took an extra step or two. 'Christ, yor all useless – useless!'

Inside, forming a line along the counters, the recruits were fitted out with their gear, although 'fitted out' was a term used loosely. Size was simply an approximation. There were no tape measures to be seen, only a beady eye from the older storeman who looked recruits up and down and flung clothing toward them based on his skill at visual assessment, such as it was. Boots were handed out when recruits mentioned their foot size. Most were a pair but on occasions one boot would be bigger than the other, a problem that when raised was greeted with derision by the storeman, who thought the recruit was simply trying to be 'fuckin' clever'.

'Smartarse,' snorted the grizzled old soldier.

Frank lifted his huge, reddish-tan-coloured boots from the counter, astounded at their weight. The tread, he thought, was similar to that of the tractor tyres at home. He wasn't quite sure how his small feet would manage to lift them up so he could walk, let alone march to the satisfaction of the sergeant.

His uniform hid his skinny body, leaving not so much as a hint of muscle to define the lines. Woollen socks that reached almost up to his knees were about the best fit of anything. The worst were the standard issue underpants: large, floppy, green shorts that were a mixture of boxers and bloomers. Frank couldn't see any reason for having them – they held nothing in and for a young man with skinny legs they were a total embarrassment. But if the army said to wear them, then wear them you did.

The slouch hats were a different story, because they needed to be shaped. Issued to recruits with a round crown and flat brim, they were soaked in water, positioned on a wooden block in the shape of a head, the indentation placed in the side and the crease pushed into the crown. The flap would then be pushed up, ready for the famous clasps to be attached.

The one indication of the seriousness of their situation would come later when the recruits were handed their SLRs, the self-loading rifle that would be their constant companion, their best friend, and something that might very well save their life one day. The rifle gave them their first proper understanding of where they were. This was now real. With the rifle came something else – the truth of the job in front of them.

Once all their uniforms were stowed in their lockers back at the barracks, the recruits headed off to the barber. Frank had decided to have a short back and sides in Birchip before he left so he wouldn't need another one. He was so very wrong. The Birchip short back and sides was no match for the army barber's. A buzz or two right across the top of the head followed by a couple down each side was the order of the day. Five long strokes with the clippers finished the job in about two minutes and what was left of his fair hair was now shorter than ever – a crewcut.

The end of day one brought mixed feelings. *Shit*, Frank thought to himself, *there's a lot to be done here. What a challenge, I hope I can do it all.*

At once, it was daunting, exciting and frightening.

*

Repetition was the key to army life. They were always on the go, about 12 hours a day, with physical training and route marches with full pack and weapons. Then there was the constant stripping and cleaning of weapons; the cleaning of brass and gaiters and webbing; spit-polishing boots; doing the same things day in, day out, until they were perfected.

Drill was the first of them: learning how to march properly, how to fall in and all the different ways to hold a gun. Salute arms, order arms, stand at ease, stand easy. One after the other they repeated and repeated each activity until all the moves became second nature.

Drill was easy for some, including Frank, but there were others who found it all difficult and suffered accordingly. Frank could see there would be a few who would be picked on right from the start but he was one who got it right. *I don't want to stuff this up,* he thought.

One of those singled out for special attention was 'Jock', a Scotsman with an obvious nickname, who had been in the merchant navy for a decade; another went by the name of 'Slob', an overweight, uncoordinated bloke who was an obvious target. Jock was tough and could handle anything thrown at him, but Slob was tall as well as big, and sensitive to the barbs.

Being volunteers and not Nashos, ages in the group varied substantially. Jock was early 30s while Slob was in his 20s. Another man who was over 30 was 'Pommy', a Liverpudlian who had migrated a few years earlier. He had joined up for financial reasons. He thought it would be a source of steady income and he could do it all easily. But it was too tough for him. He'd left a pregnant wife and young child back in Melbourne, both of whom were distraught at his decision. On the third night of army life, Pommy spoke to Frank about going AWOL – absent without leave. Frank advised him to talk to his wife but not to do anything stupid. After all, Frank told him, you don't just walk in and out of the army. 'It'll be worse for you if you go AWOL, then you'll really have problems.' Frank's advice didn't register with Pommy, who about five days later left the army without permission. Frank never found out what happened to him.

After a few nights, the recruits were allowed to go to the wet canteen, a boozy venture that ended with many of them feeling rather sick the next morning. Not the best when you have an instructor ready to punish you even harder than normal, despite your head almost exploding.

Pay day was always eagerly anticipated, especially the first one. For Frank, it felt quite exhilarating: his first official pay. He had a pay book and money in his pocket. Not much, but money nonetheless.

While Frank was reasonably thrifty, other men spent money frivolously. Frank, who had always highly valued the money he made from his sheep and from his share-farming, couldn't understand some of them and the way money sped through their hands. One in particular was 'Jockey' Smith, a former soldier who had left the service and then rejoined. He had been out long enough to have to come back in through the basic training entry route. He had a wife and four kids but lost all his pay playing cards. Each fortnight it would be the same. His pay would come in and a large proportion would quickly go out at the mess. Frank wondered how his wife and family managed.

Training lasted for 10 weeks. The instructors stayed tough right to the end. The exception to the rule was Physical Training Instructor Bob Fulton, the rugby league international player and coach. One time when the Slob couldn't climb a rope Fulton, without screaming and yelling, climbed the rope next to him.

'Let's do it together,' Fulton said. 'Breathe in, breathe out.' An obvious leader, Frank thought.

Generally, there was no slackening off, even when basic drills were finally done well. The sergeant stayed true to form right to the end, regularly questioning their sexuality, parenthood and whether they wanted their mothers, all in his booming voice laced with language so profane it made the roughest, toughest new recruit flinch. One of the sergeant's favourite lines was reminding the men to follow everything without question.

'Yor not in the army to think!' he would yell at them at least three times a day. 'Yor in the army to just DO!'

*

Kapooka was home to thousands of trainees at any one time and there was a real sense of competition between the platoons, cultivated by the men themselves and by their instructors. Which was the best turned-out platoon? The best at marching drill? The best at weapons drill?

Frank's platoon was one of the best and their pride was obvious at the passing-out parade. Slob had trimmed down and got on top of the business of soldiering while Jock's toughness and resilience stood him in good stead. He was now a soldier to be admired if he was on your side and feared if on the other. Even the sergeant showed a few human traits when the platoon passed out. He and a couple of the corporals had a few beers with the men and wished them the best of luck.

Frank, although quite pleased to see the back of his initial training, had loved the experience and the challenges, even though exhaustion would get him down from time to time. There were things he considered a waste of time: the futility of inspections looking for spots of dust when the men could have been doing some more training, and the yelling and screaming when a more measured tone would have been equally effective, were just two of them. He thought of saying to whoever was yelling: 'Yeah, we get your point, calm down.' But then he could also see how and why it worked on some. Frank was proud of many achievements at Kapooka. He had changed. He now accepted that things were as they were. Everything eventually became automatic, which is what the army wanted. Don't rebel, don't question, just go with it. He knew that where he was going, it would be important.

Frank felt a bit alone on Passing Out Day. Many if not most of the men had family to watch on proudly. Frank didn't. With money being in short supply on the farm, no one could afford to get there. It was disappointing but then Frank understood. As far as the farm was concerned, he was used to disappointments.

At least he had the rising sun badge that he could attach to his slouch hat. He looked forward to the time at corps training when he could receive his infantry badge and then the RAR badge when he went to his battalion.

But that was in the future.

Chapter 6
WELCOME TO PUCKA

While Frank Hunt was training at Kapooka, young men whose birth dates had been drawn in the lottery were waiting until a brown envelope arrived in the mailbox. These contained instructions for the young men to report to a designated army barracks in their home state for induction. From there, either by plane or by train and bus, most national servicemen from Australia's southern states were taken to Puckapunyal, the army base near the Victorian town of Seymour.

The 400 square kilometre area was first used by the army during World War I and by the early 1920s an ordnance store and rifle range were built on the site. Its name was taken from the Aboriginal name for a large hill within the training area, and has been variously translated as 'death to the eagle', 'the outer barbarians', 'the middle hill', 'place of exile' and 'valley of the winds'. A couple of these would have resonated with soldiers at the base, if, that is, they ever wondered about it. Soldiers enlisted for earlier wars trained there and during the Vietnam era, recruits either went there or to Kapooka, as did Frank Hunt, or Singleton in New South Wales.

Two of those who went to 'Pucka' were Mick Storen and another young man from Adelaide, Leigh Floyd. Mick was an uncomplicated, reflective young man. He stood about five foot nine and was slim and fit. He had lived a quiet life in a seaside suburb of Adelaide and during his school years he'd joined the cadets, learning how to march properly and do all the parade ground drills expected of them. Cadets had rifle drill, there was a signal section, a pioneer section, they learnt how to build flying foxes and temporary bridges, and how to use a compass and read maps. At least twice a year the cadets would troop off to the rifle range and learn to shoot with their .303 Lee Enfield rifles, relics from previous wars.

Cadets gave Mick a sense of purpose. As he progressed through the ranks from private to corporal, then to sergeant and cadet under officer, he began to form an interest in the army as a career. When he left school he applied to the army to do the tests that would give him entry to officer training at Portsea, but he was not selected.

Mick had other plans, though. He wasn't put off by not being selected, he thought he'd start at the bottom and work his way up. He was now of the age where he would soon be required to register for national service. He knew that if any young man wanted to, he need not wait for his name to be called, he could volunteer. That way he could spend two years seeing what the army was like and whether it was for him. The alternative was to sign up for three or six years as a regular or take his chances in the national service lottery. To that end, Mick registered as a volunteer Nasho.

Neither of his parents thought his idea was any good. They had different reasons: Mick's father Wally, being a World War II veteran, knew about the dangers he could potentially face and while Nancy, his mother, did not have that experience, she had the usual mother's instincts. Both were worried that he might be wounded or, worse still, killed.

After receiving the official document telling him what to do, on 18 July 1968, at 19 years of age, Mick Storen joined the army in the 13th intake of national servicemen.

*

Leigh Floyd didn't want to be in the army. He had been taken out of a great life in the Adelaide Hills and dumped, by dint of a date embellished on a wooden ball, into military service. A shortish, thin youngster, Floyd was a deep thinker. He was against conscription, the war in Vietnam and anything that came with it. Like many of his contemporaries at the time, Floyd, philosophically, didn't understand what the war was all about.

He'd known a Nasho who had returned from the conflict and had gone for a drive with him. The former soldier had thundered along the tight, twisting roads through the hills with no regard for his — or anyone else's — safety. Floyd thought the bloke had a death wish, or that, because he'd come back alive, he thought nothing could harm him. Floyd had also heard of a regular soldier who had been shot in the head in Vietnam, so he wasn't keen on being told he had to face the same risks. However, he reasoned that if it was to be that way, he needed to make the best of it. He had no choice in the matter so he decided to do the best he could, more for his own sake and satisfaction than the army's. He knew that anyone who answered back or couldn't take it would be targeted as an example. Floyd made a pact with himself to keep his head down and mouth shut, putting up with what he needed to put up with.

Floyd and Mick had not met when they arrived at Pucka, having been allocated to different training Companies. Shortly afterwards, Floyd's head was spinning when his group was assembled in three rows on the road outside their barracks. A bit of a shuffle here and there after some almost indecipherable words from a rather large Khaki Uniform, creased to perfection, and they were marched up to the Q Store – the Quartermaster's Store – for their uniforms.

For the first time Floyd heard the distinctive sound of hobnailed boots clipping rhythmically on the bitumen and the Khaki Uniform's loud, gruff voice yelling 'Eff roit eff roit eff roit eff!'

I'll learn to play their silly games, Floyd thought to himself as he marched along the road.

As the weeks passed, the soldiers came to understand more of what they were doing and became better at it. Inside each hut, where 16 of them lived together in four-person cubicles, was a varied group. There were some who needed a bit of prodding and others who took to army life well; some who didn't care where they were; some who liked it because it gave them a sense of purpose, and a couple who didn't think much at all. After a little while all were committed. They had no other choice.

They shared a common philosophy of wanting to do the job well. Mick found it easy as he could rely on the years spent in cadets while at school. In his company, Floyd took to it with aplomb and even though he didn't want to admit it, he had the makings of a genuine soldier. He had a couple of problems, though, one of which was being left-handed. While shooting left-handed was easy enough, doing drills with a rifle right-handed was very difficult. Shouldering arms, presenting arms and all the rest was trying and Floyd, usually in the middle of the front row, heard and noticed the despair of the instructors.

'That man, what are you doing?' he heard many times as he battled to remember which side was which.

Floyd would think to himself, 'I'm doing the best I can; I didn't ask to be here.' Eventually he got it right even though it was a struggle.

During initial training there was no time to be homesick, as their days were fully occupied. Time management was another skill to be learnt. Boots polished, uniforms washed and ironed, lockers arranged neatly, hut cleaned and dusted, everything needed to be in order in the evenings as the day began around 6 am. Inspections were frequent and if things weren't exactly as required, a nocturnal visit was assured and vengeance taken by the instructors. These visits were called 'jumps'. Anywhere between midnight and 2 am was the usual time: 'Up you get, on parade with SLRs in one minute!'

Panic ensued. The men had no time to dress, just to grab a rifle and stand at attention at the end of their bed while listening to a dissertation on what was wrong with the hut, the men, the kit, the world, and anything else that might take the fancy of the NCO doing the yelling. Jumps could be for one night or for several in a row, depending on how the instructor was feeling at the time.

Parade ground drill was the main activity for the first few weeks. That and physical training to toughen them up. Sit-ups, push-ups, climbing ropes and jumping off tall fences were all daily pursuits. While some found it easier than others, it was a grind to all. There were long route marches and runs in the company of drill instructors who were obligated to be obnoxious and ruthless and who took their obligations seriously. Recruits had to repeat the drills over and over again until they achieved some degree of excellence. Those who just didn't get it or those who were slow in learning and couldn't do it properly were, in extreme cases, back-squadded. That was dreaded. To be kept back was embarrassing and having to join the next lot of recruits was deflating.

Each day was spent either on the parade ground or in the gym where there were variations on a theme – boxing being one of them. Training in the soldiering aspects needed to be absolutely correct but as with the physical training, what was expected in boxing was the ability to make a good attempt and not shy away. Backing away could not be tolerated either in training or where the men were headed.

Recruits could see the point of it all after a while. It wasn't something that was obvious at first but gradually they came to understand why the instructors were tough on them. In fact, after the overwhelming initial few weeks were completed, most of the NCOs were admired by the recruits. Most had seen action in Vietnam on earlier tours and knew what was required to make it as easy as possible for the recruits.

At the end of the 10 weeks, the men had all changed. They were disciplined, organised, time-conscious and fitter than they ever had been. They proved that if the system was followed and orders obeyed, then everything, as much as it could be, would be alright. What had been a motley crew of different heights, weights, backgrounds, beliefs and personalities, was now working as one. While many fundamental things about them didn't change, they were now a unit with men, young as they were, who could be relied on by their mates. They were proud of what they had become.

One night before Passing Out Day, the NCOs took up a collection and headed with a couple of recruits into Seymour to buy beer and a few supplies, including huge steaks, for a barbecue.

That night on a road out the back of Pucka, they all drank and ate and talked and became even closer. The men realised they were now privates, not just indifferent, lowly recruits with no ranking. They were nearly real soldiers. While the passing-out parade would be a big day, in its own way this was a bit more special.

A song doing the rounds had been picked up by a few of the men. It had been popular for some years. No one knew who wrote it but they all enjoyed it as they sang to the tune of 'Bye Bye Blackbird'.

Pack up all your bags and kit,
Puckapunyal's up the shit,
Bye-bye Pucka.

Stew for breakfast,
Stew for tea,
No more bloody stew for me,
Bye-bye Pucka.

No more hiking over bloody mountains,
We'll be drinking Foster's out of fountains.
No more blanco, no more brass,
You can stick them up your arse,
Pucka, bye-bye.

*

As Passing Out Day approached, the officers in charge decided what corps the men would be assigned to. As usual, the decisions were made with regard to army needs not the men's preferences. Floyd had turned out to be the best shot in his platoon, so when he selected the service corps as he wanted to be a driver and thought he might learn a bit about maintenance and mechanics, he was duly assigned to infantry.

Mick's path was similar. He'd asked for infantry, following his father. Because Mick wanted infantry, he was allocated to armoured corps. Almost straight away he went to his company commander, who happened to be in the armoured corps.

'I put infantry down twice, sir, how did this happen?' Mick asked.

'We need men like you in the armoured corps,' was the reply, 'but I'll see what I can do.'

A couple of days later, Mick's allocation was changed. He got his wish and was scheduled to join infantry. He mused that all the men who didn't want infantry were sent there while the one who wanted it, wasn't. That was the sort of thing he was still coming to terms with.

The passing-out parade in September was marked by the attendance of Malcolm Fraser, the newly appointed Minister for the Army, who was the guest speaker and who made the most of his time at the microphone.

The day was very hot for that time of the year, very unseasonal, and for the men who were still in heavy winter uniforms, very uncomfortable. While Fraser droned on and on about things the men were not interested in at all, some of the troops collapsed and fainted. Seeing the men's discomfort, a small section of the crowd began to clap when Fraser took a breath. That applause grew louder and louder, extending through the crowd that had come to witness the occasion – the audience obviously thought Fraser had gone on long enough. Fraser soon relented and quickly finished his speech.

Afterwards, Mick realised he'd seen 'people power' in action and discussed it with his mother, father and sister Denise, or Denny as she was known, who had driven over from Adelaide to watch the parade.

It had been a long 10 weeks, hard at times but gratifying.

Chapter 7
TO THE REGIMENT

From Kapooka, Frank Hunt was sent to the Ingleburn Infantry Combat Training Centre on the outskirts of Sydney. There he would learn the finer details of becoming a real soldier, although not in the way he wanted. At the time of passing out from Kapooka, Frank was asked which corps he'd prefer; what he'd like to do in the army. Frank requested engineers or signals, so they sent him to infantry. Another waste of time, Frank thought: *Why bother with all the bullshit, why not just allocate and get it over?*

Frank arrived in late February. The weather was stinking hot and soldiers were living in tents with duckboards – the floor and the canvas not only accentuating the heat but creating that distinctive smell only found in old, thick, canvas tents. The men eventually moved out of the tents and into huts that accommodated about 30 men in each. Communal living called for each person to get along harmoniously with the others and if one was not up to the mark, all 30 men in that hut would suffer. That in turn called for measures that weren't straight from the army training manual. Teamwork was the key and anyone who stepped out of line was not only punished by the platoon NCO but by the men. If you didn't bathe properly you were scrubbed with a hard broom till your skin turned red, and if you were in trouble for not presenting yourself properly on parade, other punishments followed. The men knew that where they were headed there was no room for passengers or those who wouldn't fit in. Everyone depended on everyone else.

Training at Ingleburn was all about team cohesion. The difference between this training and rookie training was marked. This is where they all changed from being lowly recruits to soldiers with a degree of respect from those in charge. This was about knowing what your mate was going to do when the shots were fired – from you and at you. It developed automatic thinking, automatic responses. Frank's corporal had already completed a tour of Vietnam and his experience was invaluable. He was very tough but fair with it. He knew what the recruits faced and was determined to pass that knowledge on to those in his charge.

While marching around was still prevalent, constant rifle practice and weapon cleaning kept the men occupied. Recruit training had already included the importance of having a clean rifle, but this was more intense and could result in big trouble for any miscreants. The worst offence of all was to have a dirty weapon. Your weapon was your friend, your protector, and to have it in anything other than perfect working order was lunacy.

Ingleburn was the place where everything was explained in detail. The men were told why things were being done a certain way and the consequences when they weren't. Instructors taught them constantly about patrolling in arrowhead formation and single file, about setting up night harbours, and about fire lanes.

Training was intense and time off was rare, but occasionally there was an opportunity for fun.

*

Frank became friendly with Spike Jones, a tall wiry bloke who came from the northern beaches area of Sydney. Jones once tried to set up a date for Frank with a friend of his girlfriend, but the girl's father was a squadron leader in the RAAF and didn't want an ordinary 'grunt' – a lowly infantry soldier – to have anything to do with his daughter. Frank wasn't particularly worried and concentrated on the training. When they did get weekend leave after about six weeks, Jones, Jock McKeenan and Frank headed to Kings Cross. They took a train to Central Station, strolled along George Street, then proceeded with a long walk up William Street towards the gigantic neon Coca-Cola sign.

The Cross was a revelation to Frank. Coming from Birchip, the Cross was something he'd never seen the like of before, even allowing for a few escapades at Kapooka. Bars and clubs like the Bourbon and Beefsteak, the strip club Pink Pussycat, Whisky à go go and the all-male revue Les Girls were packed with raucous and drunk Australian and American servicemen. Ladies of the night and the way they dressed were a provocative surprise, although with little money, any feelings of temptation for the ladies were quickly put to rest. In a side street off Darlinghurst Road, Frank and his mates watched as, with sirens wailing, police cars descended on one establishment. It made for interesting viewing, with men and women dashing frantically in every direction and in all states of dress and undress. After a minute or so, Frank's group took off, racing back to the main street, lest they became embroiled in it all. It was the highlight of their trip.

In the days after his escapades at the Cross, Frank developed a toothache. It worried him for about four days until he found the courage to report to the dentist. It wasn't that he was scared of dentists in particular, he simply didn't trust them. Not only had he suffered in Birchip when he was 15, he had also had a tooth out during his time at Kapooka and the dentist's pliers had slipped off the offending tooth and crunched into the roof of Frank's mouth. Several stitches later, Frank had gone back to his hut not being able to talk. He'd also heard a horrifying story of one young soldier at Puckapunyal reporting for a dentistry check during his recruit training. The recruit's name was Cunningham and when he went in, the dentist reached into his filing cabinet, took out a chart, ummed and ahhed and then removed six teeth. He told Cunningham to return in a week, at which time he removed a few more teeth after consultation with the chart. He went a third time for some more removals. The next time, Cunningham, with just a few front teeth left on the top and bottom gums, asked why the dentist was removing all his teeth.

'Well, because your chart says so, Private Birmingham!'

Frank thought about that each time the ache flared again, but eventually he went to the dentist and a small filling procedure was carried out easily, safely and with no unwanted consequences.

*

The weather had cooled once autumn and winter rolled around and exercises became the norm. One took place near Mittagong in the New South Wales Southern Highlands in weather that was wet and freezing cold. The 10 day operation was not only severe in terms of weather conditions but it was the first time the men had been sent out with just packs and small tents, the way they would have to when fighting.

After 12 weeks, training finished and postings were handed out randomly, men going to different battalions stationed at different places around the country. Frank was sent to 6 Battalion RAR based in Townsville. Thirty of the men headed north together. They travelled by train all the way – Sydney to Brisbane to Townsville – two and a half days of bone-rattling. On arrival in Townsville, the men were bussed to Lavarack Barracks, where Frank was allocated to A Company, 3 Platoon.

*

Before Mick Storen and the other recruits left Puckapunyal, it had been made known that the 6th Battalion in Townsville was calling for volunteers to do infantry corps training with the battalion instead of going to Singleton in New South Wales. The idea was that this group would remain in the battalion for the whole of its next tour of Vietnam. Mick was one who raised his hand, an unusual move for most in the army. Leigh Floyd had been noticed by those who made decisions. He had developed into a very good soldier and with his ability as a marksman was bound to be selected. In line with the old army mantra, he didn't volunteer but was sent anyway. While Floyd objected, his sergeant advised him that it was the best option. 'Go with your mates,' he said. 'Trust me, it's for the best.' There were five positions available in Floyd's company – four were filled by volunteers and the fifth by Floyd. The sergeant's advice was correct as, after more rigorous training with 6 RAR, Floyd went to Vietnam with men who came to know each other well.

There were four volunteers in Mick's platoon. However, there were only two spots after the other places had been filled by other training companies. Mick's sergeant suggested they draw cards for it. Mick drew a queen, the highest, and his future was set.

A couple of days later the men boarded a bus for Melbourne, after which a civilian flight took them to Brisbane and then on to Townsville.

At Lavarack Barracks in Townsville, Mick and Floyd became good mates. One of the soldiers already in the platoon when the volunteers arrived was Frank Hunt, who greeted Mick and the others warmly.

More training awaited but it was now a lot more intense. This was about real soldiering. Corps training normally took 10 weeks but because of time constraints, 6 RAR had it compressed into six weeks – 6 am to 10 pm every day. It began each morning with a five kilometre run. Other training included how to dismantle and reassemble weapons quickly, what a properly cleaned weapon was, and how to work as a team in simulated battle; there was also a limited amount of parade ground drill. They handled most of their tasks clinically and competently – except for the time Floyd was charged with accidental discharge. He'd been cleaning his rifle when it went off. He had forgotten it was loaded with blanks. A lesson was learnt by the whole group, not just Floyd: know everything about your weapon and treat it with the utmost respect.

Training was intense and unforgiving. Plenty of time was spent in the jungle-like rainforest. One night the instructors called a tactical withdrawal exercise. The platoon was in a night harbour position in the rainforest in the middle of the night and was told they needed to leave. So all the gear was packed and the men, in pouring rain, walked down the track in the pitch-black night before being told to head off into the forest and camp 50 metres away while watching the track as much as possible. That night was miserable, wet and muddy.

On another occasion, the men were conducting a night exercise at Mt Spec, in the tropical rainforest some 100 kilometres north of Townsville. They assembled at the edge of the rainforest and one of the NCOs, a tall, slim, West Australian corporal named John Needs, spoke to the group.

'Tonight you're going to find out what the jungle's like,' Needs said. 'What you're going to do is hang on to each other and go in single file 60 metres, turn left and go 60 metres, turn left again and go 60 metres and come out again.

'All that stuff you've heard about snakes and that isn't true. There's no rattle snakes, there's none that hiss, they're all quiet. There's no spiders that'll harm you but you might come across some. And there's also clinging vine called "waitawhile". Don't pull against it because you'll end up with lacerations, so stop and take it off you.'

The next 30 minutes were sheer hell. Nothing could be seen of the moon or stars, there was nothing but complete blackness, and as the men walked into the thick jungle, hands on the shoulders of the man in front, they found it eerie and quiet. By the time the men emerged, they were absolutely exhausted – from being careful, from being scared and from being in a totally foreign environment. The lesson was that if anything untoward happened, it happened, and they had to make the best of it. They had to work out how they would get through it by relying on their mates to help.

As the men were recovering, Needs told them they'd probably never encounter anything quite like it again. He explained that it was a practical lesson. 'That's what the jungle is like. You're all alive, you helped each other and no matter what you find or what happens to you from here on, just don't worry about it and keep going.'

Needs was a constant, the one all the men looked up to. He was a sport-loving type who could also be quiet and reflective.

He was a leader; quiet, intelligent, with no need to be loud or appear tough. He didn't pretend to be an expert on drill nor was he overly concerned with it. Instead his strength was a command of the practical part of soldiering. He gave tips on weapons, on patrolling, and he taught by example, not by yelling at the men. He was tough and solid – a friend when he could be, a leader all the time. The sort of man others wanted beside them.

Mick chatted to Needs one night and in the conversation discovered that their fathers had both been in the same machine gun battalion during World War II.

*

Another exercise at Mt Spec didn't go quite as well as some of the others. It involved being flown to Ingham on Caribou aircraft in temperatures of well over 40 degrees. The men came off the aircraft, marched to the end of the airstrip and were told to 'dig in'. There was no shade, not enough water, and only a three-strand barbed wire fence line. Frank grabbed his small shovel and began trying to make his way through what consisted more of rock and concrete than soil, to no avail. After a time, an old farmer arrived.

'What are youse doin' here?' he yelled. 'This is my fuckin' land! Nobody's asked me if you can be here. Where are your officers?'

After being told of the commotion, the officers arrived and made peace with the farmer, who told them, 'You and your men can fuck off!'

The men filled in whatever they had dug up and, after a few trucks arrived, were taken across to the foot of the nearby mountain. There had been no resupply of water organised and after camping overnight the climb started. The group that had just joined the battalion, which included Mick and Floyd, made their way up the mountain with ease, while those who had been there for some time struggled. The men who had been mocked about being 'newbies' had shown their worth. On the next ridge a water resupply had been sorted out and the newbies volunteered to go across to get it. Bringing the water back to the rest of the platoon was significant. From that moment the men were together as one. They could rely on each other.

At the end of the corps training period, 3 Platoon, A Company was complete. The men were not necessarily all the best of mates. Some were, and among the rest there was comradeship and tolerance, but the biggest feeling of all was trust. Even though the bloke next to you might not be top on your list of mates, the main thing was that you could rely on him, that he knew and understood his job and that when the chips were down, he would be there for you. That's what counted, nothing else, and that would be proved to them all.

Chapter 8

PREPARING FOR WAR

A Company, one of three rifle companies in 6 RAR, was nowhere near its full strength of some 110 men when Frank Hunt arrived. Many of the soldiers that were there had just returned from Australia's involvement in Malaysia. Some were veterans of the previous tour by 6 RAR and were waiting for their time to be up so they could leave the army. Others were on leave and had not yet returned. It would be several weeks before everyone either returned or arrived and the company was complete.

As the men had finished corps training, they were now entitled to be officially accepted into the battalion. A formal graduation parade was held during which the men received RAR shoulder flashes for their uniforms as well as the official 6 RAR lanyard. This moment was a proud one for all.

3 Platoon, one of three in A Company, was led by Lieutenant Peter Hines, who'd been in the army for some six years. A fit man who loved surfing in his home town of Newcastle, Hines

had originally been a private in the signal corps. After being promoted to corporal, Hines had undertaken officer training at Portsea and this was his first command. The men knew he understood them. He knew what it was like to carry a pack, what it was like to dig a latrine after a route march, knew the pressure his men were under. He was a natural leader and the men grew to love him.

Gerry Newbury, an older, tough and battle-hardened soldier, was platoon sergeant. Newbury had completed a tour of Vietnam with 1 RAR and served in Malaysia as well. The men called him 'Mother' behind his back because he cared so much for them and looked after them. Another of his nicknames was 'Sheriff' after the Sheriff of Mayberry in the popular television show with Andy Griffith. The men always knew exactly where they stood. Instant obedience was always called for. Newbury and Hines worked extremely well together, which meant a happy platoon, something that would also be gratifying when times became difficult.

Each of the platoons in a rifle company was supposed to comprise 34 men: three sections of 10 men – sections 7, 8 and 9 – with three overall leaders and a medic that constituted Platoon Headquarters (PHQ). In 3 Platoon they were: Lieutenant Peter Hines, Sergeant Gerry Newbury, Signalman Rod Ballard and the medic Graeme 'Doc' Davis. Each section had a corporal in charge – Corporals Greg Cooper, John Needs and the third, let's call him 'Smithy', who was not at all popular with his men. However, 3 Platoon was missing a few men. Seven of the men had been dropped from the platoon for various reasons, sickness and injury being the main ones. The platoon would later arrive in Vietnam short of a full complement. After recovering, those men who had left the platoon would became 'Reos', reinforcements who were on standby to fill vacancies left by wounded or killed men, or by those incidents such as happened to 3 Platoon. When ready, the men who dropped out would be sent back to 6 RAR and, along with the battalion's advance party, were there waiting in Vietnam when the others arrived.

The leaders had varying effects on the men. To Frank and the other men Needs was brilliant, a man who had been with them for a while and one whom others would follow without question. Cooper was good and fair, while some in Smithy's section thought he left a bit to be desired. Frank was in 8 Section under Smithy. Frank thought the contrast between Smithy and the section's second-in-charge, Lance Corporal Jim Kelly, was marked. Kelly, who was still 19 and had been promoted earlier than would normally have happened, was everything Smithy was not – someone the men could talk to, someone whose nature men could relate to, someone to be trusted and followed. Kelly and Frank struck up a close friendship. The two young men who had lived in rural areas were billeted in the same room, they thought the same way, they were a similar age and were interested in the same things. It was a natural affinity.

After a few weeks Frank decided that he needed a car to travel around the area with ease. He still had some money in his bank account, so he looked around Townsville's second-hand car yards and forked out $300 for an FJ Holden. Although the car was owned by Frank, it was a car that anyone in the platoon could use, as long as they paid for petrol and drove carefully. While the car was used by others on occasions, mostly Frank and Kelly drove it around on the weekends they had leave. Another mate, John Goslett, would go with them, sometimes using Goslett's car, and the three young men would go to local dances, where Frank was in big demand when the ladies saw the way he moved on the floor. Kelly watched and wondered whether he would ever dance the way his mate did. He was never jealous, rather he looked on in admiration, sometimes attempting a few steps but wondering what he looked like in comparison.

They often made the 130 kilometre trip to Charters Towers for the local dance, and one time Frank fell in love with a local girl there. The relationship was doomed from the start and didn't last long. One weekend, after taking the girl to the movies, Frank drove out to the girl's farm to pick her up but while he waited under the huge peppercorn tree at the top of the dirt drive to the farmhouse, he saw her father approach, armed with a gun and with two huge dogs straining at their leashes.

'She don't want no fuckin' army types, so piss off!' the farmer yelled.

Frank quickly did as he was asked, the FJ skidding and sliding through the dirt track on the way out.

Some of the men wondered why Frank chose those old-fashioned dances and not the loud, noisy pubs with rock 'n' roll on the agenda. Frank didn't discuss it much but they were the dances he'd been brought up with and learnt. And always in the back of his mind was the way he had been exposed to alcohol through his father's problems. He worried that it might be hereditary. He had no real cause to be concerned and anyway, even though he occasionally went to pubs with the blokes and got as drunk as they did, he loved ballroom dancing so he followed his passion.

*

While Mick had known about Vietnam and the war for quite some time, Frank had only heard vaguely of the country before army life. Now it was all they heard about, all they trained for. Everything was geared towards it. And they were happy to go.

For a young bloke from the Mallee, it inspired dreamy fantasies of a tropical paradise and was something to be looked forward to. The news was exciting. Frank was fit; he had grown and put on weight. He loved his mates and what they had gained from each other, he was keen and he was ready for the world, more so than he'd ever been in his short life.

Mick felt much the same. He'd read a lot about Vietnam and keenly studied what was happening there. He had been particularly interested in the Battle of Coral-Balmoral, the two Australian fire support bases in the northern part of South Vietnam. These battles had taken place in May and June of 1968 when the Viet Cong and the North Vietnamese Army (NVA) attacked the bases. During the battles 25 Australians were killed and 99 wounded. That was a sobering thought, although not something to dwell on, even though it came a few months after the Tet Offensive, when North Vietnamese troops attacked over 100 cities and towns with 80,000 men during what was traditionally a cease-fire for the Tet Lunar New Year celebrations.

When Frank had been at Kapooka, at times he thought about what he was heading into, what he was in for. How many casualties would there be and would he be one of them? Now he didn't have time to pause and reflect on his decision to join. This was no time for second-guessing. That was the way it was; that's what happens in a war, there are casualties. Any thoughts or feelings of trepidation were not constant, even though there were always newspapers lying around the place telling stories of the dead and wounded. There was no time to spend worrying about the news; spare time was limited and, anyway, the corporals and the sergeants wouldn't talk about it, they were too intent on training the men properly to avoid casualties. Besides, those matters didn't seem real and were for another time.

In most cases the men looked forward to going. They were excited but knew they faced a formidable challenge and there were a few hurdles to overcome before that happened. The battalion had a lot of serious training to do and besides that, Frank, along with a small number of the other volunteers, was still not 19, the age they had to be before the government would let them go to the war. No matter that in 1968 they couldn't vote or legally drink in Queensland pubs until they were 21, they could still fight and be killed in an Asian war. Like the others his age, Frank knew that he wouldn't be going anywhere until at least January the following year when he turned 19, but that didn't concern him or any of the others unnecessarily.

Training began in earnest in June 1968 with an expected departure date some time during May the following year. It was a long time to prepare, but very necessary. Early training was at Mt Spec, which Mick had already experienced, and a place called High Range, an open plain some 30 kilometres to the west. The vegetation of both places was similar to that found in Vietnam, especially the rain-soaked jungle environment of Mt Spec.

Soldiers were severely tested in training. They were on the go for most of the day with everything learnt at corps training being put to the test. At times they would be out in the jungle area of Mt Spec for weeks at a time, practising how to set up camp at night, how to set up for ambush, setting up harbours for the night, tactical manoeuvres and so much more. Maintaining fitness was extremely important, as they would need it later. Everything was done over and over and over again. It might save your life; it might save your mate's life. There were very few protests. Not that it would have made any difference anyway, and by now the soldiers, young as many were, had become hardened and committed to their cause.

Mick wrote home about one of the company's exercises:

... It was painful from start to finish. It began in over century heat and finished the same way. The last two days can only be measured in sweat as we trekked 2000 ft up a ridge through the J [jungle], climbing up and slipping down carrying full packs, weapons, etc. The last day nearly saw me out, the heat was fantastic. It was so hot that I didn't see any leeches, the ticks had taken over still I only got one in me ...

For a few days, the men of A Company did some helicopter training with RAAF Hueys providing support for aerial assault practice and transport. 6 RAR were supposed to be the most efficient air assault battalion of all. It was a questionable title to the men as when the helicopters weren't available for training, the Company Commander Major Belt organised for them to leap from the back of jeeps with weapons at the ready. Real choppers and the sound of their rotor blades would become a signature background sound to them in Vietnam and, at one stage during training, provided a glimpse into the future. One day at Mt Spec, Frank lost his footing and fell down a ravine, hurting his kidneys when his canteens thrust into his back. He needed to be evacuated, so a simulated dust-off was called in and a casualty evacuation undertaken at night, with everyone in the whole platoon taking turns carrying him on a stretcher to the evacuation point. After a few days in hospital, Frank was soon back in the platoon. Neither he nor Mick could possibly have imagined what the ensuing year would hold for them both.

All the training was important but perhaps the most crucial was in using weapons. Marksmanship skills needed to be as close to perfect as they could be but, more than that, those skills needed to be achieved under pressure. A soldier needs to be able to shoot properly and accurately, particularly when the enemy is shooting back at them. It is one thing to shoot accurately on a rifle range but another entirely in the jungle when bullets from the Viet Cong are zinging around your head from someone you can't even see hidden deep in the jungle. That's where fitness and mental strength play a big part in a soldier's survival and the survival of his comrades. There are times when a soldier, carrying a pack and sweating in the sweltering tropical heat, adrenalin pumping through his body, heart racing, has to sprint into a firing position and engage the enemy. All the practice on a rifle range doesn't give him that experience, it has to develop in training that simulates as much of the real thing as possible.

*

Christmas was fast approaching and the men were granted leave. Frank was keen to go home but it was a long trip. To accommodate travel time, Frank was given six days more than those who lived in Queensland – three for the journey down to Birchip and three for the return – while Mick and the other South Australians were given ten extra days – five home and five back.

Like many things in the army, the trip didn't go as planned. Those going south headed off on a bus to Brisbane but some four hours into the trip the bus broke down, which resulted in a four-hour wait on the side of the road for a replacement to appear. In the early hours of the morning they arrived in Brisbane but had to wait all day for the train to depart that evening. The train took all night and the next day to get to Sydney, all the next night and day to reach Melbourne before another all day and night trip to Adelaide. Ten days later it all happened in reverse. After the initial bus breakdown, Frank's journey in both directions went smoothly but for Mick and Leigh Floyd, the last leg back to base was not as easy. In Brisbane the men found their bus bookings to Townsville had been overlooked. They were stuck and worried they might be considered AWOL when they eventually returned so they headed out to the army barracks at Enoggera to confess what had happened. The duty officer was somewhat sceptical of these two but allocated them a room where they left their bags before heading back to the city.

'Let's go to Surfers,' Mick suggested to Floyd, who agreed that seemed like a good idea. So with about five dollars between them they caught a bus down to Surfers Paradise on the Gold Coast, shared a salad to keep the pangs of hunger at bay, slept on the beach and were roused by the local cops before dawn. They returned to Brisbane on the first bus, caught another bus out to Enoggera to grab their luggage and a third to get back to the city, where they finally boarded the bus to Townsville. They arrived exhausted.

*

The battalion reassembled after Christmas leave and set off for the Jungle Training Centre at Canungra, just near the New South Wales border in south-east Queensland. Canungra had been a training centre since World War II, for soldiers preparing for battle against the Japanese in the Pacific region, and for those who went to Indonesia and Malaya. All but a handful of the men who fought in Vietnam went through Canungra, all of them benefiting from the experience, although some didn't think so at the time. Canungra was tough but it needed to be if the men were not only to feel as though they were properly prepared for jungle warfare in Vietnam, but to survive.

There were drills, drills and more drills. Contact drills, fitness drills, ambush drills, harbour drills, and any other drill that could be thought of. Most were conducted in silence, using only hand signals. All were extremely demanding and needed immense concentration.

Early every morning the men had to complete an obstacle course that included jumping over a two metre high wall into the 'Bear Pit', a smelly, muddy pond of dirty water. The men would be under logs, over logs, in water and out of it, through muddy holes and all in debilitating heat and humidity. Designed to get the soldiers familiar with obstacles and to overcome them no matter what, it was made more difficult by simulated artillery fire, smoke bombs and grenades exploding, after which they'd have to climb up a small wooden ladder to the top of a ten-metre tower and take a plunge, while fully packed and laden, into the local river. Days would bring long marches through jungle where figures cut from metal and painted to look like VC would jump out from behind trees, with instantaneous responses needed. Then at night there'd be ambushes and sentry duties and more jungle work the next day. There was no respite.

Frank's section was the first to do the battle efficiency course (BEC), in effect becoming the guinea pigs that would show the rest of the company what not to do. The BEC included what was called section fire and movement, and what they needed to do when nothing could be heard because of any battle noise. Carrying full packs and rifles, the men spread out in a line and moved forward in a mock assault, crawling at some stages, crouched over at others, through lanes of long grass, barbed wire entanglements, and other obstacles. All the while a Vickers machine gun fired live rounds over their heads and mines and artillery fire exploded around them covering them with mud and dirt and creating anxiety.

This training was the closest to real combat that any soldier would experience. On its completion the men were exhausted, physically and mentally. Their exhaustion was exacerbated by the section leader, Smithy, who had made a mess of the drill, with men going all over the place under his instructions. Smithy's stories were patently either not true or at the very least enlarged and he was not liked by his men. He rode them unmercifully and, worst of all, unfairly. At the end of this exercise, he did nothing to endear himself to them when he told his men he wanted a magazine check to see if any dirt was in them.

The men knew they'd have some dirt in their magazines but they suspected Smithy was doing it to deflect blame from himself for not conducting the drill properly and not having control of his men. Smithy must have got wind of the men's mood, as nothing further happened. The magazine inspection was abandoned. Later, a few of them spoke to Smithy and told him of their concerns. The corporal listened intently and promised to fix things. Nothing ever changed.

On their return to Townsville from Canungra those men considered unfit for service in Vietnam due to injury, or for any other reason, were culled from the platoon. It was necessary but it meant there were vacancies in the platoon that were not filled by the time they headed off on exercise at Shoalwater Bay. The men were still expected to carry a full complement of weaponry, ammunition and suchlike but with fewer men. Those extra responsibilities extended to sentry duties, patrols and everything else required by a platoon.

*

The battalion flew to Rockhampton and from there were transported by truck to the training area. Operation Bright Armour was the completion of everything the troops had done, the final piece in the puzzle that began when they arrived at Kapooka and Puckapunyal. It included using armoured personnel carriers (APCs) and helicopters in cordon and search missions, plus ambush techniques, reconnaissance and assaults on fortified camps – in fact just about anything they could reasonably expect to be engaged in Vietnam. The one drawback to the whole exercise was the weather. In the two weeks they were there, some 300 millimetres of rain fell, drenching the whole place and making things extremely difficult. It was wet all the time. Wet when marching, wet when stopping, wet when sleeping – or rather, when trying to sleep. It was the toughest time of all.

One night when things were low and men were beginning to think being selected for infantry might be the worst thing that had ever happened to them, a few of them sat around with Peter Hines, their leader and their skipper, who recounted the story of his journey from where they were currently to where he now was. Skip told them he had suffered doubts about what he was doing, but he knew he would get through it. A natural leader, he reassured the men about what they were doing and told them as long as they all stuck together, everything would be alright. The men who talked with Skip had their spirits lifted and took to their training with renewed vigour.

By the time the exercise had finished, the battalion was becoming restless. The waiting was monotonous. They were sick of repetitive training and needed an outlet for everything they'd learnt. They got their wish. At the end of March the men were sent on pre-embarkation leave with a departure date set for early May. Mick went home to Adelaide and Frank went to Birchip.

Frank was keen to see his family. He wanted to share stories of the young girl he had met while in Townsville. He had briefly told his mother about her in a letter after they'd met:

I'll be home before I go overseas Mum and I'm looking forward to talking to you and Dad. I suppose it's cooling off down there at the moment and not so hot. We've been doing some exercises and they've been really hard. It is so hot and humid up here and we're all struggling but it's good really. I'll be able to tell you more about Constance and the plans we have made when I see you all.

Frank, 19 at the time, had met the 17-year-old Constance a few weeks earlier and they were determined to be married. To that end, the young couple had recently become engaged. Frank was eager to tell his parents about his future and of the grandchildren they could look forward to.

The army flew them home this time. Mick caught up with his mates and spent a lot of time with his family. While there was no specific talk about the war, an unspoken worry was always in the air, more on his parents' part than his own. Mick's step into war was inevitable, so he had come to accept it: it was something to which he looked forward. When the time came to go back, he looked forward to being back with his mates. He'd done all the training and now it was time to put it all into action.

Frank's time in Birchip went quickly and on the night before he left, the town held a going-away party at the local hall, a real country 'do' with ladies bringing a plate of supper. There was dancing and plenty of chat, most of it either about the war or about Frank and Constance, and the presentation of a wallet full of money that had been collected from those attending. Alcohol was banned so Frank, his uncles and his dad had visited the local pub beforehand. Frank was a little bit the worse for wear and slurred his words while responding to the presentations.

Before dawn the next morning, Frank was driven from the farm to the station by his mum and dad, the trip undertaken in silence. The train left at 4.20 am bound for Melbourne and while his dad quietly shook his hand, his mum broke down. She said later she knew, with a mother's intuition, that something was going to happen.

'Take care, son,' she said through freely flowing tears.

'It's OK, Mum, I'll be right,' said Frank, hugging her close.

Family friends Jack and Emily Smith had also turned up and gave Frank a thermos of tea and a brown paper bag holding homemade sandwiches to keep him going until he reached Melbourne.

*

On 1 May 1969, 6 RAR marched through the streets of Townsville and was given a rousing reception. It was an impressive farewell. The battalion was due to leave for Vietnam on the troop carrier HMAS *Sydney* in a week's time. With their green uniforms ironed to perfection, boots polished, brass shining, they marched through the crowds lining Townsville's streets. The onlookers were four or five deep as the men marched, chests out, proud of who and what they were. Frank was exceptionally proud. He had grown from the introspective youngster he had been a year previously into a fit, confident soldier.

He could now use an M60 machine gun that spat 7.62 mm bullets at the enemy at about 600 rounds per minute over 1000 metres; he could fire an M16 Armalite rifle which would send 5.56 mm rounds towards the enemy at a rate of some

800 per minute on automatic fire; his personal rifle was capable of 700 rounds per minute of 7.62 mm ammunition. He had learnt how to lob hand grenades that might blow up several enemy at one time and to set a Claymore, a concave mine that, when triggered, released 700 small ball bearings flying forwards to stop anyone in range. Not that he dwelt on it too much but it gave him pause for thought. Frank Hunt and the other young men who had such diverse earlier lives were, if and when they were required, highly trained killing machines. And that, after all, was the point.

Frank was still naive in many ways. The reality of what he was about to undertake was not completely apparent to him. How could it be? Newspapers and television reports of the war seemed to be far removed from normal life in Australia. Even reports of killed and wounded men had not really hit home. Frank was 19 and the big adventure, as he termed it, was about to begin.

Chapter 9
ON THE WAY

When 6 RAR boarded HMAS *Sydney* on 8 May 1969, protests in Australia had been increasing for some time. Before and during the battalion's training period, the public and political scene had changed. While the majority of people still supported the war, the number of those against it was growing quickly. The media, the press in particular, led the charge. In the early days of the war newspapers ran stories of the mateship and hero-worshipping type – almost propaganda. But when the casualties mounted and places like Long Tan and My Lai became household names, and when television began showing disturbing news footage as families sat down to their evening meal, opinions started to change, and discontent with what was going on in Vietnam grew.

Through 1968 and 1969 there was a harder edge to the commentary – and to what was happening in the streets. Young people were embracing 'flower power', peace and love. Music with protesting lyrics, and drugs like LSD and marijuana were prevalent, and the youth were not afraid to voice their discontent at what they saw were the injustices of whatever the government was doing. It might well have been the Age of Aquarius but the nation was dividing. Not evenly but significantly. Not only was it dealing with turmoil in its own towns and cities, it was also contemplating the assassinations of Martin Luther King and Robert Kennedy in America. The world was a messy place. Australian Prime Minister Robert Menzies had gone, his replacement Harold Holt had drowned and now the new man, John Gorton, was viewed by some as disappointing in the extreme. Like Holt before him, pandering to the Americans was not, despite what anyone believed about the war, a good idea, according to most Australians. The Labor Party, now led by Gough Whitlam, began to make political inroads.

What was happening in Vietnam became the focus of discussion played out everywhere – dinner parties, pubs, hairdressers, workplaces, in families and among friends. Opinions on either side of the debate, unless the parties were like-minded, could almost guarantee an argument and, in many cases, vilification. Young men burned their call-up notices in public, protesters chanted such things as 'One, two, three, four, we don't want your dirty war' and, copying the Americans, 'Hell no, we won't go'. Many of the protesters, especially students and younger left-wingers, openly supported Ho Chi Minh and the Viet Cong, some even raising money to send to Hanoi, until such activities were banned. This was a bridge too far for most Australians. Even if they didn't agree with the war, sending money to the enemy was treason.

By this time the National Service Act had been beefed up, with those who burned their notices fined $200 on the spot, and anyone who refused to serve sentenced to two years jail. Anyone who failed to report draft dodgers could be fined $400, a proposition that enraged most Australians, who believed that 'dobbing in' was anathema to the culture of the country. That, in turn, led to more draft dodging and more burnt cards. There were still those who joined as volunteers, and, while the vast majority obeyed the law even though they might have preferred not to, there were those who didn't mind being called up.

For the men of 6 RAR, protests in Townsville were rare. There were a few problems with local bikie gangs and there were some locals who didn't want the army around because of the American connection, but overall Townsville was a military town and had been for many decades. Trouble was generally limited and, on the occasion of the soldiers' march towards their destiny, non-existent.

*

HMAS *Sydney*, known affectionately as the 'Vung Tau Ferry', was anchored in the Townsville harbour as weather conditions meant it was unsafe at the wharf, so most of the men had to be ferried out – literally. The ferry that took people between Magnetic Island and the mainland was pressed into service and made its way out to the ship full to the gunwales with soldiers. Scrambling nets had been thrown over the side of the ship and soldiers, carrying their packs with rifles tied to them, climbed up, slowly and carefully lest they tumble into the sea, as sailors watched with amusement. Dropping rifles or soldiers' packs to the bottom of the ocean would have been frowned upon.

This was the *Sydney*'s fourteenth trip to Vietnam and many of the sailors had made the journey several times before. The navy's role in the Vietnam War was downplayed by many, who thought the army was the only service that mattered. Soldiers dominated the public's perception of who was involved, but the navy also played its part and those who made the journey to and from Vietnam recognised the *Sydney*'s contribution and that of her men.

When Frank clambered his way up the nets and stood on the deck he joined the ranks of thousands of other soldiers who had been transported safely to and from Vietnam over the years. He was at once excited and apprehensive. He followed directions down the steep stairs to the deck where he would be sleeping and stowed his gear. By the time he returned to the upper deck, the ship was on its way, shadowed by its escort, the destroyer HMAS *Vampire*.

Frank quietly bade farewell to Australia as he watched the land recede from sight, not really sure how or if he'd be returning. He didn't dwell on the thought for long.

The trip to Vietnam was no luxury cruise; in fact it was hot and uncomfortable. In a letter home Mick Storen called it 'HMAS Sauna Bath'. A former aircraft carrier, HMS *Terrible*, bought from the British Navy after World War II, the *Sydney* was rusty and noisy. It had been built for conditions in the North Atlantic, not Asia, and air conditioning, such as it was, worked only some of the time and even then not to every part of the ship. Many soldiers slept on camp stretchers – if they were lucky enough to get one – in passageways and in little nooks and crannies wherever they could find air that moved. Those who slept on the mess decks were mostly issued with hammocks, which all found very difficult to tie up – or to 'sling', as sailors called it. When they were all slung properly it was wall-to-wall hammocks with very little room to move; the only way through was to go underneath. Many gave up trying to get the ropes – or the 'clews' – in the right place and slept instead on the tops of boot lockers that ran around the steel walls of the mess. Sailors helped soldiers to sling their hammocks as much as they could, but there was a limit to what soldiers could absorb in such a short time.

When he was walking through the mess decks, Frank, short as he was, kept hitting his head on the hammocks. Most soldiers suffered from that until they discovered they needed to drop their heads lower as they walked around. And everywhere they turned there were pipes of varying sizes and shapes, all covered with asbestos lagging. Narrow passageways had doorways between the bulkheads which had to be stepped over rather than walked through. The doors had strange-looking handles on them called 'dogs' which clipped the door safely into the closed position when needed. Woe betide anyone who walked through a 'dogged down' door and didn't 'dog' it down again. The trip was hot, humid, uncomfortable, claustrophobic to many, and different from anything they had experienced and anything they could have anticipated.

Soldiers enjoyed the food on board and they looked forward to the nightly beer issue when they received a large (750 ml) can of, usually, Foster's or Carlton Draught. The men would line up when the announcement was made about the beer issue and be given the can after a sailor spiked a hole in the top with his special rope spike. The regulations allowed 'one can per man per night . . . per haps'. Non-drinkers and those who felt a bit off-colour made quite a bit of money selling their ration.

Although they could have a rest at night, the soldiers could not completely relax, as during the day they were kept busy with physical training, rifle drill, volleyball in the lift wells of the aircraft hangars and tug-of-war on the flight deck, leaving time for only a bit of lounging around in the sun. Target practice off the end of the flight deck was a constant: coloured balloons would be released and shot at either floating through the air or when they landed in the ship's wake. There was piquet duty on the flight deck, lit only by the stars if there were any, and the ship's red and green steaming lights.

For most the *Sydney* provided a pleasant enough way to train. When the ship sailed over the Equator, the traditional 'Crossing the Line' ceremony was held, with King Neptune rising from the deep and welcoming the soldiers who had never before ventured into his kingdom. Many memories of the journey faded but if there was one thing the soldiers never forgot about their trip on the *Sydney* apart from the heat, Neptune's appearance was it.

There was not a great deal of contact with sailors but when it occurred it was mostly cordial and friendly. One night soldiers were woken by what turned out to be a man overboard exercise, although no one knew that at the time. Soldiers were quickly mustered and counted while the ship slowed down. They had a lot of time, as the *Sydney* took some eight kilometres to slow to a stop. It gave the soldiers some idea of how big the ship was. Sailors more or less kept on doing what they were supposed to. The man overboard was never confirmed but the soldiers were all accounted for. Frank and a couple of his mates laughed. After all, it didn't really matter if a sailor went missing, as long as a soldier didn't!

Ever the thoughtful son, Frank had managed to organise a telegram to be sent to his mum for Mother's Day. On board he was often lost. Even after seven days he could still not find his way through the rabbit warren of doors, passageways, offshoots, ladders and other obstacles that constituted the inside of the big ship. He got to know plenty of sailors during that time as he was constantly asking for directions. He fell for the trick many novice sailors fall for when at sea for the first time. He managed to sling his hammock near a scuttle – or porthole – through which any small breeze would be funnelled in and across his hammock courtesy of an air scoop attached at times to the hole. But he didn't think about the ocean just outside his mess, which was on the fourth deck, and when the ship subtly changed course, sea water swept up the ship's side, in through the scuttle, and soaked him and his bedding. Generally, the weather was good all the way, with balmy nights on deck spent watching a sky full of stars and picking out the Southern Cross as it got lower and lower in the sky.

For amusement during the voyage, concerts were held in one of the aircraft lift wells where the navy band played and soldiers could show off their diverse range of talent. Frank and his mates – Norm Brown, who played guitar, John Goslett, Jim Kelly, Owen Cook and Alfie Lamb – made up a group called The Foundations. They sang a variety of songs including '500 Miles' and 'Johnny Won't Be Coming Home Again', which brought a rebuke from one of the officers who told them such songs had the potential to lower morale, as a result of which the men could be charged. When they had finished their songs Lamb provided the highlight of the evening with his recitation of a poem called 'The Red Robin', the story of a bird which lands on a window-sill tweeting that morning has come. The bird looks and sounds happy but the man in bed isn't and the poem ends with a punch-line that tells of disposing of the bird with the slamming of the window on his head. Not a right and proper poem but hilarious to soldiers heading to war. Lamb became famous for his poem and was asked to recite it many times in the ensuing months.

One evening, close to their destination, Frank was talking to a sailor as they gazed at the unspoilt heavens from the flight deck.

'Been a good trip,' he said.

'Yeah,' the sailor replied. 'Glad about that, you lot can be a pain in the arse at times, getting in the way, but we try to make it a bit friendly because some of you mightn't be coming back with us.'

After 10 days at sea and nearing the *Sydney*'s destination, the escort HMAS *Vampire* assumed a state of 'defence stations', with the next step 'action stations' if needed. *Sydney* would be in a state of 'darken ship', in which all the portholes – or scuttles as the navy called them – were closed and all doors were either closed or had black curtains hung across them so as to cut the light out when sailors made their way through. Two navigation lights were all that could be seen of *Vampire* and not much more on *Sydney* and if they weren't careful, on a dark night absent-minded soldiers taking a turn in the evening air could wander off the end of the flight deck.

After 11 days, the *Sydney* anchored in Vung Tau harbour and began unloading. As the American Chinook helicopters hovered above the ship and lifted up trucks and guns and other equipment with their giant claws, other smaller craft and barges secured themselves alongside, taking other bits and pieces ashore.

Then it was time for the soldiers. The LCMs had been lowered and the men scrambled carefully down the nets, into the craft and headed for land and to whatever else awaited them.

PART TWO

Chapter 10
HERE WE ARE: VIETNAM

Vung Tau was a busy harbour on 19 May 1969. In addition to numerous transport ships, there were several American warships, helicopters buzzing around like a swarm of bees overhead and, at times, flights of Phantom fighter planes flashing across the sky on their way to deliver napalm, rockets and other assorted means of killing. The sea was murky and navy divers often had difficulty checking for mines that had been dropped in the water by the Viet Cong. Scare charges were continuously dropped over the side of ships to counter any underwater activity by the enemy. The sky was generally grey but days and nights were never cold. The big thing that struck those who had not been there before was the humidity – the stifling heat that brought instant sweat, with no breeze at all to moderate it. Out in the middle of the harbour it was bad enough but in the jungle it would be much worse.

This was the scene as the LCMs carrying the men of 6 RAR headed toward land. The soldiers could not see much of the shoreline from the *Sydney* and even less from the inside of the landing craft. Lieutenant Hines and Sergeant Newbury stood in the middle of the craft while Frank, waiting expectantly, was at the back. As the LCM churned across the sea, 3 Platoon's Corporal John Needs told the men to be ready for anything. This was a war zone, he yelled above the roar of the sea, the wind and the engine, so they should be geared up to counter whatever they found. The men grabbed their SLRs a bit tighter, hitched their packs into a more comfortable position and waited, breathing steadily. They were Australian soldiers, ready for whatever was waiting for them.

The LCM crunched onto the shore, the ramp was lowered and there before them was, well, not much. Only a couple of Vietnamese women clad in their traditional white dresses and big wide-brimmed straw hats riding bicycles along the nearby road.

Needs laughed. 'Welcome to the Funny Country. Not what you expected, boys?'

'Fuck you, Needsy,' came a voice from the centre of the cluster of men. Frank and a few others joined in with other disparaging but good-humoured remarks aimed at their corporal.

From there the men jumped into trucks and were taken to where American Chinook helicopters had arrived with the men of 4 RAR who would board HMAS *Sydney* to make the return trip to Australia, their tour of duty over. As they boarded the choppers the men of 6 RAR were issued with ammunition for the trip that would take them to what would be their new home for the next 12 months: Nui Dat.

Nui Dat – meaning 'small hill' in Vietnamese – or 'The Dat' or 'The Big Red Dat', as the soldiers knew it, was the Australian military base in the centre of Phuoc Tuy Province, the region allocated to Australia by the Americans in 1966 as its area of responsibility.

It had been chosen because it had room enough to build an airfield and enough flat ground around to make it defendable. Nui Dat was surrounded by multiple, almost circular 12 kilometre barbed wire fences with M60 machine gun pits every 50 or so metres as well as Claymore mines set up at varying intervals just outside the wire. The trigger mechanisms – or 'clackers' – for the Claymores were at the end of long wires that ran back to the gun pits and lay next to those men on duty who could set them off easily.

The base had been hewn out of the jungle and rubber plantations with bulldozers ripping away trees, some of which had previously been defoliated with chemicals, including Agent Orange, so named because of the orange stripe on the drums in which it was contained. The nearby villages of Long Tan and Long Phuoc had been cleared of 4000 civilians in 1966, a 'resettlement' decision that was resented by the Vietnamese, even those who were not involved with the VC.

Nui Dat was virtually a town, albeit a military one. There were still plenty of rubber trees inside the wire that gave protection to the rows and rows of tents surrounded to half their height by sandbags. These were 'tent lines' or just 'lines' as the army knew them. There were parade grounds, flagpoles, canteens, workshops, sheds, and signposted bitumen and dirt roads with trucks and Land Rovers and APCs rolling along them every day. There were several areas for helicopters to take off and land, the largest being the 'Kangaroo Pad'. There was also an airstrip: Luscombe Airfield. Nui Dat was, at different times, hot, humid, sticky, wet, muddy, dry and dusty. It was many different things to many different soldiers. Even though the time spent there would be brief in between operations, to all soldiers who served in Vietnam, the Dat was a sort of home. It was the same for the men of 3 Platoon, A Company.

As 4 RAR had moved out, 6 RAR moved in. Lockers, beds and other assorted paraphernalia were waiting for them. Their lines were close to the perimeter wire, just a short distance from the jungle about 300 metres away across a cleared area. Frank, along with Mick and another young private, Col Renehan, were allocated a tent adjacent to the wire, with other tents running back from theirs. For these young men, the excitement they had felt on the journey up, the feeling that all the training was over and it was now time to put it into action, had been replaced by a certain degree of apprehension. They didn't know what was in front of them; they couldn't imagine what they would face, but they were keen enough to find out.

The close proximity to the jungle was something that played on Frank's mind. 'Shit, they could come close and drop something over the wire at any minute,' he thought.

Those thoughts disappeared soon after when the company was told what they could and couldn't do in the camp, and what their duties would be. The men stowed their gear and were put straight to work, fixing up the tents and cleaning up the entire area, including the leftovers of 4 RAR – beer cans, general rubbish and some ammunition left lying around.

From the weapon pits the men could use their guns and be protected from incoming fire so keeping them clean was most important. The machine gun bunkers were always manned but if an attack came and a 'stand-to' was called, the men would jump into their allocated pits, which needed to be clear of any obstructions.

As it turned out, very late on the first night the battalion arrived a mortar attack was carried out on another part of the base and a stand-to was called. When Frank responded and landed in his pit, it became quite apparent that some work needed to be done and the pit cleaned out.

While the mortar attack gave the men cause for concern that night, in the first few days there was no time to be overly reflective or worried. It was a very busy time, with much to do. Scrounging was a high priority. A wander around the area would occasionally produce valuable finds that could be turned into something to make the tent more comfortable. Boxes that would make rudimentary tables or chairs were always sought after. Pin-ups were fixed to lockers and personal effects stowed neatly – anything to remind them of home.

One evening when the men had finished for the day, Frank went for a short walk to see what was what. This was all new and fresh to him and the rest of the platoon but he came across those who had been there a long time, some with over half their tour completed and others nearing the end. Those men were more grizzled, more fixed on going home and more inclined to assume an air of indifference to all things military. Voices came at him from the grey-faced veterans whose jungle greens were not so green, whose brass was unpolished, whose boots were not so shiny and whose bodies and eyes showed the effects of their journey. 'You'll be sorry. You've got another year, we've got four weeks.'

Frank asked one what to expect. 'What's it like?'

'You'll learn, mate, you'll find out. It's nothing like training, the Nogs will show you that.'

That worried Frank and he talked about it later in the tent, but in the end he knew their training would serve them well; after all, surely the trainers knew what they were doing?

There wasn't much time to dwell on it though, as it wasn't long before 3 Platoon was ordered to undertake an orientation exercise. APCs took them out into the rubber during the day and they stayed out overnight. The APCs formed up in a sort of 'circle the wagons' way and the platoon camped in the middle. The exercise was designed to indoctrinate the men into the jungle at night: the blackness of the dark and the sounds, mysterious and unidentifiable.

A couple of days later the platoon was sent on a tactical area of responsibility, or TAOR, patrol. Now they had taken over and replaced 4 RAR as a fighting battalion, these patrols were assigned to the men of 6 RAR. Designed to deter the VC from attacking the base by creating activity in the jungle, the patrols were also intended to prevent the enemy from moving into the nearby settled areas without fear of being engaged by the Australians, and to make it more difficult for them to move as they liked from their bases around the area. The patrols didn't last long at all, but gave the VC something to think about.

The TAORs were an introduction to the jungle or, as the soldiers called it, the 'Jay'. It was also an introduction to fear. It wasn't so much the Jay that worried them, it was the unknown, the silence and the sounds they knew they'd need to get used to fast.

Frank worried about becoming edgy, about how that edginess would affect him and the others. Safely back in the Dat, the fear subsided, but in the back of his mind he was thinking about next time. What would happen then?

Chapter 11
THE REAL STUFF BEGINS

O n 30 May 1969, some 10 days after 6 RAR arrived in Vietnam, Operation Lavarack began. This was the battalion's first operation, a month-long reconnaissance mission aimed at restricting the VC's use of its main communication roads and tracks around Nui Dat and in the rubber plantations and farming areas. The battalion was told there were no significant enemy forces in the area, in particular no strong combat forces. However, unbeknown to the commanding officers, the VC had gathered in greater numbers than any since the Battle of Long Tan in 1965. Operation Lavarack was supposed to be an introduction, a warm-up before any major operation so the battalion could have everything working properly under combat conditions. It turned out to be nothing of the sort.

The monsoon season had started by the time the battalion headed out. The rain would increase in intensity and volume throughout the operation and the ground would become more waterlogged and muddy and small creeks would either flood or spring up as the water ran freely the longer it went. A fire support base (FSB) named Virginia had been set up where supporting artillery fire could be given to the patrolling platoons over most of the area of operation (AO). When the FSB was completed, A Company was taken by APCs to the base to begin its own operation close to a rubber plantation, and patrolling began. From there A Company set out to ambush the VC at the junctions of the jungle tracks and find out exactly what they were up to.

*

Patrolling was the day-to-day routine of the infantryman, moving stealthily through the landscape to locate enemy patrols and to find and destroy their camps or supply depots. Most patrolling was done in the jungle, the Jay, on tracks where it was thick and dense or in the 'bush or scrub' as the men knew it, which was more open with small bushes, smaller trees and large clumps of elephant grass every few metres. Whether the patrol was in the open or on the tracks there was the danger of mines or booby-traps or of the watching VC.

Men were attacked frequently by ants and in the wet season by leeches that seemed to appear from nowhere and attach themselves to any piece of skin they could find. When patrolling in the thick jungle there were always gaps or, more rarely, tracks that were followed. Sometimes, when they were needed, machetes and bayonets were used to slash a way through but that was extremely noisy so was kept to an absolute minimum. In the open areas the humidity was as big a concern as the rain. Men struggled with the huge loads they carried, sweating and at times gasping for breath with the humidity. In the wet, mud clung to boots and the vegetation reached out like green sticky fingers to grab at the body. It was a debilitating and dangerous existence.

Some of these areas had been defoliated by the Americans using chemicals including the destructive and toxic Agent Orange. While this denied cover for the VC and destroyed food crops, it was only partially effective as the trees and scrub grew back and after each wet season the spraying needed to be done again. The use of Agent Orange was so widespread that there were not many, if any, soldiers who were not exposed to it. The chemical was in the water they bathed in and on the ground they lay on at night. Some even drank it when they filled canteens from streams or waterholes that were simply rain-filled bomb craters. The water there quite often had a slightly milky white appearance and even with purifying tablets added would still prove to be a dangerous concoction. Over the years, some soldiers had the experience of American helicopters or planes flying overhead and spraying the trees above them. During the war, America used over 75 million litres of Agent Orange.

It wasn't only the jungle that was sprayed with chemicals; the use of dieldrin in Nui Dat was extensive in combating disease-carrying mosquitos and illness borne in the latrine pits of the 'long drop' toilets. Several times a week a jeep with fogging equipment would drive through the lines, spraying and fogging chemicals over anything that moved and every-thing that didn't. Soldiers in Vietnam were exposed to many risks, not only bullets or mines from the enemy, but other menaces such as this, most of them from their own side.

*

Frank was a forward scout, the soldier who heads out in front of his section of the platoon, checking out the landscape, looking and listening for sounds, smells and whatever else he might find that would alert him to the presence of the enemy. In 8 Section

Frank was the lead scout and Mick was the second. The two men would change places and take the lead in rotation. Forward scout was a dangerous position. Contacts could come at any time. The man in the lead was the one most vulnerable; he could be the first to die in any action. Across open ground he might be 20 or more metres ahead of the spread-out soldiers, in rubber planta- tions just 15 metres ahead of the men in single file. On the tracks through the dense jungle and where the forward scout needed to machete his way through, the men were closer together still while always in sight of the scout ahead of them. The forward scout was his men's eyes and ears, alerting them to lurking danger and at the same time being in the most perilous position. At times the men would speak in low murmurs or whispers but mostly silence was paramount, with hand signals telling those behind what was happening. About 30 signals were used along with others devel- oped by each platoon. All knew what they meant.

Frank and Mick had trained for the job in Townsville and Canungra but on the ground it was completely different. Some scouts were circumspect but Frank had been a bit cocky before he actually arrived. He thought he'd have no problems, that it would be the same as training, to an extent. He soon discovered it wasn't the same as Canungra, no matter how much he told himself it was. Canungra had metal dummies that jumped out at you from cover. You knew you were safe. Canungra didn't have VC some- where around you, hidden from view, who wanted to kill you.

Out in front of a section, Frank was vulnerable, always on edge, the tension almost intolerable as he waited and wondered if and when a contact would come. There would be relief after a couple of hours or so when either Mick, or the next section of the platoon, would go to the front of the patrol, but there would never be any respite from being alert, no respite from the worry of missing something. Then, after the break and seemingly too soon, Frank had to go back to the front again, watching silently, listening closely.

*

Each morning Platoon Commander Lieutenant Peter Hines would tell the section leaders what the aim was for that day: where they needed to go, what they would try to find. The leaders would then relay those messages to the men. Patrolling would continue until Hines called for a night harbour and the men set about the established routine, working in pairs digging a shell-scrape for the night – a shallow pit some 30 centimetres deep that almost hid their prone bodies and provided rudimentary protection if they were mortared or attacked during the night. They'd pitch their two-man tents, unsling their thin swag mattresses and then cook their evening meal, all of it to be finished by sunset when each man would 'stand to' in a position of readiness to defend their position against attack. Then they'd search for whatever sleep they could find. They'd be up in a short while doing their turn as piquet on one of the machine guns at the ends of the harbour with the 'clackers' to trigger the Claymores close at hand. Two men at a time would be there for two hours, with relief staggered. At one stage the army issued a pneumatic blow-up sort of mattress but those were chucked out quickly. They made too much noise when the men moved while sleeping. 'Useless' was the general assessment.

The jungle was dark at night, and on Operation Lavarack it was wet – horribly, constantly, mind-numbingly wet. Monsoonal rain nearly all day and most of the night was depressing, debilitating and frustrating. Light from the moon or stars never poked through the dense covering.

At night, whatever the weather, the jungle came alive. Many times Frank found sleep difficult. His imagination kicked in, his mind wandered, his eyes flicking through the darkness and his ears alert to every sound. *What's that? A cricket or a lizard? Do they even have crickets here? What's that rustling beneath the crap on the jungle floor? Fuck those whining mozzies! Bloody hell, that artillery's loud tonight. Wonder what's going on over there, that's an M60. Wish I could sleep. Bloody rain, doesn't it ever stop? I've got piquet in an hour. Gotta have a piss. Gotta remember to go past the gun pit and tell 'em. Don't want the pricks shooting at me out there. I'd have a shit too but the soldier ants'll get me. Geez, it's dark. Dawn soon, then we'll stand-to and be off again. Wish I could sleep. Fuckin' rain!*

*

As this was the first operation, the men were more tired than usual, not only because of the unfamiliarity and the weather. Hines, the Skip, had ordered an extra week's rations to be carried and 2000 extra rounds of ammunition for the machine guns. He was concerned that on the first operation there might be a bad firefight and he didn't want to be caught short. If everything worked the way it should there would be a resupply every five days but it was better to be safe. Resupplies were conducted by Hueys flying in everything the platoon needed to stay in the field. The load was hauled out of the chopper as quickly as possible, as the Hueys were always exposed to the possibility of enemy fire.

Normally men would carry one belt of ammunition for the M60 but with Hines' order now they had to carry two, a total weight of over 10 kilograms. With their own ammunition and the extra, and their pack, each man was lumping a combined weight of about 50 kilograms. The difficulty was amply demonstrated when waiting for the APCs to take them out. The men in the platoon were of varying shapes and sizes, not all of them scrawny, but not overly muscular either. But they were all very fit. Standing around was making one of the lance corporals tired so he decided to conserve a bit of energy. He sat down with his pack and all the extra gear he was asked to carry still on his shoulders. When the time came to leave, and much to the amusement of his mates, he couldn't get up.

After only a few hours out from the FSB, the rain had seeped into every crack in the soldiers' gear and every pore of their skin. A few days later it had rotted their jungle greens, which became weaker and consequently tore easily when caught on a tree branch. The knees on some of the men's trousers were holed, the crutch hung down to about where the knees should have been, shirts were torn and everything was caked with mud. For whatever reason, the 'resupp' that was supposed to happen every five days had been extended to 10. On each resupp the men would send back their greens to be washed communally and a second lot would be sent out. This time no fresh clothes arrived. When a new lot eventually was sent and the old ones arrived in Nui Dat, sometimes they were not washed, they were just taken out and burned. Underwear was never a problem because no one, or at least very few, ever wore it. If it wasn't sweat rash and sand rubbing in the nether regions it was rain, so the vast majority of soldiers let it all hang out. Tinea and crotch rot were always a concern and it wasn't long before Frank's crotch started to show signs of it. His skin was red raw and painful.

'Have a look at this, will ya?' he asked Platoon Medic Graeme Davis one evening.

'Shit, Frank, I'll have to do something here. Drop your greens.'

In the jungle in the middle of a sweaty, humid war, there was no room for embarrassment with the blokes you were fighting with. Frank did as he was told and Davis treated the affliction with the cure-all Condy's Crystals, mixing it with water to form a pinky-coloured solution. Davis applied it front and rear and when Frank bent over so the task could be completed, he painted a 'W' on either cheek of Frank's behind, whispering 'Wow' and chuckling to himself at his cleverness.

*

In early June, some two weeks into Operation Lavarack, B Company was involved in a significant contact that resulted in a huge firefight. A Company, being the closest, was ordered to go in as reinforcements. They headed off mid-morning with 3 Platoon in the vanguard. Frank led them out into extremely dense jungle but on a well-defined track. Moving carefully and watchfully through the trees, Frank's progress became slower and slower. He was worried and kept signalling to Mick behind him that he could hear the sound of rifle bolts.

The jungle is difficult for scouts, hard to read. There's the rustle of the trees, bird songs, dropping twigs, all manner of sounds. It can be very quiet at other times and when there is a little bit of noise, that noise becomes more obvious. What those noises are can be hard to determine. There are noises that are not easily defined, certainly not by young men two weeks into a foreign country's thick landscape.

Frank was careful; he would never lead the men into anything he was suspicious of. It was his responsibility, he thought, to make sure they were as safe as they could be. This was no different but the company had been told to get to the fighting without delay. This was a delay. Hines had been asked in no uncertain terms by CHQ what the holdup was, so he went forward to see for himself.

'What's going on?' he quietly asked Mick.

When told what Frank had heard, Hines dismissed it out of hand.

'They don't have rifle bolts. Just get out there and get going,' he told Mick.

Mick took over from Frank and went as fast as he could, hoping no VC were out there lying in ambush – or if something or someone was there, that he would get his shot off first. Mick was as careful as Frank, but this time he had been told to 'get going', so he had no choice. He'd made a conscious decision: if shit happens, then shit happens. There wasn't much he could do about it; he just hoped that if he did run into anything he could get down or get a shot off. As always, his finger was poised, ready to pull the trigger of his SLR. When the platoon eventually reached B Company, they found men who were drawn, grey and dirty and looked physically and emotionally spent after an extensive firefight with the enemy. Mick had heard the expression from the French war in Indochina: 'Like Christ on the Cross'. That's what sprang into his mind.

The enemy had left well before 3 Platoon arrived; the firefight was over, so new orders sent them off into the Jay again.

Chapter 12

TESTING TIMES

Most days were repetitive. The platoon would cease patrol about half an hour before dark, which the men thought was too late for all they were required to do. The night harbour would be set with an M60 at each end and an ambush-type configuration of men who had set Claymores ready to be activated if need be. Shell-scrapes were dug. There was little time, or inclination, for talking. Or at least not for meaningful talk, as the men were either digging scrapes or making their meagre evening meal from their ration pack. Like most things between the two men who were paired up, it was done alternately. One would be digging while the other was in the kitchen, so to speak. By this time darkness was usually approaching and the men were tired and would be more so after their night duties had finished.

Orders had arrived before the operation began saying that the Reos, the men who had joined the platoon in Nui Dat, were not allowed to do piquets and man the M60s. While the Reos had finished training in Australia, those higher up the chain of command thought that as they had not been trained with the battalion, they didn't know the way the battalion or the platoon worked. Reos were said to be inexperienced. The orders also said they could not be teamed together; they had to be with someone from the original platoon. Frank was separated from Mick. They would still patrol together but Frank was now teamed with Peter Hoskin for a few days before he and Jim Kelly became a pair.

The men thought all that was 'bullshit. What would they know? And anyway it's really stupid.'

Nonetheless, orders had to be obeyed. It meant there were extra duties for all the other men, something less than pleasing. In between sentry duties, digging scrapes, making a meal and spending two hours on the M60, the men were supposed to have time for sleep. But extra of everything made it difficult for any continuity of sleep. The nights when heavy rains came were even worse. While men managed four or five hours a night on average, it was usually broken into blocks of two hours at a time. The sleep that did arrive for the exhausted men was deep. Unless it rained. They'd be wet, then they'd dry out in the warm night, then they'd get wet again.

Night time brought mixed emotions for all the men. Some took what was happening in their stride, others worried. Some were confident, or at least appeared to be to the others. All had more than a little fear. Frank admitted as much to Jim Kelly, hoping others felt the way he did.

Daily routine started a short time before dawn when stand–to was called. The men would be in combat position, still, silent and ready, for about half an hour before stand-down. Then weapons were cleaned, breakfast was eaten, scrapes filled in and the camp cleared. At daylight patrolling began and didn't stop until setting up camp as the light faded. The stand-to routine was again followed.

Mick, Frank and a few others talked about the pressures they felt. They knew there was simply not enough time to get everything done when they were patrolling until dark and then beginning again before daylight. The men's moods were starting to become ragged at the edges. They knew what they were expected to do was too much, too dangerous. Too many men were affected. It wasn't as if they were slacking off at night. Nothing was being left to chance, but with the Reos not being allowed to do anything and the full day occupied with patrolling, the strain on too few was too much. None of the men considered it was their fault; it was the army's. It just made an already difficult life that much harder.

Mick knew first-hand how tiredness was causing problems. After a resupply the men were all in their clean jungle greens and when they came to a small creek, Hines didn't want them to wade through the water, thinking he'd protect the clothes for at least a short time. He ordered the men to cross via a tree that had fallen between the banks. Mick was in the lead at the time and cautiously stepped his way across the slithery, lichen-covered log. He'd almost reached the other side when he slipped and fell into the mangrove-type roots of the jungle trees. Had his head hit one of the roots he could quite easily have been killed. He began trying to disentangle himself, weighed down by his pack and the extra gear he was carrying. He was almost exhausted trying to extricate himself from his predicament when Hines, at the rear, relayed a message asking what the holdup was and if everything was OK.

Frank, crouched in the shrubs, called out quietly, 'You right, Mick? Skip's asking if it's OK.'

Mick was exasperated and muttered to Frank that he thought it was bloody impossible.

Frank, not aware of what had happened to Mick, innocently but without thought, relayed that message to Hines.

'Mick says it's impossible.'

Not surprisingly, nothing is impossible in the army. Even if those asking the question thought something was impossible, they'd still ask the lower ranks to achieve it. Under the log, stuck in the tree roots, Mick was almost in a state of shock. He didn't mean it was impossible in the literal sense, just that his position was impossible. That was not how it came out. When the platoon finally crossed the log, Hines unloaded on him.

'What's wrong with you? Don't tell me it's impossible! Straighten everything up; put those rounds on your shoulder in your pack!'

Mick was utterly drained. He was tired, his strength had gone and he was speechless. He saw it was pointless trying to tell him what had actually happened, as Skip was in no mood for explanations. He sat on the ground, saturated, took the belts of 100 M60 rounds off his shoulder and shoved them in the bottom of his pack.

After the month-long operation had finished, in an unusual move, the Battalion Commander, Lieutenant Colonel David Butler, held a meeting with the troops, excluding the NCOs and other officers. He wanted to know how everything was going, whether there were any problems the men wanted to raise or things that could be done better. The men spoke up, telling Butler that they were patrolling too long in the afternoon, too close to sunset. They explained their concerns and said they were run ragged with the extra duties caused by the policy around the Reos. Butler agreed and changed the routine. Reos ception...

could and had to do everything in the platoon, they could not be hidden away any longer; they would do their share. The men were happy; they knew it would make a big difference to morale. After all, it wasn't as though they were knocking off for the day and going back to base when they harboured up for the night; they were still out there in an ambush situation and prepared for a fight. But they would be better prepared for the night if they had more time, so a more even-handed approach to duty was taken.

*

It wasn't long before A Company swung into action. In the first week of June they'd come across a large VC bunker system, the entrances disguised by rudimentary bamboo-thatched doorways and protected by a large force with RPGs (rocket propelled grenades) among their weapons. 1 and 2 Platoons had engaged the enemy while 3 Platoon was sent to wait in reserve behind a ridge until needed. Holding a firm base, 3 Platoon did not become directly involved. As darkness fell, 1 and 2 Platoons disengaged from the fierce firefight and returned to the base held by 3 Platoon. The company had a 50 percent stand-to during the night due to the closeness of the bunker system, which was abandoned by the VC during the night.

It was a week later when 3 Platoon's first direct contact with the enemy came while ambushing one of the many tracks in the area. This ambush site, offering a small clearing, was what the soldiers knew as a selected 'killing ground'.

A machine gun was set up at each end with 7 and 9 Sections as the ambush group facing the site and 8 Section set as rear defence. The first two sections had managed to dig shallow shell-scrapes and faced the ambush site. 8 Section had no time for digging, they were facing the other direction, and simply waited in case the enemy came around the side to the rear. This section was to be used as the sweeping party, so when the contact was over they would get up and sweep through the area to make sure there was no enemy left, pick up weapons, check for bodies and generally make sure it was safe. The other sections had put Claymore mines out and set up the M60s. Soon a group of about 10 enemy came down the track but, from a distance of some 20 metres away, sensed something was amiss, turned and ran.

Leigh Floyd fired a bank of three Claymores and the machine gunners fired long bursts into the jungle. Even though two of the enemy were killed, the rest stayed to fight, firing back towards the ambush and keeping the platoon at bay.

Frank and the rest of 8 Section were facing the other way, so they had no idea what was happening. All they could hear was the din of exploding mines and chattering machine gun fire. Even from short distances and shouting at the top of their voices, it was difficult to hear what their mate was saying. The only thing they knew was that they were sweating more than usual, their blood was pumping and their hearts galloping faster than they could ever have imagined. Enemy fire was still landing in the vicinity, with bullets zinging and cracking in the air across their heads. Dirt was kicked up, bark flew off trees, small twigs dropped broken from the trees, and all the while the men had to stay where they were and hope they were not shot up the backside.

Jesus! Frank thought to himself. *I hope that doesn't get any closer.*

The packs the men carried offered some protection, but they were trying to press themselves into the soft earth of the jungle floor as well as keep their minds active and hoping they would not be attacked from behind.

The firefight carried on for half an hour or more and the small group of enemy was holding the platoon at bay. Hines didn't want it to go much longer; he didn't want to be pinned down. When he thought it had gone on long enough, he yelled to 8 Section: 'Right, get up and start the sweep now.'

That meant coming from the rear of the action and sweeping through the ambush 'killing ground' – an area with no cover, no place to hide, no protection when bullets started flying, a place that you wanted to get out of as quickly as you could – earlier than would normally have been the case. But this was no normal sweep; the enemy was still there. Frank, hunched over and treading gingerly, headed off through the thick vegetation, followed by the others. All he knew was that there were people out there who would be more than happy to kill him and his mates and were looking to do just that. Frank led the section in single file. When they reached the killing ground, they would form an extended line then spread out into a clearing next to a huge tree about five metres in front of them.

As the men moved forward, a huge explosion split the air – the thunder of an RPG that had been fired at them but luckily had hit a big tree instead. These were no small arms. RPGs were Soviet-made weapons that had to be held across the top of the shoulder to be fired and could stop Centurion tanks. The mess they made when hitting infantry was devastating.

The noise as the grenade exploded was almost deafening. The VC had tried to bounce it off a tree so that it exploded in the midst of the section, sending shrapnel everywhere and damaging as many as possible. This time it didn't work.

At the front, Frank had just moved into the open space of the killing ground. He dropped to one knee and yelled, 'Contact, front, get down!' He fired off a burst from his Armalite and then, a few seconds later, let off another burst.

'Bloody shakin' legs,' he said to himself as he realised what was happening to him. 'Stay still.'

He was trying to steady his body but he couldn't steady his heart.

'They're over there, I can see 'em!' he said to no one in particular as he fired another short burst.

Frank had seen movement behind a tree about 50 metres away across the clearing and after he fired he believed he'd hit two of them. There were only about five of them but Frank was convinced one was wearing a tiger suit.

A tiger suit? he thought. *What the fuck's going on?*

Why he saw that, he had no idea. What was it that caused his mind to see that? Was it really a tiger suit? Was it stress or anxiety, or was it real? Either way, he'd thought about it for only a few seconds.

'Get down, Frank, get out of the way,' came the desperate cries from the crew that Frank had blocked from using the machine gun. Frank was supposed to be prone so the M60 could fire over the top of him. The noise from the guns had blocked his ears and when they cleared, he grimaced inwardly, relieved that he was still alive. He began to crawl backwards, knowing he was in the way and he needed to get back to the relative safety of the jungle cover. As he crawled slowly back towards the rest of the section, he knew he had given the enemy something to think about.

The firing kept up, bursts of AK47s from what seemed out of nowhere. It was a stalemate; the action was going nowhere, so Hines made a decision. 'Right, we've got to finish this!'

He ordered the whole platoon to stand up and move forward. This action flushed the remaining VC out of their positions, with one wounded as they fled. The ambush had resulted in two VC killed and several wounded. No one from 3 Platoon was wounded.

This was the platoon's initiation. Frank knew nothing could be any clearer. This was all very real and whether you were killed or wounded or escaped unharmed was all a matter of luck. The enemy couldn't be seen, there was nothing ahead but jungle. All he was doing, all that any of them were doing, was going on instinct and their training. Hopefully that would be enough, but the nerve ends were fraying long before any contact came and the reactions kicked in.

The platoon came out of the jungle and headed off down the track. More patrolling was the order. Potentially, more of the same but certainly more rain, more darkness, more unknowns, more anxiety and sweating. More fear.

That night, Hines called a 50 percent stand-to, which meant it was shared. While one of the paired men slept in their meagre shell-scrape the other was on sentry duty. There was little or no talk among the men. In each hootchie men were lost in their own thoughts, trying desperately, to no avail, to stay dry or, at the very least, not to get soaking wet – another almost impossible task.

Frank was exceptionally tired but did his share. In the short time allowed for sleep, Frank lay awake for a while and suffered the drips on his head while he thought about it all. He thought about whether he'd made a mistake, whether he'd 'fucked up'. He knew he should have gone to ground and he knew his Armalite would not have had the impact an M60 would have. Maybe the whole lot of the enemy would have been killed by the M60 if he'd gone to ground when he should have. But to some extent he justified what he had done and he was happy about his reaction. He didn't freeze, as he had heard some in other actions and tours had done, and he didn't 'shit himself' as others had admitted to doing. He did his job.

Frank thought about the men he'd shot at. As much as he was full of bravado and thought he could do his job well, the last two weeks had brought home to him in no uncertain terms where he was and what he was doing. This was another world. He wondered if the men he'd shot were alive, if they had families. Right from the start he had prayed that whoever he came across while scouting they wouldn't be a woman or a child. He knew they posed as much of a danger as any grown man and that many women and children had been used as decoys and grenade carriers. If he was called on to fire at them, he hoped he'd make the right choice – his mates or the enemy. He slept fitfully, thinking about a man in a tiger suit. He also knew that in the morning he would get up and he and his mates would go out and do it all again. For Frank, Birchip seemed so far away.

*

Two days later, 3 Platoon were patrolling along the edge of the jungle when they came to a rubber plantation – rows and rows of trees with the ground cleared underneath them. Moving closer, the men started to enter when a group of local people began walking towards them. Frank watched them carefully. The rules of engagement for the Australians were very strict, in order to prevent civilian casualties. You could not fire unless you clearly identified an enemy by his uniform or a weapon he was carrying, or if you were fired on. But not all the enemy wore uniforms. One of the instructions the men had been issued with on arrival was to watch out for the enemy, as they would be wearing black pyjama-like clothes. The problem was, as Frank had pointed out in frustration, 'All of 'em over here wear them; how are we supposed to tell the difference?'

As Frank was in the lead at the time, he dropped to his knee and prepared to shoot. He thought it was a VC force and his duty as lead scout was to warn and protect the platoon.

'Hold on, Frank, hold your fire!' Hines yelled.

Hines had received information that something was happening in the village of Binh Ba and civilians were heading out. He was told to check the identity of those people and to make sure they were all civilians. They were and the group shuffled away as quickly as they could, scared and leaving the little they had behind. A local company of the North Vietnamese Army – the NVA – backed by Viet Cong had infiltrated the village and were beginning to slaughter all those who were seen as enemy collaborators, and those who did not wish to succumb to the Communist regime.

The 6 RAR warm-up operation was by now heating up. In the first two weeks there had been 55 contacts across the battalion. While 6 RAR kept patrolling along the tracks leading to Binh Ba, looking for and engaging any enemy that tried to escape, the reaction company from Nui Dat D Company 5 RAR and the Centurion tanks of 1st Armoured Corps were sent in to clear the village. VC survivors came out of hiding, mixing with the civilians who were fleeing the village as well. It was extremely difficult to determine who was who. The fighting lasted two days and nights and was to become the longest battle of the war in which Australians were involved.

*

A Company returned to Nui Dat on 2 July, tired, dirty, dishevelled but happy with how they'd performed. Weapon cleaning, body cleaning and fresh uniforms were the first items on the agenda, followed closely by a trip to the company 'boozer' to wash away some internal complaints.

The men's stinking jungle greens had been sent to the wash. Hopefully they'd be burnt. Frank had showered and changed, trying to clean off the jungle feel and, most of all, the smell. The Jay had a smell of its own, as did Vietnam in general. It never left you. You could forget the names of the towns and villages you went through, the areas, the dates you were there, the names of other soldiers you came across sometime, some-where. But the smell you never forget. It's the smell of dank jungle, the smell of decaying animals and plants, the stench of open sewers in the villages or the smoke of rocket fire and phosphorus. It's the smell of death, either imagined or at hand.

Wash as they might, the smell either stayed or, if it did go, was soon replaced by another smell. There were solutions, though. As long as you weren't scheduled for piquet duty, a trip to the boozer would fix it. There, a good dose of VB or XXXX or, for those who didn't have tastebuds, Tooheys, would sometimes wash away thoughts of the jungle and the smells. The reprieve was only temporary, though, because when morning came, when sobriety reared its head, it all came back whether you admitted it or not. There were other things to think about then, as it wouldn't be long before you and your mates were all back out in the jungle.

Operation Lavarack, while supposed to be the usual quiet introductory operation, turned out to be something much more than that. There had been 85 contacts with the enemy and 6 RAR had cleared Phuoc Tuy province of many VC and NVA units. The operation was meant to test the battalion in each of its elements under hostile conditions. They were sent to what had been thought of as a relatively quiet area with no reason to suspect it was any different. However, 6 RAR spent the whole month in testing conditions. They'd been in Vietnam just six weeks and later it was said to be the most intense introduction to Vietnam of any unit at any time.

Chapter 13
PLEASURES OF A 'FUNNY COUNTRY'

After settling back in at the Dat, there were a couple of days to enjoy the delights of Vung Tau, called an R&C, rest in country leave – or a '36-hour rec leave', as the soldiers knew it.

Frank and the others from his section headed off in trucks to the decaying port town which once had seen the splendour of the French colonial period. While vestiges of the architecture were still obvious through the ravages of time and war, Vung Tau was a place where just about anything and everything was on offer. The men could lie on the beach or surf if they were inclined to, they could wander around the dirty streets filled with stalls or they could avail themselves of other delights. 'Vungers' was another world.

The streets were a maelstrom of movement: bikes, minicabs, pedicabs, trishaws, carts, cars both rusty and newish, and people, including exotic women, walking everywhere. The men were free to do as they wished, and most did: beer, beach and brothels, not necessarily in that order. The first taste of Vungers was freedom to those young men brought up in the restrictive, conservative world of Australia. Vungers was like living in a fantasy, albeit one that they could never have imagined.

On arrival the soldiers were lectured by senior officers, doctors and even the battalion religious leaders about the pitfalls of Vungers: about how they were visitors and not to bring Australia into disrepute; about those who were married remembering their wives; about making sure they were in before curfew otherwise they'd be in trouble and, most of all, about using condoms. But it all fell on deaf ears. This was no time for lectures on moral standards and dangerous diseases. After all, the men had taken chances a lot more serious than these and when let loose went for it with endeavour. Many paid a price, not only in money, with a high rate among the troops of venereal diseases of varying degrees of seriousness. These were ordinary young blokes looking forward to extraordinary times – which were what they found.

The men mostly stayed in the Peter Badcoe Club, a beachside resort a short distance from the town centre, named after the major who won a Victoria Cross in Vietnam. In a typical Australian way, after Prime Minister Harold Holt drowned, an Olympic-sized swimming pool was built and named, appropriately, the Harold Holt Swimming Pool. It was at the Badcoe Club that men stored their rifles, dressed in civilian clothes and headed out for the town. The club was somewhere safe for all those who needed safety at night, and somewhere they could rest in the knowledge that others around them were their own kind.

There was much to be wary of, though. Vung Tau was not immune to Viet Cong infiltrators and there were instances of grenades being exploded in bars or indiscriminate shootings in the back alleys and streets. Some of the bar girls were reputed VC informers but it was impossible to tell who they were. Then there were the 'White Mice', the Vietnamese National Police, who would often shoot first and ask questions later if they felt it was warranted.

Virtually anything that was to someone's liking could be found in the town. Vungers boasted plenty of shops with souvenirs for those who were so inclined, plenty of bars with plenty of beer, and plenty of young, sensuous Asian women who offered services beyond the wildest dreams of most of the young soldiers frequenting these establishments. The women also had souvenirs, but not of the kind any of the men wanted. The welcome from the bar girls entailed pleading to be bought Saigon tea, basically a coloured soft drink, in return for their attention and later, after he was drunk enough and an agreed price was struck, anything the men desired.

'You want sucky suck? Fucky fuck? Number one short time? Long time?'

And, with hands placed strategically on the young soldier's crotch: 'You come with me, beeg boy!'

Rejection was frowned upon by the girls. A ditty emerged from the bars and became a favourite of the soldiers. Anyone who served in Vietnam knows it. Called 'Cheap Charl-ee' or 'The Bar Girls' Lament', it is sung to the tune of 'This Old Man'. *Uc dai loi* means 'Australian' or 'men from the south'.

Uc dai loi, Cheap Charl-ee
He no buy me Saigon tea
Saigon tea cost many, many P
Uc dai loi he Cheap Charl-ee.

Uc dai loi, Cheap Charl-ee
He no go to bed with me
For it cost him many, many P
Uc dai loi he Cheap Charl-ee.

In other verses Cheap Charl-ee would try to 'get one for free', upset the mama-san, leave the woman with a baby and go home across the sea.

Another popular attraction was '100P Alley', a place where a 'short time' against the wall or with a girl kneeling in some shadowy doorway could be had for that price, a bargain when you consider that one Aussie dollar was worth about 1200 piastres.

If you wanted a haircut, then you could sit in the barber's chair and have your hair trimmed, your fingernails done, your feet massaged and, if you paid a few more P, one of the girls would lift the protective sheet and attend by various means to other more sensitive parts of your body.

*

Frank and a squad of mates made the journey into town and spent many hours in the bars, enjoying the facilities. One time Frank and four others, including the battalion's padre 'Tank' Nolan, were drinking VB stubbies in a bar with two black American medics who had a most unenviable job, probably the worst of all. They would rise before dawn and head out into the previous day's battlefields in the jungle to bring in the bodies of their dead comrades. They wore hospital masks dipped in vinegar but the smell of death was constant. Sometimes they'd find someone alive, but it was rare. And they were always afraid that the VC were watching and ready to open fire because they were not quite done. Drinking helped. The drinks vanished swiftly and more were ordered. The process continued: order a drink, swill it down and get another. That way the stories became surreal. Even Padre Nolan had no answers from his area of expertise as to what it all meant.

Later in the night, two white American MPs came through the door and wandered over to where the men were drinking.

'What are you doin' drinkin' with these black cocksuckers?' one said to Frank.

It might have been the bravado of the drink or the change in his personality brought on by what he'd recently seen and done, but to Frank, the small but indignant Australian soldier, it was something he'd never experienced. Quixote-like, he flew at the MPs and an all-in fight – which included the padre – began. Punches flew everywhere, with the MPs backing off and trying in vain to restore order. The fight was soon joined by everyone in the bar and the Aussies managed to hold their own while the two medics escaped, leaving the others to explain the chaos. The padre spoke to the MPs, eventually convincing them to leave well enough alone, and they departed the scene.

The next day, in the Grand Hotel, a resplendent old-time building in the centre of Vung Tau, Frank and a few others sat around drinking 'tinnies' and discussing the night's activities before they dispersed and headed off to follow their own agendas. Frank should have stayed. He had to rush to beat the 10 pm curfew at the Badcoe Club. The illogical nature of army life was on show at curfew time. If you were going to miss the deadline it was better and easier to stay somewhere safe in town if you could, because if you arrived back at the Badcoe too late, you could be up on a charge.

Frank and a few others from the platoon were wandering around the streets laden with cartons of beer when they spied some MPs looking for miscreants. They scattered and Frank found himself opposite the Rest and Convalescence Club lying on a verandah of the local funeral director among the coffins waiting for bodies – of Vietnamese dead, not Australians. He'd heard the story about two soldiers trying to hide from the MPs and White Mice while making their way back to the R&C

Club after curfew. The men were so drunk they had snuck into two coffins, pulled the lids over them and fallen asleep. In the morning the funeral director's wife and daughter were on the verandah when the lids were raised and the two bodies sat up. The poor ladies ran from the place screaming and frantically waving their arms.

Somehow Frank and his mates met up again and, weaving a zig-zag course through the streets, they eventually caught one of the last taxis around. By the time they returned to the Badcoe any semblance of order or decorum had disappeared. On their return, a party was still in full swing. The company commander, Major Peter Belt, formed everyone up and tried to march them into the pool. Many followed orders but others stopped at the edge, much to Belt's chagrin.

*

The trip back to Nui Dat was quiet. The rec leave enabled the release of all the anxiety accumulated over the first operation. No matter whether they realised it or not, the men were filled with tension and apprehension about what was happening and in Vungers it had, for a short time, disappeared.

Heads were aching, bodies were tired and minds were not where they wanted to be. As the trucks bumped along, wind whipping across their faces, wooden seats uncomfortable and the heat penetrating every pore of their skin, the men were silent, each thinking about the next time they went out.

Chapter 14
INTO THE UNKNOWN

On 14 July 1969, two weeks after returning from Operation Lavarack and only two months since arriving, the battalion was scheduled to head off on another operation. Apart from the visit to Vung Tau, the fortnight had not been restful. The other two battalions that occupied Nui Dat were away on operations of their own so defence and security were left to 6 RAR.

Apart from maintenance issues and replacement and cleaning of equipment, the men conducted TAOR patrols, manned the guns on the fence line, and were on stand-by to react to any problems arising in the AO. There was virtually no rest, only the time spent after hours – mainly in the boozer. However, for these two weeks, the rifle companies were not constantly on guard against, or looking for, contacts with the enemy. That, at least, was something.

After one TAOR, A Company was sent out on a short operation to an area near the village of Thai Thien that was full of mangrove swamps and creeks and an agricultural area that provided a major food supply to the VC. Frank's second scout was now Tony Muir as Mick was on light duties because of a rash he'd found on his skin that needed treating. Muir, a Tasmanian called 'Shorty' because of his diminutive size, was a Nasho and when his call-up letter had arrived he knew he had to do what he was told. Philosophically he was against the war, but knew he couldn't really get out of it.

3 Platoon was again at the forefront of the action when they found a bunker system that had been occupied the previous night by what was estimated to have been around 80 VC, an unusually large force. Once the bunkers were cleared and destroyed after they'd seized mines and AK47s from them, Frank and Muir led the men carefully and slowly towards the village. They slogged their way through rice paddies and low scrubby vegetation, and finally into fishermen's huts. As they searched the series of thatched huts it was obvious how the people lived: in abject poverty. The villagers milled around, all sounding and looking the same. Most were simple farmers who didn't want to be involved in the war but an undertone of duplicity was evident. Frank wondered who was to be trusted, and how they could work that out.

In one of the huts a family huddled, scared, in the corner. Frank went over to them.

'What the matter?' he asked, trying to speak in a way they would understand. Using broken English and the smattering of Vietnamese he had picked up, he found out one of the children, a girl, had a badly ulcerated leg.

'Here, let me put some of this on you.'

Frank applied some of his tinea powder to her leg. The girl said she felt relief, which may or may not have been true, but the mother smiled and bowed and scraped before Frank in a display of gratitude he had never imagined was possible. Before the platoon moved on the mother gave Frank a bag of bananas to eat along the way when they had a chance. But the fruit was not ripe and later, when the men scoffed them, it went through their digestive systems like the proverbial dose of salts.

The village wasn't all safe, though. After leaving the family, Frank's section found another hut with men standing around suspiciously. In baskets and on the rudimentary tables and cupboards were radios, cassette players and Seiko watches, not something that ordinary villagers would have. Three large drums of rice out the back were an indication that the people in the hut were VC sympathisers. They were taken prisoner and interrogated.

The platoon was out for a week before returning to the safety of the Dat on 10 July. There had only been a very short respite from Operation Lavarack and in another four days they'd be off again on Operation Mundingburra. Short as it was, Frank was glad of the break. He wrote home saying as much:

> . . . Everything is going well over here. Had a bit of fun on a couple of the patrols but nothing much so don't you worry about me, mum. We're having a spell for a couple of days which is good, although it doesn't seem much like it, there is still plenty to do around here. The officers make sure we don't have much time to ourselves. We're going out on another Op again soon so that'll be good. Don't like sitting around much. Hope all the crops are in and the rains come for you. I wish I could send some from here, there's a lot to spare . . .

When he'd finished the letter Alfie Lamb, who was sitting near Frank, said he wished he had someone to write to him. In his next letter to Constance, Frank, ever the helpful mate, asked if she knew anyone who would fit the request and she did: her friend Jenny. The two corresponded throughout the tour and were married afterwards.

Frank had also received mail from home. His mum had written wondering how he was going . . .

> Not too frightening I hope Francis. They showed on the TV last night that four Australians had been killed and another group moving in on a hut. Our prayers are with you and the boys all the way . . . and are you getting enough to eat? . . .

Two other letters arrived at the same time for Frank, one from the Birchip RSL Ladies Auxiliary, who sent a postal order for the princely sum of $3, the other from one of the Birchip nuns, Sister Francis de Salis who wrote:

> I hope you've found your legs in Vietnam and how are your nerves withstanding the rockets etc. Do write to your mother often Francis, even if it is only a few lines. Mothers just can't help worrying and those few lines help to keep the ripples of anxiety down. She has great trust in God and now it is up to you to be everything God wants you to be, which at the moment is a good soldier doing His work . . .

Frank read those lines questioningly. Was he doing God's work, he wondered?

The day before heading off on Operation Mundingburra, Frank attended Mass. Catholic and Anglican church services were conducted for anyone interested before each operation, even in the jungle on occasions. Frank attended this time, taking

Communion from the battalion padre. He had no particular reason to do so but something had told him he should. Whether or not it was the letter from Sister de Salis he wasn't sure, but he felt content and peaceful afterwards. He'd told his mum in the letter he'd just sent that he was going to Mass. He knew she'd be happy.

*

Rumours had been flying around the battalion as to where they were going next. Some said it was back to where they had already been, while others said they were headed to the Horseshoe, a fire support base in the south which was in a protected area, although still dangerous. Neither of these turned out to be true. This time the battalion's operation was to be conducted to the east of the Long Hai hills, the most dreaded area of Vietnam for Australian soldiers. This was near a VC minefield that had been established after what would later be judged as one of the worst decisions in Australian military history.

In 1967, Brigadier Stuart Graham, who was considered to be an officer of the highest calibre, ordered about 20,000 M16 Jumping Jack mines to be laid over an 11 kilometre stretch of Phuoc Tuy province, from the area around the village of Dat Do to the sea. The minefield was to be a barrier that would supposedly protect the local Vietnamese population in the south-west from advancing Communist forces. It would also, Graham considered, cut off food supply lines to the enemy forces and restrict their recruitment of locals to the cause. Graham and others in high command underestimated the abilities of the VC and the way they had already infiltrated the villages of the province.

While it was laid properly, with a barbed wired fence that ran along both sides of the minefield, there were not enough troops to guard it. Graham had been promised the use of South Vietnamese troops to supplement the Australian men but when that was not forthcoming, the minefield was left open to enemy infiltration, which the VC gratefully did. It would prove to be a tragic mistake. Even though about half the mines were fitted with anti-lifting devices and one in four with trip-wires, the VC still managed to lift thousands of the mines and re-lay them in areas where the Australians were active. Graham was warned not to proceed because he had insufficient troops to guard the minefield, but even though he knew this, he still thought the anti-lifting devices and the promise of help from the South Vietnamese Army would suffice. They didn't.

Jumping Jack mines were cylindrical objects about the size of a tin of fruit with three prongs at the top that, when disturbed, primed the mine. When any degree of force was placed on the prongs, there was a two second delay, during which time the person who stepped on it moved on, before the mine 'jumped' unhindered out of the ground to somewhere between knee and waist height. Inside was half a kilogram of high explosive which destroyed the steel casings inside and out, and sent red-hot fragments with bullet-like intensity in all directions. A Jumping Jack is lethal to around 25 metres and has been known to wound up to 200 metres.

Between 1967 and 1971, some 10 percent of all Australian casualties were a result of these mines exploding. During 1969 and 1970, the percentage had increased dramatically, with about half of all casualties during those years caused by re-laid Australian mines.

Before 6 RAR left Nui Dat, talk was rife of casualties flowing into Vung Tau hospital because of the mines. The VC minefield ran right through the area where 6 RAR were headed. The re-laid mines could be anywhere underfoot as the VC used them to protect its guerilla bases in the Long Hais. This was what the men of 3 Platoon faced as they headed off.

*

The Long Hais were full of caves, known as Hy Hom Secret Zones, that provided a haven for the VC. Not far inland from the coast were areas of Long Green, gradually changing into Light Green. The VC could move to their bases securely through the Long Green as well as having almost unhindered access to the minefield.

The object of Operation Mundingburra was to provide a screen around the villages in the area and to stop the enemy freely accessing them. Most of the operation would be in the Light Green with just the occasional foray into the Long Green. The task was complex with so many villages and hamlets as well as the farming areas that were worked during the day. It was difficult to know whether those moving around were VC, their sympathisers or legitimate farmers going about their daily routine.

Operation Lavarack had opened the eyes of the men and, even after just eight weeks in Vietnam, to some extent they knew what to expect. Now, they were to be deployed on reconnaissance and ambush missions in the Light Green to search for mines in bunkers and other places where the VC might have hidden caches of weapons and ammunition.

As had happened many times, the men were taken by Hueys to the area of operation. Frank and the rest of 8 Section, 3 Platoon sat quietly in the chopper, wondering what was ahead of them, and whether they would be able to tell the difference between innocent civilians and the enemy. Frank gazed out of the open side of the chopper at the beauty of the countryside, wondering how it would look after the war had finished and what would happen to the people.

Corporal John Needs looked around at the men and, like them, pondered what would happen this time. He'd had a chat over a beer with Frank the night before and there was a different air about him. Needs, on his second tour of Vietnam, was careful as well as confident about what he had to do. He was the soldier the men looked up to and would follow without question. As Frank watched Needs in the chopper, he shut out the negative thoughts swirling around in his mind and focused on the task at hand. He heard Needs say the same thing he said whenever they went out.

'The biggest thing, boys, is that even though it might be diffi-cult at times, you gotta stay calm down here. It won't be easy to do at times, but we'll all help each other. Just stay calm and rely on your mates.'

The men nodded in acknowledgement.

Needs was totally different to Corporal Smithy, who had not been out much with the troops. Instead he'd had quite a few things wrong with him during operation times and had to stay behind at the base. This didn't endear him to the men, who all wondered about his problems and whether they were legiti-mate or not. Those thoughts intensified when Smithy had to miss Operation Mundingburra because of some illness or other. Frank's other concern was the load that fell on Jim Kelly, who had to take over as corporal when Smithy was not around. None of it impressed Kelly at all. At times he was so livid with Smithy that he resorted to extreme measures: before one TAOR patrol when he couldn't wake Smithy to help with rounding up the section, he cut the ropes of their tent and let it fall on him.

'Fuckin' stay there then,' he said scathingly as he left.

*

While there was a certain degree of knowledge among the men about what to expect following their experience of Operation Lavarack, Frank's role in the platoon was completely new. In the short break between operations, Platoon Commander Peter Hines had called Frank to his tent.

'Rod Ballard is going home soon, so we're going to train you and make you the sig,' he told Frank.

Ballard was the platoon signaller whose tour of duty was finishing up in a couple of weeks, so a new radio operator was needed. Frank was shocked. He loved being a forward scout despite the anxiety it caused him. He'd never been much good at anything during his short life, but here in the jungles of Vietnam, he'd found something he could do well and he wanted to continue. He didn't think he'd done anything wrong, which Hines later confirmed.

'Hell, Skip,' he said to Hines, 'no, I'm a forward scout, why me?'

Hines snapped into officer mode, his tone instantly different. 'Because I told you to, Hunt.'

Frank knew the real answer. Hines knew that Frank had volunteered to do a three-day signals course back in Townsville while waiting for the rest of the battalion to arrive. Volunteering was something Frank had done quite often back then, if only to learn new skills and make his name known among the hierarchy. He thought he was being clever by volunteering. Now, assigned an unfamiliar role, he felt his 'cleverness' had been misplaced. Here was proof that volunteering never got you anywhere. And the training hadn't been ideal: three days in theory and just two days on the practical side of things. Not much when he considered where he was going.

Frank's place as lead scout was taken by Mick, who retained Tony Muir as his second.

Frank wrote home on the first resupply.

> ...they've made me the signaller and taken me off scouting. I wasn't very happy with Skip and I told him that. He wasn't impressed with me then. I asked if I'd done anything wrong but he said no. I hope that's right. Not sure whether this job will be any good for me. I don't know if I can do it but I'll try. I think that changing things around is not good but I suppose I'll just have to wait and see. I'll be right ... at least we're off to a drier area so that's good ...

*

A Company's foray into the Light Green included the usual single file patrolling through the sandy scrub. As always, the forward scouts were out the front of their sections trying to spot signs of the enemy before they spotted him or anyone else.

All scouts were nervous, anxious, scared occasionally, but in the main none had the time to think about it much. They felt it but it didn't overtly register with them. They simply concentrated on the job at hand. Each night they went over things in their mind, then when they started again the next day, it was like a switch flicking back into scouting mode, their eyes sharp, ready for what the day would bring. They needed to be that way as they searched for tracks and anything else that indicated the enemy.

Scouts also needed to warn those following them about snakes, ant nests, wasp swarms, booby-traps or trip-wires attached to pitchforks. Punji pits or spikes were the worst. The spikes were sharpened, needle-like bamboo sticks that were dug into rice paddies or tied to bent-over saplings where soldiers would tread. They were intended to wound the legs or other parts of the body and were planted where soldiers might throw themselves during a contact – in long grass, behind logs, in ditches; anywhere they would land with force. Small humps on tracks where spikes were laid could cause men to stumble and fall onto them. The VC dug punji pits to a depth of about 30 centimetres and set bamboo spikes in the bottom, usually smeared with excrement, then covered the holes to make them look like just part of the track or the jungle. The spikes had been designed to penetrate the latest steel-soled infantry boot. If men dropped into the pit, the spikes would either kill them or the excrement would infect them. Either result was what the VC wanted.

Being an accurate, quick shooter was essential for scouts. The ability to drop or take cover, warn the men behind and get off shots was essential. The responsibility was stressful. Mistakes could cost your life and that of your mates following you. If you were ambushed, you could be the first to die.

For Frank, the differences were stark. Although he was no longer out the front, there was still potential for death. He tried to concentrate as hard as he could on his new role as signaller, but at times he knew that wherever he was positioned in the section each step could have been his last, each heartbeat and each breath.

Every day brought more of the same as the company had been given detailed plans for a slow, methodical search of its designated area and the scrub – the more open areas – loomed, as did mines. This was the beginning of 3 Platoon's destiny.

On 15 July, CHQ had a contact with three VC who headed off in the direction of 3 Platoon. Hines immediately set an ambush and two of the VC ran straight into it. Both were wounded by 3 Platoon fire and dived onto what they thought was the safety of a bunker. While 9 Section gave covering fire, 7 and 8 Sections spread out in an extended line and swept through the area, searching for more VC. While the rest of the platoon avoided an open patch of sandy ground, Mick and Tony Muir found themselves isolated and only five metres from 7 Section, whose commander yelled that the bunker with the VC in was in front of them.

Initially Mick couldn't make out the bunker, as it was very low and completely covered in sand. Then he saw the front sight of an AK47 poking out of the entrance. He took aim with his SLR and asked Muir to grab a grenade while he covered him. Muir was having none of it, telling Mick to get his own grenade out. The impasse was solved when Mick fired a tracer bullet at the back of the bunker entrance, lighting it up brightly. Immediately Hines raced forward and lobbed a grenade into the bunker, killing both VC.

*

Several AK47s as well as an RPG were found in the bunker. Three days later, 1 Platoon and CHQ were moving across the Light Green towards the ocean on the left while 2 Platoon was in the centre of the patrol. 3 Platoon was on the right and harboured with 2 Platoon that night. That way they wouldn't need so many machine guns set up or so many soldiers to man them. The soldiers could have a bit more rest than usual. Talk during the evening was about what was happening in outer space. Not too many of the men were really impressed or that interested, but it was something different to chat about. A few days earlier, it was estimated over one million people had gathered around

Cape Canaveral to watch the launch of Apollo 11. In this part of South Vietnam, there were about 30 men with varying degrees of interest in the whole event.

'It's a long way up there,' Frank murmured to no one in particular while having a brew and looking up at the sky. 'I can't see the point of it, really, but I hope they go OK and get back.'

Frank took radio messages with orders for Hines later in the evening, but apart from that the night was regular. They were in the open area, so there was no jungle roof covering the sky. The moon shone brightly. There were no more than the normal weird sounds, nothing to be overly alarmed about. It was just another night at war.

*

It had only been a few days but by now, Frank had gained a little self-assurance as a signaller after initially having doubts about his ability. He had wondered if he could handle the sig set and the pressure associated with it – whether or not he could use it properly as well as using his weapon if needed, and not put his mates in danger by switching to the wrong channel or getting the message muddled. He asked Hines how he was going on one break, whether Skip was happy with him.

'Don't worry about it, Frank,' Hines told him. 'Your messages sound clear to me and, anyway, if I was unhappy or anything was wrong you'd be the first to know.'

Ballard came to Frank when they stopped a couple of times, encouraging him but giving him some tips, including a reminder to watch for the aerial being hit on trees. Being constantly physically close to Hines gave Frank a better understanding of the operations and how Hines' mind worked: how he saw things unfolding and the decisions he made as a result.

Frank had gained self-belief. He was now more confident in his abilities. He knew he had changed once again. He'd changed ever since he went to Kapooka straight off the farm. He had changed when he undertook training in Ingleburn, then again in Townsville. Canungra had changed him even more. In Vietnam, the four deaths and many wounded in the battalion had shown him the death and destruction of war, and the tension and fear of the unknown had changed him again. Frank thought he was a good soldier and had been told that by Needs. He worshipped Hines and Newbury, and his mates. He had become harder and believed what they were doing was right and that the soldiers were doing a good job. He thought they should be there, in Vietnam. Even though he suspected what was said at home was mostly propaganda and misinformation from politicians, Australia was part of the alliance with America and, as such, should be there to stop the spread of Communism. His conservative Catholic upbringing was playing a part in his beliefs: that he should follow without question; that there was always a greater good that he shouldn't query. Everything that had been drummed into him in his formative years was now coming through.

Later he would see things a lot differently, but for now he was looking at the situation through the eyes of a 19-year-old. He was doing a man's job but with a naive mind.

Chapter 15
LIVES ARE CHANGED

In the distance, the noise of the American B-52s dropping their bombs could be heard as 3 Platoon stepped out just after sunrise on the morning of 21 July 1969. 2 Platoon had gone north and 3 Platoon was heading south, parallel with the minefield and in an area where there was no doubting that mines had been re-laid. Nothing untoward was happening; everything was quiet. There were no unusual moves by the enemy. Indeed, the VC didn't really need to do much at all. The mines they had lifted and re-laid were doing their terrible job.

While Neil Armstrong and Buzz Aldrin were making their way from Apollo 11 down to the moon in the Eagle with the world watching, the men of 3 Platoon finished their stand-to at dawn. They cleaned their weapons, prepared and ate breakfast and waited to be advised of the day's activity by the section NCOs who relayed Lieutenant Hines' orders.

They patrolled across country, not following any defined tracks, until Mick came to a 'foot pad' which they crossed, when

Skip called a halt and ordered a harbour position astride the track. They were not to know that in a short while, as much as the Americans were making history, so, in their own way, would they.

*

The explosion came out of nowhere. Platoon Commander Peter Hines had trodden on an M16 Jumping Jack mine.

The almost deafening noise split eardrums and the blast knocked soldiers onto their backs, even from their prone positions. A thick black cloud of greyish-brown jungle dirt surged 20 metres into the sticky, humid air, while sticks and leaves and rubble floated down through the dust. Jagged shrapnel sliced through the air and tore into the soft, sweaty flesh of nearly all the men. A shot was fired from an SLR, more as an instant reaction than at the sight of any enemy. Hines had both legs blown into a twisted, mangled mess and somehow, with blood leaking from his wounds, in the immediate silence that followed found the presence of mind to call out to his men, 'Do your mine drill, do your mine drill!' The agonising cries of men in pain shattered what had been a short period of silence.

Corporal John Needs took control, as Platoon Sergeant Gerry Newbury had also been severely wounded, and called for everyone to shut up. It brought instant silence. He then began organising for a 'dust-off'– an emergency casualty evacuation – and for anyone able to help the wounded.

Near PHQ when the mine exploded was the two-man engineering splinter team, Corporal Phil Baxter and Private Dave Sturmer. As the harbour position was being set up, the two sappers had been told by Hines to head forward with their mine detectors to see what was around, to check if there were any mines on the track. Baxter and Sturmer had gone about 10 metres when, from behind them, the blast knocked them over and riddled them both with shrapnel.

Frank, who had been the closest to Hines waiting for messages that needed to be sent, was now a couple of metres away, lying on his back where he had landed after being thrown helplessly like a leaf in the wind. He was bleeding profusely, his left leg shattered, his face, arms and chest burning with pain from shrapnel wounds. He thrust one of his hands down his trousers to check whether his testicles were intact but all he could feel was wet, sticky blood.

He looked down at his legs and saw a gaping hole through one of them where a large piece of shrapnel had entered and exited. It had penetrated the special jungle boots he was wearing and ripped through his calf muscle and bone. Gathering strength from somewhere, Frank tore off the field dressing from the butt of his rifle where soldiers kept it for ease of access, and thrust it into the hole, winding whatever bandage he could around his leg to reduce, if not stop, the bleeding. The pain he could do nothing about.

Private Alfie Lamb, who felt searing pain in the centre of his back, had been blown over. He managed to pull himself up onto his knees and when he did the flow of air through his shirt brought immense pain from other wounds to his ribs. He knew that when shrapnel enters the body it is red-hot and when cool air blows on it the pain is accentuated. Lamb was bleeding from his chest and back.

'Fuck, your guts have been blown out!' one man nearby yelled. The comment was a far cry from what they'd been taught in basic training, which was that soldiers should reassure their mates when and if they were wounded. Lamb then heard a voice calling for men to assume a firing position and for those that could to cut saplings for splints to help the extremely wounded.

The call was unnecessary, as anyone who was able had already thrown themselves prone, ready and waiting. The sapling cutting needed to wait for a while. Even in pain, Lamb had his weapon ready, his eyes darting here and there, watching anxiously.

Lamb thought the voice giving the orders belonged to Hines, but Doc Davis, who was also terribly wounded, thought it belonged to Sergeant Newbury, whose legs had been shattered by the blast.

PHQ had taken the brunt of the explosion. Davis had two broken legs and shrapnel wounds in his neck and chest; one piece had even entered the sole of his foot. Most of the damage consisted of hot metal burn from small pieces of shrapnel which, when they entered, sealed the skin again. The larger open wounds bled. He couldn't move by himself and no one could help him, most being worried about their own condition. Davis checked himself over when he could, his mind kicking into survival mode. He knew he'd survive, or at least he hoped he would. He desperately wanted to see his wife again; today was their first wedding anniversary. Davis couldn't move, couldn't even crawl. He felt useless. He was the medic and could do nothing for his mates. He could hear them calling out, yet all he could do was lie in the jungle, trying to overcome his own immense pain.

Davis watched as three metres away Hines died. Lamb watched as well.

Lamb thought Hines' action during the few minutes he survived was the bravest thing he could ever imagine. He knew that adrenalin had kicked in and kept Hines going enough for him to yell out to his men to do mine drill. He thought he heard Hines try to issue other commands but really all he heard was the gurgling in Hines' throat as his life slipped away. Lamb couldn't understand it, didn't want to understand it. Why the Skipper? The men all loved him, this man who led them, who had been with them since training and had invited them into his home back in Australia – who had been Peter off-duty and Skip when the business part started.

Lamb consoled himself with the knowledge that Skip had died trying to look after his men; that he was a soldier to his last heartbeat.

From close by, Frank had managed to turn to stare at his Skip, who was lying face down and no longer moving. He saw the lance corporal of his section and his best mate, Jim Kelly, writhing in agony, his legs and ankles full of shrapnel. Kelly had been squatting near Newbury and Hines, just a couple of metres from PHQ, and almost in slow motion had watched the mine as it leapt from the ground. Automatically, his reaction was to turn his face sideways as it exploded, throwing red-hot shrapnel into the back of his boot and along his leg, face and arm, tearing them to shreds.

Frank yelled into the radio without regard for protocol or his wounds: 'Alpha 3 to Alpha 6. The Skip has hit a fuckin' mine and has been killed. Sergeant Gerry Newbury is wounded and Corporal John Needs is now in charge!'

The response from Company Headquarters came back: 'Alpha 6 to Alpha 3, use correct procedure and protocols to relay messages.'

Frank's reply was straight to the point: 'Fuck procedure, fuck protocol, a mine's gone off. There are lots of men down!'

Frank had been training as a radio operator for just four days. He knew what he was doing was not correct procedure, but he knew he had to do something. Ballard was close at hand but had also been badly wounded.

Despite his severe wounds and ignoring the pain, Frank now stayed as calm as possible and forcefully called in gunship helicopters as well as air cover and demanded Medevac helicopters, giving the co-ordinates concisely. Frank understood his responsibility was to keep CHQ aware of what was happening for as long as possible and to make sure he did what he could to see his mates 'dusted off'.

The explosion had wounded 18 men, many seriously. Newbury was one of the worst, suffering severe leg and stomach damage, which had left the only unhurt NCO, Needs, in charge. A cacophony of noise rose from the scene. Wounded men were groaning in pain, some were calling out.

Needs yelled to the men, 'Shut up! Everyone shut up!'

Order was restored and there was silence again. Needs yelled again, repeating Hines' earlier order: 'Do your mine drill, do your mine drill.' Mine drill meant that all soldiers stayed where they were and dug around themselves with their bayonets, pushing them into the ground at a 45 degree angle so as not hit the detonator point on top of the mine. A metallic clunk told them when they found a mine. A short sharp intake of breath was followed by a sigh of relief. Even though all the training they'd done back in Australia was now kicking in, the men knew this situation was different, this was the real thing. They just hoped they were doing it right.

From five metres away, Newbury managed to call out to Frank, asking how he was going.

'I reckon I could've lost my balls!' was all Frank growled through the pain.

He hadn't, although shrapnel had split his scrotum and blood was running down the leg of his sweat-stained, damp jungle greens, congealing with the detritus of the sandy ground. Davis' wounds meant he was unable to help, so field dressings were applied by anyone who could manage it, some by mates, others by the wounded on themselves. It would not be too long before the Medevac helicopter arrived with morphine, another doctor, Trevor Anderson, and Battalion Commanding Officer Colonel David Butler, who had decided to fly in to check on his men when he heard the news.

Mick Storen and Tony Muir had dropped their packs and were sitting on them when the mine exploded. They fell off their packs into firing positions. Mick felt a piece of shrapnel hit him and blood trickle down his back, but he was not in pain. He asked Muir to look at it and was told there was just a small piece that had torn through his shirt.

As those who could attended to the wounded, Needs called out to ask if anyone could see an area that could be used as a landing zone (LZ) for the helicopters, and Mick responded that there was one in front of him. Even though the helicopters could not land for fear of triggering a mine, they needed to have an LZ to hover above as close as possible to the ground.

With no regard for his safety or the rules of mine drill, Needs then walked across to the two scouts and threw a smoke grenade onto the proposed LZ. Mick looked at him quizzically, as if to say, 'What the hell are you doing walking through a minefield?' Needs could see the question in Mick's eyes. 'Sometimes you have to take a risk, Mick,' he said. Needs had just demonstrated the risk and now it was their turn.

Mick looked at Tony Muir, who looked back at him, both their gazes steady. There were no words, just an acknowledgement of the extreme danger of what they were about to do. The place for the LZ was some 30-odd metres across the minefield. Their expressions said not only 'Good luck, mate', but 'Goodbye'.

They began their walk and started work, forgetting about the danger, simply thrashing with their machetes as hard and as quickly as they could. Any step could have brought death to either of them. Exhaustion was the antidote to anxiety and fear, and exhaustion came quickly as the two soldiers pounded the scrub into submission.

In the meantime, Frank had managed to position himself where he could best work the radio. All over his body he could feel the tacky, hardening blood. He tried to wipe the sweat and dirt from his face and eyes with hands crusted with blood and dirt. He thought he was dying. The pain was intense. In between calling in on the radio, he started saying to himself, 'I'm fucked, I'm fucked.' But he also thought that if he was going to go out, he would do his job properly first – or at least as properly and thoroughly as he could.

He still had only a field dressing on his leg and the five canteens he carried on his belt had been holed by shrapnel and his water was draining out. He knew he was losing blood fast and that to survive he had to act. In case he later wanted to move, he dug around him with his bayonet to see if there were more mines. Once he had secured a small amount of space around himself, he ripped pieces of material from his shirt, which had been shredded by the blast, poked them onto the shrapnel holes in his chest and arms and side and, to stop the bleeding, covered them with mud made from dirt and water where his canteens had leaked. Most of the patches fell off again but he consoled himself with the fact that at least he had tried. He couldn't reach his legs, where most of the damage was, but the worst wound had the field dressing, which was reducing the blood loss. Although the radio was close to him, by now he was screaming his instructions and information into the handset, partly with pain, partly with frustration and partly because he had no real idea what to do. He was nothing if not determined. 'I can't fuck this up,' he kept repeating to himself through the pain and the waves of dizziness. 'I can't fuck this up.'

Frank kept radio contact up until the dust-off choppers were on their way, guided in by Frank's instructions and Needs earlier releasing a grenade of an identifying coloured smoke so the choppers would know where to go. Four more followed later, all of them needed to evacuate the wounded who waited, by now mostly silent, simply stunned.

As the choppers hovered about 10 metres above the LZ, the men below went about their duties. The familiar 'whoop, whoop, whoop' of the rotors, and the rush of the downdraft of air, brought a sense of some relief to the wounded, who knew they would now be safe. Prior to the first chopper arriving with Dr Anderson, Corporal Needs had called out to see if anyone was protecting the LZ. As Mick was the only one on the landing zone, he moved across to the other side to allow another man to help in that space. Once there, he realised it was a pointless action, as he was still the only one there.

He thought better of it and carefully returned to where he had been and helped with the dust-off. Needs was now going from man to man, calming them down, seeing what they needed and, with Dr Anderson, judging who should have priority in the evacuation.

*

Earlier, in the moment right after the explosion, adding to the instant cries of 'Mine drill, mine drill!' from Hines and Needs, was the voice of Sapper Phil Baxter, who was ignoring the pain from the shrapnel wounds he'd suffered. It was his job to find clear paths to the wounded, to make sure that there were no more mines in the way and that everyone understood they were not to try and move any further than the length of their bayonets which had cleared the space around them.

'Stay still, stay still! Don't anyone move,' he yelled out. 'Just do your mine drill around you and stay put!'

Baxter had suffered shrapnel wounds right down his back while Sturmer, who had covered Baxter somewhat, had been wounded as well. The men tended to each other's wounds, reassured each other about what their job now was and began their task. Some of the men were near small trees, others partially hidden behind low shrubs. Others had moved as far as their bayonets told them they could, which was only a metre or so, and taken whatever cover they found: logs, mounds in the soil, behind their packs. None of them was near to Baxter and Sturmer; a few were more than 25 metres away.

The sappers could not use the mine detectors as the shrapnel lying around would have given false readings and not only made the task more difficult but increased the risk of hitting another mine. They had to use their bayonets. The men were helped in their endeavours by Needs and the three of them went about their work. Bent over and crouching painfully, they poked and prodded their way to where the wounded men were. The process was slow and methodical and as they worked through the area, they strung white tape along the cleared line where it was safe to walk.

Baxter's heart was racing. He could almost hear the pulse beating in his throat, which was dry. He hoped he wouldn't hear the dreaded 'clunk'. If he did, he prayed he wouldn't have hit it hard enough to move it even a fraction, as that could detonate the anti-lifting device. His legs ached, his back was stinging, his head hurt, his wounds were oozing blood and throbbing but he crept along, as did the two others.

Leigh Floyd had come into the harbour as 'Tail End Charlie', the last in the single file of men, guarding against any attacks from the rear. He'd done his mine drill and as he wasn't wounded, he began probing in towards the centre of the harbour so as to do what he could to help. At one stage he came across a mine, the metallic 'thunk' stopping his heart momentarily. He had to take a detour, marking the place by putting something, anything, over it. He heard Needs' voice calling out to him.

'If you're going OK, Floydy, get over to Roddy Ballard and see how he is.'

Floyd had no idea where any other mines were but hoped the taped track was done properly. He knew he had to get Ballard, who was disoriented. Floyd was concerned that Ballard might stand up and try to stagger away, thinking he was going to safety, but then be injured further. Floyd wanted to get to Ballard quickly but he took his time, knowing the danger of being too hasty. Ballard was only 20 metres away but those were the longest 20 metres Floyd would ever cover.

'It's going to be OK, Roddy,' Floyd told the wounded man as he sat down next to him. 'We'll get things sorted for you.'

Floyd stood up and led Ballard back along the taped track.

When Ballard was safe, Floyd was told by Needs to help Private Merv McInnes, who was wounded and away from the main group at the back of the harbour.

'That area's not cleared yet, Needsy,' Floyd called back.

'Well, the chopper's coming, you'll just have to go and get him,' was Needs' reply.

Gingerly stepping on small tussocks of raised grass, Floyd made his way safely out to McInnes, who had wounds to his arms and chest and was in shock. He told McInnes to place his hand on his shoulder and follow him on the tussocks. Halfway back Floyd turned around and saw that McInnes was walking anywhere his feet hit the ground. Floyd knew he could do little, except say a small silent prayer that those feet would not hit another mine.

Needs was still barking instructions to all and sundry and gradually, with Baxter and Sturmer, the three of them managed to stretch the tape to all the men, even those who weren't injured – not that there were many of them.

Tony Muir was one. When the mine exploded, he had gone straight to ground, heart pumping and eyes darting through the scrub ahead. At the blast, an involuntary scream of 'Fuuck!' was all he could manage. He had fired a shot from his SLR into the scrub, more as an automatic reaction than because he'd seen any enemy. After cutting the space for the landing zone with Mick, he heard the familiar sound of the first Medevac chopper's blades swishing through the air before it came into view. Louder and louder it sounded, signalling safety was at hand.

The drone of the helicopter motors was one of the many things soldiers in the field could be assured of: if they were wounded and made it to hospital, they had a 95 percent chance of surviving and they were never more than 45 minutes away from a dust-off. The word 'dust-off' came from the Americans: Dedicated Unhesitating Service To Our Fighting Forces. It was the call-sign for rescue helicopters in the US Army and it was what was needed now.

Muir watched the first chopper arrive with Dr Anderson, Colonel Butler and another with four more sappers. All were winched down carefully into the area Muir and Mick had cleared. Mick told Colonel Butler that Corporal John Needs was in charge and pointed him in his direction, whereupon Anderson received a briefing from Needs. Anderson treated the other

18 wounded men who hadn't yet been attended to because of the limited supplies that had been used on others.

The sappers began their work after talking with Baxter who, by this time, looked like he needed to be dusted off himself – he was dazed and obviously in pain.

Butler walked where he could to reassure his men, talking to those who were waiting for the choppers and doing what he could to help while not interfering. Even though the carnage was obvious, the men were calm by now. There was more stunned silence than anything else.

*

The first to be dusted off were the worst wounded and those who might not live. Frank was one of them, along with Jim Kelly and Graeme Davis. Frank had long since dropped the radio and through wave after wave of pain and disorientation looked around at the mess. None of it really registered. He was some-where else. Somewhere in his mind was the thought that he had done his job. His wounds were desperately in need of proper attention. Needs walked over to him, picked him up, threw him over his shoulder and, semi-crouching, made his way steadfastly through the clumps of waving grass to the stretcher that swirled back and forth in half-circles after being winched down from the hovering helicopter.

The morphine that Frank had been given by Anderson was by then almost useless and, because of his blood loss, he had to be flown out as soon as possible. Needs' method of getting him to the helicopter was rudimentary to say the least, but necessary. This was no time for niceties. Frank's legs dangled uselessly, the smashed bones scraping and grating against each other, the last pieces of his shirt caked with mud dropping from his wounds as he hung over Needs' shoulder. Each agonising step sent pain spearing to every nerve and fibre of his body. His chest burned, his groin and arms felt as though they were being torched. Frank's agony was obvious and he shrieked with pain at every step as he was being carried. Through it all his mate Leigh Floyd yelled out, 'Hang in there, Frankie, hang in there!'

Mick and Alfie Lamb were under the chopper and steadied the stretcher as Needs carefully lowered Frank onto it. Needs grabbed Frank gently on the shoulder in a combined gesture of support and farewell, then stood back. The chopper crew began to winch the stretcher up but Frank had grabbed Mick's wrist and wouldn't let go. As the stretcher rose towards the chopper, Frank's grip on Mick was broken.

The helicopter's downdraft threw the stretcher around and around and around. It spun faster and faster as it rose to the chopper, rolling it from side to side and bouncing Frank as he lay there. The pain caused by Needs' method of carrying him was nothing compared to this. Frank's screams echoed through the jungle.

As the door gunner made way at the chopper's open doorway, a huge black American medic pulled the stretcher inside and gave him a shot of morphine. Frank could hear the helicopter blades and the voice of the pilot somewhere in the background. By now, he was indifferent to the pain. It had gone past the stage where he could feel anything. He was calm and warm and peaceful, floating on the painkiller. He was ready to die, and was convinced he would.

The medic could see Frank fading away, both from the pain and what was by now the loss of between a third and a half of his blood. He started slapping Frank on the face. 'Don't you go to sleep, you motherfucker,' he yelled in his Southern drawl. 'You stay awake, ya hear?'

Frank's eyes opened slightly. He slowly raised an arm as though to aim a pathetic punch at the medic. The American laughed, his smile showing rows of gleaming white teeth. He had made his point and done his job. He moved to another wounded man.

Above the trees, as the helicopter banked and turned, Frank saw the blue of the sky and somewhere in his subconscious he knew he had left the turmoil below. Not much at all was registering, if anything. It was just his mind imagining what he could see – a drug-induced nightmare. Below the chopper his mates – most of them wounded – were now just tiny figures. In flashes of light his thoughts turned to those who would not be going home. He thought about his life. He remembered the farm and the Mallee. He could see his parents, his brothers and sisters. He thought about dying. That was OK. If that was to be, he was ready. Everything was a blur.

*

As the first chopper departed, Dr Anderson called out, asking if anyone else needed medical attention. Mick put his hand up and said he had a piece of shrapnel in his back. Anderson treated the wound. Colonel Butler saw the activity and pointed up in the air, indicating for him to be dusted off.

It was the last chopper and while he was the only wounded man in the helicopter, sitting near the open door, he wasn't alone. Next to him was the body of Peter Hines, wrapped tightly in a blood-soaked ground sheet, covered apart from his boots sticking out from the end at odd angles. Emotion welled within Mick. He was angry and he swore at the Vietnamese working in the paddy fields below. The door gunner motioned for him to sit in the centre of the chopper.

The chopper turned and banked away, the pilot happy to leave. Dust-off chopper pilots had their own bravery. Holding a hovering helicopter above the ground while wounded men are being winched up, and all the while with the possibility of being blown out of the sky, takes some doing. There's nowhere to hide 10 metres above the earth.

To those still on the ground, the familiar sound of the blades gradually faded away to silence. Somewhere in the sky Armstrong and his mates were making their way back to the spacecraft, their exploration almost over. The world was watching them while here, with not many knowing what was happening, the men of 3 Platoon were mostly going to a war hospital. It all seemed rather surreal.

A short time later, on the ground, Dr Anderson, Colonel Butler and Needs were walking along a taped line to the LZ. All the wounded had been evacuated and Butler had decided he needed to leave; he had a war to fight. The other men were going with him to see him off. Somehow, while escorting him, Anderson either stepped outside the white tapes or brushed against them. Whatever he did, his foot landed on another mine in close proximity to where the first had gone off. The explosion ripped through the scrub again, echoing the first, only this time it sounded even louder in the silence.

In the explosion, both Anderson's legs were smashed and he was blinded. Colonel Butler caught shrapnel as well and was knocked out. Two unharmed soldiers raced to the spot. They saw Needs sitting motionless on the track without a mark on him. Anderson was just a bloodied mess; Butler was prone. Needs' mouth was full of dirt and as the men rushed towards him they wondered why he didn't spit it out or clean it away as he sat there. What was he doing? When the others reached Needs and opened his shirt they saw a thin red mark under his heart where shrapnel had entered. The man who had done more than anyone to save Frank's life, and who had looked after his mates without care for his own safety, died a few minutes later.

Another dust-off was called in and it wasn't until the new casualties were admitted to the army hospital at Vung Tau that Mick and the others who had been dusted off learnt about the second mine and what had happened to Anderson and Needs. Lamb, who was in Needs' section, broke down. The loss of such a brave man was unbearable.

CHQ was about 500 metres away when they saw the black smoke of the first explosion rising towards the sky. When CHQ found out what had happened the company medic, Corporal Rob Laurent, asked if he could go to help as the platoon medic would either have his hands full or might be wounded, which would mean help was needed even more. Permission was refused and not long after he heard the dust-off choppers in the air. Soon enough the second explosion rent the air and more smoke curled above the trees. Again, Laurent asked if he could go. Again the answer was no. Laurent began fretting. For the rest of that day he worried that as the medic he could not do what he was supposed to, which was to help the wounded.

Fate, chance, luck, destiny, fortune, providence, or whatever anyone wanted to call it, prevailed that morning. It was bad enough that the mines had been activated and bad enough that it resulted in carnage, but the fact that they were Australian mines hurt to the point of disbelief. Any number of men had walked around the area up until then. Why does one foot make contact at that precise point? Why that man's foot? Why at that time, at that moment? It remains one of life's imponderables. Hines had taken innumerable steps in the many, many kilometres he had walked during his time in Vietnam. Like Armstrong's, this one step was to echo through the years.

Within four hours that July day, one that would live in history as the day man made one small step and one giant leap, a small platoon of Australian soldiers saw two of their number killed and another 23 wounded, many of them severely.

In hospital, Frank was triaged, operated on and stabilised, ready for evacuation to the RAAF base at Butterworth in Malaya. Davis saw Frank on the operating table when he was sent in and stabilised. He would be evacuated as well. They were both still 19 years old.

Mick, just 20, was only slightly wounded and could move freely around the ward. He helped other wounded men by reassuring them. As he made his way around the ward, the news was played on the small television mounted precariously on a stand in the corner, displaying flickering black and white pictures of Neil Armstrong walking on the moon.

Chapter 16
WHAT NOW?

After helping with the wounded men from the first explosion and realising he could do no more for the time being, Leigh Floyd had gone to the machine gun position, lying prone to make as small a target as possible, ready to protect everyone. He knew he had been lucky and he was not about to press that luck any further. He remained there, heart beating fast, eyes darting everywhere, watching, waiting and hoping the enemy would not come. If they did, he was ready. That action saved him, as he was only some five metres away when Anderson trod on the second mine. The blast soared over him.

The second mine explosion was a cruel blow, a final indignity to 3 Platoon. Six more men had been wounded, as well as Anderson and Butler. The only NCO left after the first mine was Needs and now he was gone too. Two of the sappers brought in to help were also wounded. Butler directed the second dust-off despite his wounds, only accepting treatment when all the men had left. Tony Muir and Floyd helped with the wounded until the last man was flown away.

After the sound of the choppers' blades had again drifted away to silence, a sense of disbelief and hurt and sorrow engulfed the men. It hung over them, a cloud of bewilderment. Skip was dead, Needsy was dead, Frank was nearly dead and quite possibly could be for all they knew, and 23 others were wounded.

None of those left spoke. They couldn't; there was not a great deal to say and even if they wanted to, they couldn't find the words. Floyd was thinking 'What now?' He felt a sense of relief that all the wounded had been dusted off safely and would be looked after, but what was going to happen to the rest of them?

An hour or so later, a Huey came and took the five remaining men to A Company Headquarters. Again, there was silence inside the chopper. Waiting for them at HQ were reinforcements who had been flown in: a new sergeant, new corporals for the sections, and a new platoon commander, Lieutenant Marks-Chapman. The reinforcements had been seconded from wherever there were spare men. It was the nearly all-new 3 Platoon.

The survivors of the morning mayhem met the new blokes and they headed off. Evening was falling, so before too long they established a night harbour. The next morning Marks-Chapman gave a brief, morale-boosting talk. The new platoon leader was a tall, likeable man who was fair but was totally different to Skip. His talk to the troops didn't do too much for Floyd and Muir and the others. It wasn't his fault, quite simply the men were still numb, still getting over the previous day. They didn't need a captain's talk. They knew what was expected of them, what they had to do. They had to accept what had been thrown their way. One concession was granted to them – they weren't required to stand gun piquet that night.

Even though there was no sentry duty, there was little sleep. Some looked at the sky, seeing the million pinpricks of light surrounding the glow of the moon and thinking about men walking around on it. Time spent considering the moon was fleeting. More than anything, they thought of their mates.

Floyd, who had quietly shaken his head in amazement when told of the piquet concession, remained a rifleman. Muir became a forward scout once more. He had done the job, so it was something he was used to if not comfortable with. He knew he needed to be especially alert now. At times he was scared stiff. Scouting was more nerve-wracking than ever, especially when he knew the VC were about and now that he'd had first-hand experience of mines.

On hearing the news that they were to be re-formed, the men initially felt the decision was unfair and a brutal way to treat the few men who were left after such an incident. At least they could have been given a day or so to catch their breath, so to speak, to check on their mates to see they were OK. But that wasn't the way the army worked. Butler said, quite rightly many thought, that a war was still going on. As much as the mine blasts were shocking, sadness and emotion needed to be recognised but put aside and the job at hand attended to. Butler made his decision. He knew he had a whole battalion to monitor, other companies, other platoons. They needed him as well. He could not afford sentiment.

Later that day, replaying the incident in his mind, Tony Muir felt strange, staying out in the bush when nearly everyone else in the platoon had gone. It was a weird feeling but before too long he knew it was the best thing that could have happened. If he had gone back to Nui Dat he would never again have wanted to venture beyond the wire. The best thing was to get straight back into it.

The memory of that day, those hours, would always be with him, no matter what. This re-formation meant the platoon was different, it would always be different. Most of the old platoon had been together for more than eight months, including their time in Townsville, and knew all they needed to know about the other men alongside them, which ones they could trust and who might need a bit of guidance. That was 3 Platoon; this was something else under the same name. Now they had to go through all that learning again. The new blokes were good blokes but they weren't the others, they never could be. It wasn't their fault, it was nobody's, but the survivors felt that way.

The new men were a disparate lot, flown in from all over; anyone who could be spared from other companies, other platoons or from Nui Dat. How would they go? Muir wondered. Floyd felt much the same but his apprehension was exacerbated by an experience shortly after.

At CHQ the men had been given a fresh set of greens and the old ones were placed in the bag to go back and be washed communally. A few days later a resupply came in and greens were tossed towards each man. Floyd picked up those chucked his way and noticed the name on the shirt. There on the pocket patch in bold letters: HINES. It stopped Floyd cold. Visions of Skip flashed into his mind, visions of the incident. How could he wear these? Of all the places Skip's greens could have gone, they ended up in his hands. Each day he thought about why it happened and now this. He knew he needed to force himself to get over it. Somehow he managed to. It might have been easier had they known how their mates were going back in hospital. Were they alive? But there was no news.

Due to the severe depletion of the platoon, Floyd was called on to act as section 2IC and at times as section commander during the ensuing weeks. It was a whole new experience for him and he gladly stepped aside when the replacements gained the knowledge necessary for the job. The battalion continued to suffer casualties from mines throughout the operation. Only a couple of days later, a VC officer surrendered to A Company and led them to a clearing where he showed them 19 more mines. A bunker with yet more mines and weapons was next. In all, 211 mines were found and destroyed during Operation Mundingburra. But how many were left undetected to inflict more damage on more unsuspecting soldiers was not known. The minefield that had caused so much damage when the mines in it were stolen by the VC was discussed endlessly. A Company's commander, Peter Belt, called laying it 'the most stupid act of the war'. Belt said that A Company had changed physically and psychologically. He was right: they had been unnerved by the incident. They were exhausted mentally and physically. Mines played on their psyche. They could be the best soldiers possible, but they had no control over what could happen if someone else stepped on one.

These men left behind knew that 3 Platoon would never be the same again.

PART THREE

Chapter 17

HOSPITAL

Frank had been rushed from the dust-off chopper as it landed on the 'vampire pad' (the dust-off landing area so named after the blood-sucking bat) into the army hospital in Vung Tau, which had increased in size during the preceding years as casualties mounted. At first it was a 50-bed hospital that consisted of a series of tents with sandy floors. The overflow of wounded were sent to the American medical facility, also in Vung Tau. In 1968 the Australians built a larger facility about 500 metres from the back beach and ran it themselves with Australian surgeons and nurses exposed to conditions they had never thought they would have to face. Soldiers at least had the experience of Canungra to show them conditions similar to those they would confront in the jungles of Vietnam, but the nurses, even those with experience of traffic accidents and other trauma injuries, had no preparation for what they were exposed to when helicopter after helicopter landed on the vampire pad.

After a radio message telling the hospital to expect casualties, dust-off choppers arriving with injured young men would do a low-level loop over the hospital. Ambulances would then transport the wounded the short distance to the wards. In many cases these men were younger than the nurses. Their wounds varied in severity: some were slight, others were worse, while some were badly disfiguring. Those that couldn't be treated easily in Vietnam or needed more specialist attention were stabilised and sent back to Australia. The worst upset the nurses. As one would later say: 'People see amputations as a nice neat stump. We see the ragged ends beforehand.' The traumatic experience for the men was one thing, for the nurses quite another. Yet they had no time for emotions, there was always work to be done. Any such feelings would have to wait.

The number of wounded soldiers wasn't the only issue; the complexity of their wounds also made it difficult for the surgical teams. Modern weapons were causing wounds with multiple problems, including massive tissue and bone damage, especially from mine incidents. RPGs were another source of complex wounds. Around the time of 3 Platoon's mine incidents, the hospital saw a doubling of casualties from those compared to the previous six months. Dust-off helicopters were the saviour for many of those men. The wounded could be transported from the battlefield quickly and safely. Some of those men arrived in Vung Tau barely clinging to life. Frank Hunt was one of them.

After the chopper landed, Frank was rushed to surgery with a team of surgeons and nurses hurrying around him. As the medics carried the stretcher into the operating room, a nurse put a saline drip and a blood transfusion line into his veins while another cut off Frank's jungle greens and dog tags. Through the mist of pain and drugs, Frank saw figures rushing around and heard voices that might have been real or perhaps just hallucinations.

He was in what he thought was a big shed. That was close to reality – there was just one room with two operating tables surrounded by World War II medical equipment. In the corner before he went into theatre Frank thought he saw a big drum containing cut-off uniforms and another containing boots. Somewhere else were intricate machines and piles of white cloths on stainless steel tables. The smell of the place lingered in Frank's nose: disinfectant, sweat, humidity all mixed together. It was so different to the smell of the jungle, the rain, the dirt and the gunfire.

First, the doctors needed to stabilise Frank and stop the bleeding. The larger pieces of shrapnel were picked out, as were many pieces of mashed-up bone. Any smaller bits of shrapnel and bone fragments were left to float around inside Frank's body until a later stage – or maybe forever. Then the doctors set about stitching him up, suturing wounds in his mouth, shoulders, stomach, chest, both hands and up and down both legs; there was no limb or part of his body that wasn't stitched up.

A nurse stood beside his bed. 'Keep fighting,' she said softly as she held his hand. 'Keep fighting, we'll get you through.'

An Anglican priest was in the operating theatre and came to Frank's bedside. 'I'm going to give you a final blessing,' he said to an unresponsive Frank. The priest began to pray.

Chaplain Mills, the army's Catholic padre, then arrived, made his way to Frank and began to administer the Last Rites, quietly and gently: 'In the name of the Father . . .' he began, his words not heard by many amidst the hustle and bustle of the theatre. Frank's life was slipping away. He was at peace with the morphine and the drugs and if he was to die, that would be OK. The priest had done his job.

Chaplain Mills wrote a letter to the Hunts on 22 July 1969:

Dear Mrs Hunt

I have just returned from a trip to the field hospital at
Vung Tau where I was fortunate to see your son and
some of the other poor lads from A Company. Unfor-
tunately he wasn't up to talking when I saw him but I
did my best to find out his condition. Medical people as
you know are always reluctant to commit themselves but
I noticed in the last hospital statistics he is listed as seriously ill. I can just imagine how anxious you all must be.
I sincerely hope you have some good news on your boy's
condition soon . . .

The two surgeons talked as they worked, discussing the amputation of Frank's leg. Through the mist Frank heard them and
moved slightly. The surgeon leaned over. 'Don't take my legs,'
Frank managed to gurgle almost inaudibly. He didn't know
whether he had heard the surgeons properly or not, whether or
not they had even said anything and, if they had, whether they
meant one leg or both. Either way would have been abhorrent.
Objecting took a lot of energy and it was the only thing Frank
managed to do. The rest was like a dream.

The surgeons didn't answer but, with the nurses' help, began
to prepare him for evacuation to Australia. Frank's smaller injuries
were checked and the drips in his arms secured, but his leg was
another matter altogether. The damage was horrendous; a large
piece of bone had disintegrated and the burnt flesh needed to be
cut away. A gaping hole in the bottom of his left leg was cauter-
ised but that was nowhere near enough. His leg was immobilised
by a plaster cast from his groin to his toes. That would have to do
until he reached somewhere he could be operated on properly.
The only other option was to amputate.

A nurse stayed with Frank and constantly checked the stitches for bleeding and the drips in his arms to make sure they were working. They left him for the night as comfortable as was possible. Frank stayed that way for 36 hours, drugged and in and out of consciousness, until the next aircraft was scheduled to leave for Australia. In the beds nearby were Jim Kelly, Graeme Davis and Col Renehan, also with severe wounds and bound for the same plane.

Once there were sufficient numbers to be evacuated, the men were prepared early in the morning and driven to the airport, a trip in an old converted bus that more often than not took 45 minutes, as the road from the back beach to the airstrip was in bad condition. Frank had been given more drugs to stem the pain and was still in a fog, but he was alert enough to see his battalion commander, Colonel Butler, who was in hospital also with shrapnel in both ankles and up both legs. Butler was in a wheelchair saying goodbye to his men before the ambulance drove away. He commended his men individually. 'Well done, Digger Hunt,' Frank thought he heard. While it wasn't much, it was a fillip for Frank; it showed the regard Butler had for his men and why they viewed him as they did.

The flight in the Hercules to the RAAF Hospital at Butterworth near Penang in Malaya took only a couple of hours. The journey could be painful for anyone but the walking wounded – or 'walkers', as the nurses called them – as the others could not steady themselves. Inside the plane were tiers of bunks up the sides and camp stretchers on the belly, all occupied by wounded men. Some had been shot but many were there as a result of peripheral damage from mine incidents. Nurses walked up and down attending to all and making sure the blood and saline drips in Frank's arm were secure. They were alarmed at his blood pressure as it fluctuated and was dropping more than rising. Despite the stitching more blood was going out of his body, both internally and externally, than was going in. When the plane reached Butterworth, Frank was rushed to surgery again so the plaster could be replaced, the wounds all over his body restitched and the 'bleeders' the doctors found stabilised again.

Two days passed before Frank, still being administered huge doses of pethidine and morphine, was considered steady enough to be flown to Melbourne. The flight went via Darwin to refuel, followed by a two-day stop to check on him at the Richmond RAAF base near Sydney. The harrowing trip then finished at Essendon Airport in Melbourne, from where Frank was taken to the Heidelberg Repatriation Hospital, this road journey being interspersed with agonising bumps across the many tram lines. At the 'Repat', surgeons would try to repair his shattered body.

*

Back in Vietnam, the hospital at Vung Tau was full. Another platoon had been in a big contact and many wounded had been dusted off. Medics, nurses and surgeons rushed all over the place. What seemed to be chaos was simply the result of people doing what they needed to as quickly as they could. Some of the medical team had been working for 24 hours. Combined with the attention needing to be given to 3 Platoon's wounded, there would be no rest for surgeons, other doctors or any of the nurses for at least the next 24 either.

Mick was the last to be treated. He was given a local anaesthetic and felt the incision in his back, but no pain. The surgeon prodded around for a while looking for the shrapnel, then said, 'It's too deep. I'll do more damage doing this than if I leave it there.' So the shrapnel stayed in him.

Later that day a smiling Red Cross aide handed him a pad and pen. 'You need to write home to let them know you're OK.' Mick sat down and began:

. . . Just to set you at ease I was the least wounded in the Platoon . . . I suppose by the time you get this it will have been in the papers . . . It happened so suddenly. We got off to a good start that morning, we had to travel about 1200 metres to a small hill. I was forward scout, we travelled fairly fast, keeping off the tracks, scrub bashing. We had done about 500 metres when we crossed a track . . . I was about 50 yards across the track when we got the signal to harbour up. Apparently the Skipper was going to set up an ambush on the track for a few hours so he had us and the engineers starting to clear the track with a mine detector . . . and then he stepped over a pack and blew the mine . . . Platoon HQ took most of it as did 3 blokes in our Section who were close . . .

Mick then explained about the incident and how he and Tony Muir cleared the LZ. He talked about being dusted off and how, later in the hospital, the men heard about the second incident.

. . . Apparently there is a new 3 Platoon out there. We have only seen 1 bloke from the second incident, the rest are with the Americans as this place is just about full of wounded . . . I will be in hospital about a week and I don't know anything after that, so that's it. It just happened. We thought we were on top of the world (we'd killed 2 VC on the second day) things were going well and now the Platoon just doesn't exist . . .

While the seriousness of the situation in hospital was lost on no one, there was still room for humour. Many of the blokes in the ward needed injections most mornings and one of the nurses took the opportunity to repay some of the remarks she'd fielded from one of them. The banter, mostly sexual innuendo, between nurses and soldiers was harmless, but given half a chance, the men would have lived up to their suggestions. One morning the recipient of the injection rolled over in the usual fashion and prepared for the needle. The nurse drew a cross on his backside and dropped the needle from a not inconsiderable height. The painful bellow was followed by the nurse saying, 'Let's see how cheeky you are now, soldier!'

While in hospital, Mick was asked to do a tape-recorded interview about the mine incident. At the time of the explosion Mick, like the others, had been sure that Hines had called out 'There's been an explosion, do your mine drill, do your mine drill.' Now, in the interview, he wasn't so sure. His mind was telling him something else. The trauma of being dusted off with only Hines' body for company had been so great that as Mick sat and looked at his Skipper's feet in the chopper, he had begun to think that he couldn't have yelled anything. He said to the interviewer that it must have been someone else. Afterwards he regretted his words. What he did say was that immediately following Hines' words there came a screaming and moaning. He stopped and asked the interviewer whether he was allowed to say that. He was not sure how much detail they wanted. The interviewer said it was OK. Mick then said the cries of the wounded stopped quickly when John Needs called out for everyone to shut up and then set about taking charge of the situation.

Mick spent a week in hospital and another convalescing at the Badcoe Club. He became firm friends with Phil Baxter and

Dave Sturmer, the two engineers who were also wounded and waiting for stitches to be taken out. Once that task was completed, it was back to Nui Dat.

Chapter 18
NEWS ARRIVES AT HOME

Shortly after the choppers arrived at the army hospital at Vung Tau the news was relayed to two houses in Australia.

The telephone rang early in the Birchip farmhouse. Frank's mother Eileen answered. On the line was an army priest who was ringing to convey the news of the incident. He told her that Frank had been badly wounded and that he might not live. Shortly after, a telegram arrived confirming the news. The grim-faced local postmaster knocked on the front door. He handed her the yellow envelope which contained the message: 'Your son 39701 Private Francis John Hunt has been seriously wounded in action in Phuoc Tuy province Vietnam. Further details to follow.'

Eileen called out to Maurie and after the postman left they sat down and the shock of the news started to sink in. All day Eileen walked around in a daze. Was her son about to die? How could she bear that? She had never wanted him to join the army but didn't want to talk him out of it when his mind was made up. Now this? There was nothing she could do, that was the frustrating part. A mother needs to look after her brood and she couldn't. All she could do was wait. Eileen and Maurie didn't sleep much that night. They told the rest of the family what had happened and tried to be as normal as they could be.

A second telegram arrived the next day. At the top were the words 'Urgent – for delivery between 6 am and 6 pm'. Maurie thought that was typical: an urgent telegram with a 12-hour delivery window. Still, it flew in and out of his mind almost instantly when he read: 'Your son has subsequently been removed from the seriously ill list on July 22 and is progressing satisfactorily . . .'

The family rejoiced. Eileen and Maurie could rest a bit easier now. Although it was bad enough their son had been wounded, that he was now going to be OK was something they gave thanks for. Their minds were now a lot more peaceful than they had been.

At the same time the next day a third telegram arrived: 'It is learned with regret that . . .' The words sent a chill through Eileen's heart. 'It is with regret' were the words used when someone had been killed. She read on:

> . . . that your son . . . was replaced on the seriously ill list at RAAF hospital Butterworth Malaysia while being medically evacuated to Australia. He is now in RAAF hospital Richmond NSW and will be transferred to the Repatriation Hospital Heidelberg Melbourne shortly. A progress report will be forwarded to you every seven days . . .

Later that day the family received a phone call telling them that Frank would arrive in Melbourne the following day. Maurie and Eileen quickly prepared to leave.

*

In Adelaide, Mick Storen's dad had stayed up all night watching the moon landing and his mum rose about 4 am to join him. They were enjoying a cuppa when at about 6.45 am a knock on the door startled them. Outside stood an army sergeant who came straight to the point: 'Your son has been wounded in action but not seriously.'

Mick's parents silently thanked God at the 'not seriously' part and invited the soldier in. They sympathised with the man who had the unenviable job of breaking this sort of news, and much worse, to families. He told them Mick had a wound to the 'scapula bone in his leg'. With his medical knowledge, Wally thought to himself that was rather strange. He'd never known anyone to have that bone in their leg, it was in the shoulder. But he didn't take the matter further. The soldier soon left and the couple sat down to collect their thoughts. Wally went off to work but Nancy stayed home. Later in the day she wrote to her son:

> My darling Michael
>
> How are you? God alone knows I want to really know but I answer myself and say, all will be well . . . (the) sergeant major or some other rank told us you had been wounded by a mine blast and were in hospital at Vung Tau . . . It was such a shock, it didn't take effect until about an hour later when I wanted to cry . . . I didn't go to work, I knew I'd start crying if people sympathized with me and make a nong of myself. In fact I don't think I could have driven myself there, I'd probably have dreamed off and had an accident. I've been trying to write this all day but couldn't start. I had a dream last Thursday — I called it a night-

mare. There was a group of men and all of a sudden there was an explosion and everyone was landing on their head. I was looking for you and couldn't find you. I woke up and thought my age was catching up with me at last and I'm really going nuts . . . I do hope you'll get home after this . . . it's fiendish, this isn't war as everyone knows it . . .

*

In Australia, newspapers across the country were full of the moon landing news, with photos of Armstrong wandering around the lunar landscape splashed across the front pages. Gigantic headlines in bold capital letters told the story. Up to six pages were packed with comments and editorials. Yet, proving to Australians that the men fighting a war were not forgotten, all papers carried the news of the mine incident. On page 1 *The Age* had a pointer to the full story on page 8, headlined 'Mines rip into Diggers: Heavy losses', that was next to a story about American presidential candidate Teddy Kennedy and his troubles with Mary Jo Kopechne in Chappaquiddick. The *Adelaide Advertiser* carried the story on page 10 under the headline 'Australians in Blasts' while Melbourne's *Sun* ran an advertisement calling for young men to register for national service on page 4 and on page 7 the story of the mine incident titled 'Replanted Australian mines kill two diggers'. The *Sydney Morning Herald* ran the story on its front page under the headline 'Heavy Toll on Australians in Mine Blasts'.

The stories in all the papers were the same, saying that two 33-man platoons had been cut down in separate mine blasts three hours apart and 1000 yards from each other. Two men had been killed and many others wounded. At least some of it was right but it did show that news from Vietnam was not always clear and precise. There were not two platoons, nor were they 1000 yards from each other or three hours apart.

The reassuring thing to the men of 3 Platoon, when the papers eventually reached them, was that their troubles had been recognised and that they shared a monumental day in history.

Straight from a Mallee farm, Frank Hunt had yet to turn 18 when the Army's official photographer caught up with him during rookie training at Kapooka, near Wagga Wagga, in 1967.

The assault course at Kapooka challenged young soldiers physically but was essential for fitness and teamwork. Climbing up and down without getting in each other's way was a problem for some, but not for long.

Below: Frank, 19 years old, cleaning his 'best friend' at the Jungle Training Centre at Canungra before heading off to Vietnam.

It was indeed a 'long march from cadets' when young national servicemen trained at Puckapunyal.

HMAS *Sydney*, affectionately known as the 'Vung Tau Ferry', loading up at anchor in Townsville harbour off Magnetic Island for the trip to Vietnam. The flight deck had trucks and other equipment on it and a ferry that took soldiers to the ship can be seen in the bottom right-hand corner.

Frank and a few mates performing at a concert held in the aircraft lift well during the 10-day trip. These concerts were always well-attended with seating at a premium and vantage points everywhere.

It was down to work when the troops arrived. These A Company soldiers are patrolling through heavy jungle carrying full packs.

Soldiers heading off on operations were ferried by helicopters to and from Nui Dat.

Soldiers from A Company on a day patrol through the jungle where an ambush was always a possibility. The soldier in the foreground didn't take a full pack but carried an extra belt of ammunition for the M60 machine gun.

It was vitally important that a dust-off (above) took wounded men to hospital quickly and safely. Resupplies (below) were always very welcome during operations. Ammunition, rations, clean clothes, and the most eagerly anticipated item, letters from home, were all unloaded in quick time.

On the day after Neil Armstrong walked on the moon and the mine explosions devastated 3 Platoon, the A Company Chaplain joined the men to conduct a church service.

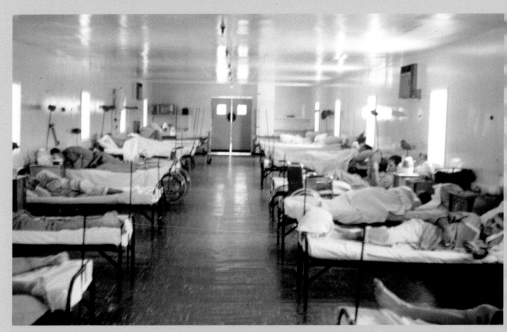

The ward in the Australian hospital at Vung Tau in 1969. Some of these men recovered and went back to their duties while the more severely wounded were sent home to Australia.

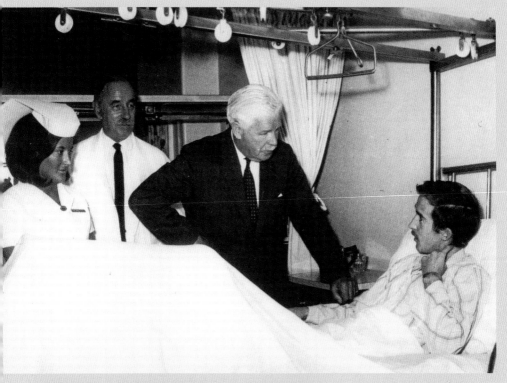

In November 1970, Frank had been in hospital for 18 months when he was visited by the Governor of Victoria, Sir Rohan Delacombe. Watching closely were Sister Ardlie and Doctor Doran.

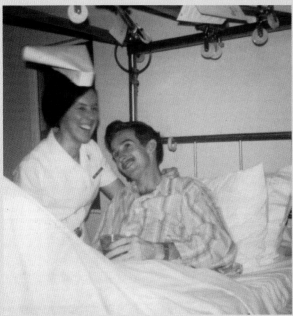

Frank's 21st birthday was spent in hospital but he had the company of his favourite nurse, Sister Mary Kelly.

Frank was asked to make a speech at the presentation of the Gold Record for 'I was Only 19'. Songwriter John Schumann said the success of the song was due in part to the hard work of Frank.

John Schumann (left) and Frank (right) in Sydney during the extensive publicity tour for 'I Was Only 19'. The song went to no. 1 on the music charts and became an anthem for Vietnam veterans.

Frank and his children were hoisted onto the stage when John Schumann sang 'I was Only 19' during the concert after the welcome home parade in 1987.

Frank attended the National Reunion and Welcome Home Parade in Sydney in 1987, pushed by his former Sergeant Gerry Newbury. Standing next to Newbury is Sue Earle, the sister of Corporal John Needs, who was killed in the mine explosion.

Among Frank's many awards, which include an Order of Australia Medal in 1988, he was awarded a Centenary Medal in 2002. Here he reflects on his memories and his contribution during the 2002 ceremony.

Chapter 19
ANOTHER BATTLE BEGINS

The Heidelberg Repatriation Hospital – the Repat, as it was known – had been a military hospital run by the army during World War II. After the war ended it became part of the Repatriation Commission in 1947, a government organisation set up to look after war veterans. It was there that, once more, Frank was stabilised, examined by a team of surgeons led by Professor Jim Hodge and prepared for surgery. He was in a critical condition, as close to death as anyone could be without actually dying.

Waiting for Frank to open his eyes when he arrived at the hospital were his parents. Eileen was clutching the telegrams she'd been sent. Reading between the lines of the clinical army-speak, Eileen knew they thought Frank was not expected to live. The hospital padre was in attendance and administered the Last Rites. While the nurses and doctors stood by watching closely, Eileen and Maurie fretted, both of them palpably anxious. Frank somehow managed a glimmer of recognition, but only for seconds, which made it all the more unbearable for the two of them. Maurie was stoic but blamed himself for not only letting but encouraging his son go into the army, while Eileen was constantly in tears, distraught. Before her, lying on the steel hospital bed in this grim place full of broken men, was her eldest son, still a very young man. She held his hand and spoke softly: 'I love you, son,' she told him.

Even though her whispered words of encouragement were heartfelt, Eileen believed her son would die. She wasn't the only one. The surgeons had no great expectations. Of course, they said they'd do whatever they could but it was touch and go whether Frank's leg could be saved, let alone his life. After Frank was taken to the operating theatre, Eileen and Maurie left for Birchip. While Maurie would return with two of his brothers to visit, Eileen returned only when she was told Frank was close to death. At those times she watched with the priest again, but apart from that she never came back. The emotion of the visits was too much for her.

In the ward with Frank were Graeme Davis and Col Renehan, who had flown all the way back with him and were having their own problems – not as bad as his, perhaps, but concerning enough for them. Davis in particular had copped a lot of shrapnel and needed operations to remove it, as well as his broken legs needing close attention. He would stay in hospital for three months. Renehan, who had shared a tent with Frank when they arrived in Nui Dat and who now shared a hospital ward, had been chopped up by shrapnel. Jim Kelly had been sent to Brisbane, his home town. Wounded men were always sent to their home states, which was the best thing for them and their families. Yet, the feeling of separation from their mates was visceral. For many, there was no contact at all for many years.

Frank needed to have his wounds restitched and checked before he was taken to the operating theatre. Before he went, the Repat's resident Catholic priest visited him and once more administered the Last Rites. Frank's blood pressure was consistently dropping and staying low; there appeared no real hope for him. The priest was taking no chances for his soul. In a lighter moment a few months later, the senior ward nurse, Harry Jenkins, told Frank that he'd had more blessings than the Pope so if he did die he'd be guaranteed a spot in heaven.

Once his wounds had been attended to, the talk about amputation continued, but again Frank tried to rail against it. Not that his protestations, such as they were, made any difference but the surgeons decided to operate and see where that led them.

Not much remained of the left leg between the knee and the foot. What wasn't missing was minced. From one side to the other was open. Hodge could fit three fingers through the hole in Frank's leg without touching the sides. The two leg bones were crushed, the muscle shredded.

The surgeons began their work. The bones couldn't be joined as the damage was so great, so the two ends of both bones were lined up the best way they could be. The bones, even though still a few inches apart, would join later, not perfectly, but at least the leg would be saved. The medical outlook for what the surgeons expected was that the 'green bone' would in time meld together. After all, Frank was just 19 and his body, like those of all young people, was still growing.

One of the many problems the surgeons encountered was Frank's damaged foot being in the wrong place: it was inclined at about a 30 degree angle. To manoeuvre the foot and, in turn, the two leg bones, into the right place, it had to be turned in. If the whole procedure worked, the leg would not only be some

15 centimetres shorter than the other, the foot would be turned in substantially. While not perfect, the only other option was amputation. The operation began, taking the surgeons all day. The leg was then encased in plaster again and weights were attached to the ankles to prevent even the slightest movement and to keep the leg, except for the foot, as straight as possible. Frank was returned to the Intensive Care ward and the wait began.

Four days later, Frank was rushed back to surgery with an infection. The plaster came off, the infection was treated, the bones were lined up again, the weights replaced, and he was taken back to Intensive Care – back to square one. It was to be a recurring theme. There were several more lengthy operations and twice during that period his parents were called in because he wasn't expected to last the night. Twice more the priest did his duty.

During the weeks and months after the operations Frank was in constant agony. The bones and the foot, even though they couldn't move, still wanted to return to their original position but were stuck and restricted by the plaster cast and the weights. Frank's body was rebelling against the surgeons moving it into an unnatural place.

Those weeks included more trips to theatre for Frank's 30 or so other shrapnel wounds. Some were minor while others were major. The larger ones were watched closely for bleeding, which happened regularly. The stitches would be removed, the wounds cleaned and, if necessary, stitched back up again. When possible, any more pieces of shrapnel or bone were removed.

The worst problem of all was osteomyelitis, the infection of the bone and marrow. When this occurred, as it did often over the next 12 months, Frank went back to the operating theatre, where the plaster was removed, the bone opened up and scraped out and new plaster put back on. Each time more shrapnel and shattered bone were removed. After each procedure, the length of time estimated for Frank's recovery, if it ever happened, was blown out. Each time there was more excruciating pain that no amount of drugs would help or, if they did, they only managed to reduce the pain from extreme to horrible.

Little by little, slowly, it became easier. Not much easier but for a couple of days at a time, in between operations, the doctors could see slight signs of Frank's condition improving. But whenever an infection was detected in the bone or the flesh, another visit to theatre showed it was all an illusion. During those operations Hodge would check on his work, sometimes needing to chip a bit of bone off here and there as it might be getting in the way. Or he would try to straighten the foot a little bit more. Whatever Hodge did, the operations usually lasted for a number of hours and, at the end, there was no real improvement, only more pain.

*

Professor Hodge was a small man, a smoker who amused Frank as he watched him get halfway through his cigarette with the ash still on its end, not dropping off. One day, a couple of months after Frank had arrived, Hodge sat on the edge of the bed and talked about the operation and the injuries, about the way ahead, what had happened and what would happen. He spoke about pain management, the way Frank would be nursed, how he would keep checking on the osteomyelitis and try to find more shrapnel and bone, even though he knew he would never find it all. Hodge explained in detail about the operations, Frank's extensive blood loss and the limited expectations for the future. He warned Frank that he might never walk again. He explained to Frank that he was lucky to still have his leg and that he was even luckier to still be alive. As Hodge was on his way out of the ward, Frank wondered aloud about the amount of time it would take for him to recover.

'How long will I be here, do you reckon, Doc?' Frank asked.

'Two years, Frank,' came the reply.

Frank was devastated. Not only a total bed case, he was now a complete head case.

Chapter 20
BACK IN THE JUNGLE

When Mick eventually left hospital, he made the trip back to Nui Dat in a chopper with a few other blokes, some of them from a 36-hour rec leave while others were also going back from hospital. There wasn't much talk, even less humour and no chiacking. The men whose wounds had healed knew they'd been lucky. They hoped that luck would hold out.

Arriving at the tent lines late in the afternoon and entering the tent that he had shared with Frank and Col Renehan hit Mick hard. Someone had come and removed their personal gear, but they had not done it gently. It had been done quickly and not carefully. Gear was left strewn over the duckboard floor. The place was a shambles. That night he slept in what he could scrounge. He found some sheets that had been left in a locker and a mosquito net. Lying on his bed just after twilight, he rolled over and spied a centipede about 30 centimetres long creeping at head height along the sandbags near the bed. After contemplating the centipede for a minute, watching it walk this

177

way and that, stop and start and look around, Mick grabbed a machete, the only thing resembling a weapon he could find; his rifle was somewhere in the Light Green. Mick struck out viciously, taking the centipede out as well as hacking the sandbag into a mess of shredded plastic with sand pouring gently onto the ground.

Mick slept restlessly, tossing and turning, and dreamed he saw a VC standing outside the tent looking in. Neither he nor the Vietnamese moved, nor was anything said. The VC just stared at Mick and then disappeared. Mick tried again to sleep but it didn't come easily.

The next morning Mick was up early, and went straight to the company clerk demanding to be issued with another rifle. He didn't mention any of this when he wrote home, but recent events still weighed heavily on him:

> . . . Needsy and I were talking about the fact our fathers had served in the same Battalion and he kicked himself because he meant to ask his dad if he knew you . . . It would be good to send a card to his wife, I don't think I could manage a letter . . . the boys are due in next week and it will be good to see them again . . .

A few days later, Mick was joined by some of the other wounded men who had been deemed to have recovered sufficiently — physically, at least — to go back to action. Three days later they were sent out on a TAOR patrol. None of the men had done anything much for more than three weeks and felt underdone. But that didn't matter. If you were back in Nui Dat, you were back to a soldier's life. The patrol was led by the Q store corporal, whose instructions were to go across the open ground from the perimeter wire into the jungle and proceed another 500 metres, making sure the area was clear of any enemy and returning the following morning. The corporal wasn't the keenest of leaders and when the men reached the jungle he said, 'Righto, blokes, this'll do us. We'll stop here and have a feed and an easy walk back in the morning.'

That sounded like a good idea to the men, so they stopped and were sitting on top of a small ridge line just inside the jungle having a meal when all hell broke loose. In the gloom of evening, tracers zinged across their heads like so many supersonic fireflies smacking into the trees above them at all angles. Mick and the others quickly slid on their stomachs down the other side of the ridge.

The firing wasn't coming from the jungle side of the ridge, it was coming from the Nui Dat side. Mick and Lamb looked up to see one of the company cooks still eating his meal, sitting upright at the base of a tree on top of the ridge, completely oblivious to the danger he was in. He was transfixed by the show until he was urged in no uncertain terms to 'get down' – an order with which he complied.

The patrol had unwittingly stopped at the wrong end of night firing practice. The corporal had the radio and was urged by concerned voices to contact the base and tell them to cease firing.

The corporal refused. 'We're not supposed to be here, so what am I goin' to say?'

One of the men warned him: 'Get on the radio or I'll shoot you!'

The corporal wouldn't back off even as tracers flew overhead and ricocheted off trees around the men. The range practice continued unabated, with bits of branches and bark and leaves flying here and there.

Luckily, a message came through on the radio from the base to the rifle range telling them to stop firing as the practice hadn't been authorised.

When the patrol returned to the base, Mick could see the farcical side of what had happened. The heaviest fire he would experience in Vietnam came from his own side. It was funny and it wasn't funny at the same time. Incompetence could have got him or someone else killed, whether it was a VC bullet or an Australian one.

*

The re-formed platoon, now containing only 10 of the original 33 and the rest made up of Reos, had finally returned. Floyd and Muir were more than glad to be back. It had been what seemed like an eternity since they had felt the safety of the Dat. Mick was happy to see the rest of the blokes, all of whom had managed to stay comparatively sane during the period after the mine incidents. The feeling didn't last, as it wasn't long before they were all scheduled to head back out. In some ways they were looking forward to going out again – after all, that was what they'd trained for and it was an itch that needed scratching.

During their break, the men read the papers even though they were days or weeks out of date after their arrival from Australia. They knew about demonstrations and protest marches but weren't all that interested. Of more concern was the fact that union activity on the wharves in Australia had caused problems with ships being loaded, causing the boozer to run out of good beer and leaving the men to drink what they called drain water – Courage. Now *that* was a problem. Bloody unions; bloody demonstrators.

*

On 17 August, 6 RAR began Operation Long Tan. The operation was designed to commemorate the Battle of Long Tan which took place on 18 August 1966 and in which 17 men of D Company, 6 RAR were killed and 21 wounded. The distance from 6 RAR lines in Nui Dat to the site of the battle is only about 5 kilometres and it is clearly visible across the low ground.

A memorial service was to be held on the site and a cross erected as a permanent memory.

3 Platoon left Nui Dat in APCs to secure a landing zone for A and D Companies who would be brought in by helicopters. The area was searched and cleared of any enemy.

Tony Muir had warned Mick that the new members of 3 Platoon were a noisy lot, something that was confirmed by the level of loud activity prior to stand-to that night.

The following day the battalion formed a square around the site, where a large concrete cross had been installed. A brass plaque of dedication was attached to it. A service was held and the names of those who died in the battle read out, after which two pipers played a lament.

For those survivors of the 3 Platoon mine incident in attendance it was a time of immense sorrow, as they remembered their fallen comrades Peter Hines and John Needs.

The Long Tan Cross site remains a symbol of the sacrifice made by Australian soldiers during the conflict known by the Vietnamese as the 'American War'. No other memorial to any allied nation has been permitted by the Vietnamese.

*

The platoon was due to go back out at the end of August on Operation Burnham, up on the Firestone trail, the third major operation in their three months in Vietnam. They'd be protecting an American land clearing team from a VC regiment known to be in the area called the Hat Dich Secret Zone at the northern end of Phuoc Tuy Province. The VC had extensive bunker systems there and were heavily armed. The Americans transported 35 huge bulldozers and graders with oversized blades that dangled from beneath Chinook helicopters, landing them where they could. These machines would be able to clear whole swathes of jungle in a short time, taking all the cover from the enemy. And, needless to say, a good drenching with Agent Orange would help.

Before he left, Mick wrote home on 26 August 1969:

> ...The Company came in on the 19th and we had a big barbecue etc then an R&C at Vung Tau the next day. A lot of Battalion duties came our way as one Company was still at the Horseshoe and one was out on a small Op. We are short on men so we were working pretty hard for a while. Thrown in on top was also a clean-up of the Platoon area, cutting grass by hand and raking up the debris accumulated from the rubber trees after a month's absence. A new innovation in the Lines has been a series of what we call 'Happenings', grogging on in one of the tents and having a thoroughly good time. It's strictly forbidden however and an automatic charge, but so far so good. As a matter of fact we were having one of these happenings when we heard a loud explosion. We kept drinking but then got the word to Stand-to. Someone had apparently thrown a grenade at the OC of the Company! When we were stood down a bloke from CHQ came down and wanted two blokes for

a piquet, so Tony Muir and I went up. Funniest night we've had for a long time. Two deck chairs were provided and we guarded (?) the scene. The incident lifted the morale of the Company greatly. Of course things have clamped down a bit. Happenings may resume after our next OP which begins on the 30th. Just as well I think as we'd had the happenings in a row and still have 3 dozen empty cans under (hidden) the table. Must remove them some time. I have my R&C on the 21st so I'll be on the OP for a few weeks and then coming in (very well timed I thought).

Not much more news. Things are ok here.

A Company air-assaulted into the area of operation with 3 Platoon under their new commander, Lieutenant Peter Marks-Chapman. On 3 September, 1 Platoon had a contact with four enemy, killing two of them. The survivors headed in the direction of 3 Platoon.

Marks-Chapman deployed the platoon on the track from which he suspected the VC would come. The enemy were heard coming through the bush immediately to the front of the platoon. The command to fire was given and two sections opened up with everything they had until they were ordered to cease. A sweep of the area was conducted with one dead enemy found, searched and buried.

3 Platoon was then told to return to CHQ about 500 metres away. When nearing the position the front section of the platoon was ambushed and Private Ian Kingston was killed. Two others were badly wounded. The rear section then went forward, not sweeping out to the flank as the platoon was caught in a mess of trees felled by the Americans. By the time they reached the front the enemy had disappeared.

Company Medic Rob Laurent arrived and began treating the wounded. 3 Platoon had already cleared an LZ for the wounded to be dusted off and after that task had been completed and as Mick headed off, Laurent grabbed him and asked him to help with the wounded. Reluctantly, Mick had to say no as the platoon was moving out and he was lead scout.

That night, after the dust-off, it rained heavily, adding to the sombre mood of 3 Platoon. Three more men were gone.

*

A week later, A Company became the close protection force for the American Land Clearing Company in their night defensive positions. Watching the Yanks try to extricate their bulldozers from the boggy, muddy ground and listening to their swearing took the A Company's minds off their troubles. Working with the Americans was an experience in itself. At the end of each day, the vegetation that had been cleared was bulldozed into a huge circle and the land clearers would spend the night inside. They didn't seem to care about the enemy, as they had all the comforts of home: lights, showers, mobile kitchens, fresh food – the lot. The Australians tended to stay a fair distance away, making sure they were silent and keeping an eye out for the enemy with sentries and patrols. The Americans spent 10 minutes each evening firing every weapon they had into the jungle away from their position to deter the VC. The noise was deafening as artillery, machine guns, M16s and the rest blasted into what was left of the jungle. It appeared to work, as there were no attacks.

The battalion had arrived in Vietnam at the start of the wet season and it had been wet most of the time since. The almost constant rain and mud were depressing. The only good thing was that no one was ever cold. It was wet then dry, then wet

again, but never cold. Staying dry was difficult and, most of the
time, almost impossible, which brought with it the challenge
of keeping associated health problems at bay. Tinea, footrot and
crotch rot were constants as feet and boots were always waterlogged. One occasion saw Chinese whispers alive and well in the
jungle when an order came down the line to say that all men
should take off one boot. In fact the order issued by Company
Commander Major Belt was that, when stopped, half the men
should take off their boots and dry them out if possible, while the
other half should do the same at the next stop.

That night movement sensors indicated a great deal was going
on in the jungle. An air strike was called in. American planes
thundered across the sky in five separate sorties. Napalm, that
dreadful substance which is a mixture of plastics and petrol and
burns to over 1500 degrees, lit up the night. Low-level bombs
ravaged the area until four in the morning. At daylight all that
was left was crushed and burnt jungle. Tracks around the area
showed that a large force had been there but had disappeared
when the planes came.

*

The familiar sound of choppers arriving with a resupply filled
the sticky air and was greeted by a happy Mick, who headed
off on the five days rest and recreation leave each soldier was
entitled to during his tour. Mick was going to Bangkok to see
the sights. Men either went to 'Bangers' (Bangkok) or 'Singers'
(Singapore), and some even went back to Australia. Many were
afraid they wouldn't want to return if they went home, so somewhere in Asia was the preference. Mick had to spend a night
in Nui Dat before leaving for Saigon and Bangkok, and was
lucky enough to see a concert at the Luscombe Bowl. A large

amphitheatre completed at the end of the Luscombe Airfield in Nui Dat in 1967, it was meant to be a place where aircraft could turn around. An extension was excavated and shaped to accommodate an audience of 1000 troops who would watch performances on a stage built from timber, steel and corrugated iron. Weatherboards lined the exterior with ply on the inside. The stage floorboards were polished until they shone. This was no makeshift arena. Earlier, concerts were held on the backs of trucks with a cobbled together canvas-covered stage. Such a stage hosted the Col Joye/Little Pattie concerts held in 1966 when the Battle of Long Tan took place. Many Australian entertainers volunteered to go to Vietnam, where they were greatly appreciated by the thousands of troops who watched the concerts over the years. The shows gave the men a taste of home and a much-needed break from everything else that was going on in their lives.

While the men were used to the conditions and the danger, the entertainers were certainly not. It was difficult for them. More often than not it was dirty, dry, dusty and uncomfortable or unbelievably wet. They suffered from the effects of the humidity, which also caused problems with their clothes. Their roadies had never encountered anything like it before, so setting up created problems. But they worked through it all and gave performances they and the men remembered forever. The entertainers also made time to give small, intimate performances to the sick and injured in the hospitals.

Performers of the calibre of Johnny O'Keefe, the ABC Show Band and Dinah Lee received rapturous receptions from the troops. There were two songs that virtually no performer could get off stage without singing: 'These Boots Were Made for Walking' and 'We Gotta Get Out Of This Place'. Lorrae Desmond's soulful performance of 'Leaving on a Jet Plane' was also a must whenever she appeared.

Lorrae Desmond was in the lineup when Mick arrived, as was a group from Adelaide – the Wills sisters. The concert was held in the monsoonal rain. Mick didn't worry about it at all. He'd been soaking wet for almost three weeks anyway so a few more hours weren't going to worry him. That was true of all those who watched; there were other things far more serious to worry about than watching a concert in the rain. Mick flew out the next day for a five-day break. He was glad to be away.

When he returned to Nui Dat the same concert was being held so he enjoyed it all over again.

Chapter 21
A NEW JOB

Mick had already been told before Operation Burnham that he would leave 3 Platoon and become the company intelligence representative attached to Company Headquarters (CHQ). CHQ was always there on patrol with the others, the pivot for the company with the commander directing the platoons, telling them where to go and what to do, relaying information they received. If they ran into any strife when they were by themselves, they had only one machine gun and limited other weapons. Staying close to the platoons was a must.

Mick was 'Tail-end Charlie', the person who brought up the rear, checking on what was coming from behind. He'd gone from the front to the back. Whenever platoons changed position or moved closer to each other, Mick hoped they wouldn't just fire at the figure on the track before they found out what was ahead of them. He was hoping the forward scout had been told CHQ was up there and they would pass them at some point. That was a conundrum. He needed to be well exposed so they could see him but he also needed to be safe from VC eyes. These were dangerous times, as much as any other. Occasionally Mick would get a surprised look from the forward scout coming towards him: 'Shit, they didn't tell me you were here,' the scout would say with his finger curled around the trigger of his SLR.

Operations flowed one after the other. Patrol followed patrol, chopper flights followed chopper flights. There were trips in APCs to different places, heavy jungle and open areas. In all of them the company moved through searching for VC installations. They found many. Small camps, weapons caches, huts hidden in the jungle, rice stores, clothing and every-thing else the VC would need to stay where they were. When the company arrived, the VC fled leaving behind all they had stashed away.

After six weeks A Company returned to Nui Dat for a short rest. The break didn't last long and after a week of relaxing as much as they could, in late November the battalion headed out on Operation Marsden. This time they went to the May Tao Mountains. The men hoped they'd be back for Christmas although the scheduled return was not until 28 December. Time was passing quickly, Mick noted. He was almost halfway through his tour.

The May Taos were an important VC stronghold, the last secret base remaining in Phuoc Tuy province. Nui May Tao was the pinnacle. This was the area from which the VC had left for the Battle of Long Tan and where they returned afterwards. The battalion had been set the huge challenge of clearing the VC from the area. The men knew they were in for a tough time but what wasn't conveyed to the troops was that the hospital at Vung Tau had been cleared out, as heavy casualties were expected. Every bed that could be spared would be needed.

Chinook helicopters flew in field artillery, skycranes delivered bulldozers and American howitzers, APCs and Hueys brought in men. All this was done at the base of the mountain, after which the long, slow climb to the summit began. The VC resistance would be fierce all the way up. A Company searched for bunkers, had many light contacts and found caches of ammunition and firearms. The company had set out accompanied by a squad of tanks which managed to become bogged only about 400 metres into the jungle where the going got a bit tough. They wanted help.

'Well, boys,' Major Belt said, 'you were going to come with us but we'll go by ourselves. You got yourselves into the mess, you can get yourselves out.'

The tank commander appealed to Belt. 'You can't leave us!'

'Yes we can,' Belt called, annoyed at the delay and how his company might have been compromised in their efforts.

As the men made their way up the mountain, Mick managed to scribble a note before a resupply arrived:

> ... At the moment the Company is 2000 metres high in the May Tao Mountains. And are they steep. Especially with all the gear we're carrying. We make the climb in dashes, going like hell for a couple of hours till we get where we have to go. Then we spend a lot of time recovering. Will probably have to finish this quickly as the resupply is coming in soon ... don't know where we'll be for Christmas, could still be bush, but won't know until they tell us ... nothing much else of interest ....

Plenty was going on. It was a long, slow process but eventually A Company reached the summit, where they set up a fire support base castle and a mortar platoon which fired over 2000 rounds on enemy positions.

*

Before the battalion headed out Mick's old scouting partner Tony Muir had well and truly regained his spirit – he wanted to get out there. They knew they had to get on with things, to have their minds right. They understood they weren't going to be sent away, told to go home; there was no clocking off or striking, so the only thing was to make the best of it. As much as he was keen, Muir had another concern. He had been told he was to be the new platoon medic. He was relieved of his scouting position and never told why. It was a toss-up which was worse, and harder on the mind. Was it better to be out the front with the heart pounding or to be on hand hoping against hope that no one would be wounded?

Muir was sent to Nui Dat for training, which consisted of a couple of days in a tent being shown how to bandage wounds and a few other things. Nothing elaborate, just the basics. The training had no depth at all, or at least nothing that Muir thought he could use to save a man's life. He didn't really understand what he needed to know but whatever the skills were that he needed, he knew he didn't really have them.

*

On 18 December, Lieutenant Marks-Chapman had taken the platoon from their base at the summit on a patrol along a spur line in heavy jungle and on very steep ground. Rocks of all shapes and sizes stuck out of the ground everywhere halfway up the mountain. The terrain was extremely difficult to negotiate. The men had even rid themselves of their packs, which they would return for later, to make the going easier. The platoon was heading along a creek when they were ambushed by a VC sentry who let off a Claymore mine, wounding one of the men.

Leigh Floyd spotted another VC approaching the wounded man.

From behind a tree, Floyd raised his weapon. He could see one of the other men between him and the VC so he held his fire, not wanting to risk shooting his mate. Bursts of fire from other SLRs thundered across the space, the barrage killing the VC just as he threw a grenade which exploded harmlessly. The wounded soldier was evacuated, which left Floyd's section with only three men. Despite being desperate for more men, the section still pressed ahead. Noting the lack of men, Marks-Chapman switched Floyd's section to the rear. Later that afternoon the platoon headed uphill toward the patrol base with one of the new men, Corporal Greg Stanford, in the lead. Stanford said he could smell the enemy and relayed that to Marks-Chapman, who raced forward quickly.

'Don't go up there, boss! Come back!' yelled the platoon sergeant. A Vietnamese bushman scout accompanying 3 Platoon at that stage had warned that there were enemy forces up the track.

Marks-Chapman had called for mortar back-up but it made no difference. When he reached Stanford and the other forward scout, Allen Brown, the enemy opened up with RPGs, machine guns and AK47s. The noise was intense, the jungle filled with the sound of death. Stanford and Brown were killed and Marks-Chapman severely wounded in the head.

Muir raced forward and did what he could to help the men, but it wasn't much. He found some cover and crouched next to Stanford, holding him in his arms. He felt helpless; he *was* helpless. Stanford had been badly hit in the chest and was drowning in his own blood. There was nothing Muir could do.

'Everything'll be OK, mate,' Muir tried to reassure Stanford in the moments before he died. 'Hang in there, mate, you'll be right; you'll be OK. There's a dust-off coming any minute.'

Muir knew it wouldn't be OK but he couldn't be silent, he wasn't going to do nothing at all.

As Muir remained with Stanford, other men managed to retrieve the body of Brown and dragged Marks-Chapman to safety.

A napalm airstrike was requested but it came too late, the enemy had gone. The platoon managed to secure its position and a dust-off was called in. An American chopper refused the request because the pilot didn't know whether the VC machine gun that had been firing at Stanford and Brown was still active. He thought it too dangerous to go in. An Australian chopper pilot, Squadron Leader Robinson, heard the conversation on the radio and simply radioed: 'Copied last transmission, will be there in five minutes.' When the chopper arrived, Marks-Chapman was winched up in what was a delicate and dangerous operation and flown to the American hospital nearby. He received as much treatment as was possible but died of his wounds the next day.

The platoon kept patrolling and drove the VC off the ridge, then harboured for the night. The bodies of the two men killed couldn't be evacuated so they stayed overnight with the men in the harbour, wrapped in hootchies, a constant reminder to all the platoon of what they were doing and the risks involved.

In the harbour, there was silence; there was nothing to say. That night Muir knew why he didn't want to be a medic but he couldn't get out of it, he had to do what he was told. He just hoped there'd not be another day like this one. He knew that until the real thing actually happened to you, no one could ever imagine what it was like to hold someone while they die. All the talk and instruction was useless then. Courses in tents were all very well but out there in the jungle, in the wet among the insects and the trees and leaves, with bullets flying and the screaming and yelling, it was very different.

Muir understood his responsibilities; he knew he had to go on. His thoughts on the rights and wrongs of what he was doing had become irrelevant, meaningless. It was only on this horrendous day with an incident like the one he had just been through and not knowing what to do, that he thought about what it all meant. Like the others, he was doing what he could for his mates, not for anyone in the political sphere.

By now, 3 Platoon had had two commanders killed, two corporals and two privates. All but a couple of the original members were wounded, together with many more wounded among the Reos. None of them looked too far ahead; one day then the next and so on, a common theme among those men who had been in Vietnam for a while. Many of them reflected on what was happening; about their dead and wounded mates. They tended to go quiet, to shut down, and to go wild when they had a chance.

When news of the contact was relayed to CHQ, Battalion Commander Lieutenant Colonel David Butler, in what was a rare display of emotion among senior officers, broke down at the utter sadness and waste of the situation and in abject despair at what was happening to 3 Platoon.

*

A new platoon commander, Lieutenant Stan Thornton, was choppered in for 3 Platoon on 21 December and more Reos joined them. Patrolling continued for them; there was little rest. The next day they came across a hospital with 30 huts that had served as wards, supply rooms and an operating theatre. The platoon captured a wounded VC and added him to the other prisoners the company had captured. These included many who had tried to escape from the hospital but couldn't walk very far. Two more had been hiding in a creek bed when they were discovered and taken prisoner. Colonel Butler congratulated the platoon for taking them all alive. All were treated by the Australian medics.

On Christmas Eve the company was flown back to Nui Dat. Mick had written home and sent it on the last resupply. His latest effort was not as profound as usual:

> ... Received this little card on yesterday's resupply – we all got one to send home so am mailing it today. We could be going back to the Dat either tomorrow or Christmas Day so that's a good bit of news. However, I don't think we'll be staying long. Everything is ok at this end.
>
> Wishing you all a Happy Christmas ...
>
> ... disastrous news heard the other day about the wharfies refusing to load the Jeparit with our Christmas beer and goodies. Hope they move the Navy in ...

Disgust was high among the troops over the union action in Australia. The *Jeparit* was a cargo ship that transported supplies to Vietnam for the government. Since 1967 it had been the focus of some anti-war protesters, with reloading in Sydney occasionally disrupted by union activity. Now, these protests came to a head when the Waterside Workers Federation refused to load or unload the ship. The government made a decision to commission her into the RAN in the middle of December. The ship became HMAS *Jeparit* and her master was given a commission in the RAN Reserve. It didn't fix all the problems, but it sorted most of them out and the Christmas parcels were there when the company came out of the jungle.

When the men returned to the safety of Nui Dat, all the tension and pressure could be released. It was like a big relief valve releasing. Alcohol steadiers tended to come into play. Memories could be wiped out for a few hours; cares would be washed away with rivers of VB.

Darts in the boozer were always popular. There'd be a big competition between sections. This was fun and not something that was readily associated with soldiers and jungles. When the boozer closed, there were tent parties to be enjoyed. Such things were totally against all orders. No drinking in the lines was allowed and any soldier who was caught risked heavy punishment, or so the rules stated. But punishment didn't really worry the men that much – they faced bigger threats in the scrub and the jungle – so parties would go on undetected, although how that happened was a mystery. Lights would be on, the tents would be full of blokes and the noise would have kept the whole place awake. Risking punishment didn't seem to matter. On many occasions even the men who were supposed to be leading the platoon would be in attendance, officers included.

One time a surprise line inspection was sprung by Major Belt. The men had hidden their cans underneath the tent's table that simply consisted of benches on top of tea chests that had one side open. The men were worried that anyone could have seen the empties. Belt stood right next to the table while inspecting the tent but didn't bend over. They got away with that, but on another occasion they weren't so lucky.

One of those tent parties was in full swing when a clever suggestion was made. Why didn't they go to the officers' mess and break in? There were no dissenters, everyone thought it was a good idea, so off they went and came back with steaks and other assorted goodies. Stealing is not looked on at all favourably in the armed services, except when junior ranks are flogging stuff from officers. That is acceptable. Not by the officers, sure enough, but by the junior ranks.

The men were caught and, when appearing before the authorities, the lies that were told by the men must have sounded so far-fetched they were given the absolute minimum punishment for being creative.

None if it seemed important in the whole scheme of things.

Chapter 22
HOSPITAL AND ANGELS

After a couple of months, Frank left Intensive Care and was put in an orthopaedic ward. It took a couple of days to adjust to his new surroundings and he slept for most of the time. When he was aware of what was going on, one of the men in the ward, Kentley Miles, who lay in the bed next to Frank's, handed him a Bible.

'Here, mate,' he said. 'Read this but hurry up because there's some poor bastard in the next room who needs it more, he's carkin' it.'

Frank took the Bible, which fell open at Psalm 23: 'Yea, though I walk through the valley of death, I will fear no evil.'

Miles had a rough way of making a point but it made Frank realise that no matter what his problems were, the bloke in the next room might have it worse. He remembered the saying the nuns would always recite at school when there was ever any whining about homework and other menial tasks they had to do: 'Boys,' the sister would say, 'I used to complain that

I had no shoes, until I met a man who had no feet. Now stop complaining.'

Frank, knowing he only had to look around the ward for someone who was not as fortunate as he, swore to himself he would not whinge from then on.

The men named their residence the 'Bay of Angels'. There were four of them, all wounded and flown in from Vietnam. There was Miles, who had been shot, Tex Aitken, who had been hit by an RPG, and Darby Munro, who had survived the Battle of Long Tan and later returned to Vietnam for a second tour. On the second trip Munro was not so lucky. He had lost both legs in a mine incident. Every time he looked at Munro, Frank considered he was fortunate.

The other beds were taken by men who came and went from time to time. Frank stayed. Newcomers were always heartily welcomed to the Bay of Angels, a practice which picked up their spirits when they looked at Frank and Munro. Everyone had a common interest: they were all in it together and, despite the differing medical problems, their deeper psychological traumas, which often dropped them into the quagmire of the mind, were similar. There were times each of them was severely depressed. Flashbacks, memories, pain, all of these things belted even the hardiest of men into a period of submission. And each knew the time to try and lift their mate out of the enveloping fug.

'Get your fuckin' act together, sort yourself out,' were some of the gentler things said. Black humour played a large part in sanity being retained. Simple, plain conversations about football, family and the meaningless dross of day-to-day life were standard topics. Mostly, talking with each other worked but at other times, the curtain would be drawn around the bed and silence ensued for a time. The darkness of the jungle at night was the same as the darkness of the mind. When the curtain was drawn back, both metaphorically and literally, no one said anything; there was just an acceptance of what had happened and life, such as it was, continued.

Heidelberg Repat was home to men from all wars. Occasionally, the ward clerk would put a really depressed World War I or II veteran in with the young blokes from Vietnam, and they'd give him a lift through their chiacking and laughter.

Most if not all of those who spent time in the Bay of Angels were smokers and when the nurses became sick and tired of the smell, the men would be taken onto the verandah, if the weather was good enough. Sometimes they'd have a radio and a nurse would organise the hospital's SP bookie to take a few bets while the men listened to the football and the races from Flemington or some other racecourse. The bets would be made after consumption of smuggled beer and scotch that played their part in Saturday afternoons that defied all the rules but gave the men a sense of normality.

The trips to the verandah were easy for those who could walk. Others could slip into a wheelchair and move themselves, but Frank, his leg still plastered but without the weights, had to stay in his bed and rely on the nurses to push him out into the fresh air. He was completely bed-bound. He wasn't being helped out of bed and wheelchaired to the toilet or the shower or anywhere else. Everything took place in bed. All his bodily functions happened in bed. All of them – even the testosterone-fuelled feelings of a 19-year-old weren't affected. Some mornings when the nurse came to bed-bathe him, she'd pull the sheets back and see what had happened.

'Oh dear, Frank, not again,' she'd chide him.

'Sorry, nurse, I can't help it,' he'd reply with a sly grin.

Frank found it difficult to absorb the fact that he was totally dependent on nurses to do everything for him – or at least help him. The nurses were wonderful in the main. Many were young girls who felt sorry for the men and couldn't understand the need for war. Those who were older were more perfunctory, the archetypal nursing sister or matron – starched uniforms and hats, clipped tones, brusque manner, but caring nonetheless. Gradually Frank became used to it all. He had no choice; it would be over a year before he stood up.

The days and weeks drifted by; some went quickly but most dragged. In between smoking packet upon packet of cigarettes, taking painkillers, reading books, talking to nurses, there'd be long bouts of monotonous nothing. The other men would be silent, the energy required to stay buoyant coming and going at irregular intervals. These were the times of thought. Thoughts that followed the theme of 'What am I going to do? What's the point of all this?'

Frank had always thought of going back to the farm at some stage but in his condition that would be difficult, without the problem of there being no money in farming. At times, he wanted to stay in the army. Or at least he thought he did. But even if the army allowed him to stay, that would entail a clerical job, which didn't appeal. Frank's thoughts were confused, they flitted in and out and around his mind in no particular order and with no particular end.

Then he thought about where he was and the state he was in. Even though he was a volunteer, he'd been sent to fight a war that he'd once thought was right because of the propaganda put forward by the government. He'd believed it all. Then he'd been blown up because of it and was lying there in hospital because of it. He thought he still believed the war was right, that Australians should be stopping the spread of Communism. But those feelings were a mixture of pride and obstinacy and not believing – or not wanting to believe – he might be wrong. In the months before he'd started to think about the stupidity of the whole Vietnam thing and how pointless it was. And how his mates had died in vain. Now, naively, he was thinking that everything would turn out well. That he'd get out of hospital soon and it would all be fine. He didn't believe that he would never be able to run again or that he would always walk with difficulty. That he'd never dance again. Those things would just happen, once he was up and about.

Christmas came and went, as did the New Year.

'Welcome to 1970, this year will be different,' Frank thought. 'Things will look up now.' He dreamed he'd soon be fit enough for a trip to Birchip; he thought about simple things like getting out of bed and showering or hobbling around. Hoping against hope he could do something, anything. But whenever a week or so went by with no problems, it would not be long before osteo-myelitis would rear up again or shrapnel would move around in his body. The next operation was always just around the corner.

When New Year had come and gone things weren't much different, the procedures still kept coming. Surgeons would check the growth of the leg bones and work out if they could extract any more bone particles or shrapnel. Each time there would be an operation and each time Frank would go through the same routine. He came to expect it – the pain, the drugs, the isolation of Intensive Care. The routine was familiar. All told, Frank would endure 25 trips to theatre, 15 of them for major operations.

After the initial surgery at Heidelberg the next biggest, towards the middle of 1970, was what was termed a cross-legged flap. This was a skin graft to try to cover the holes left by his operation and shortening of his leg. Frank's legs were placed in what were similar to birthing stirrups up to his knees with his ankles forced together and bound tight. A board about 30 centimetres long was placed between his legs to keep them apart. A 30 centimetre flap of skin was cut off one leg and overlaid onto the other. His legs were then encased in plaster, with a round lump the size of a soccer ball at the graft. There was to be no movement at all. The plaster made sure of that. If anything moved the graft would tear and the whole procedure would have to be done again.

When the operation was completed Frank was placed in a room by himself with continuous monitoring. The biggest worry was bleeding, which was a constant threat and which meant his blood pressure had to be taken at 10 minute intervals. Again, the risk of infection was always present. And blood clots.

During a routine visit by the charge nurse, Sister Murray, a World War II nurse, Frank mentioned the pain he was feeling. It had become worse during the night and while he didn't want to tell anyone he couldn't handle it, he had reached the stage where he needed some relief. Perhaps some more tablets would help, or at least a stronger dose. A small hole had been left in the ball of plaster holding Frank's legs together so Sister Murray grabbed a long knitting needle and inserted it. What she felt alarmed her.

'We've got a problem, Frank,' she said grimly.

The needle had been stopped by a large swelling and the indescribable pain when the needle hit it had reduced Frank to a quivering, tearful mess. He was rushed back to surgery and, when his legs had been extricated from the plaster, a huge blood clot was removed from around the graft. The clot was like jelly and was the size of a soup plate. If the clot had moved from his leg to his lungs, then Frank could have been minutes away from death.

The problem now was to redo the graft, so Frank's legs went back to their position before the clot was found. He was put back in Intensive Care. Not for three months would he return to the

Bay of Angels. Three months of long, long days, days of loneliness; three months of doubt, three months of wondering if it was worth it. Would he ever play sport or dance again? Would he even walk again? He wondered if he'd made the right decision; if the doctors had. Maybe he should have had done with it and let the surgeons amputate. He knew that deep down it wasn't his choice, the doctors would decide, but he thought that everything would have been over and done with if they'd taken his leg.

Frank felt despondent and he began going over the incident in his mind, replaying everything he could remember. He'd never been told much, if anything, about what had happened. There was so much confusion at the time and so little communication afterwards, that nothing was ever explained. Frank knew he had been so close to Skip that it could well have been him who triggered the mine. It must have been him, he thought, who else? His mind was so mixed up that he accepted what he thought was his guilt. He decided to write to Norma Hines, Skip's widow. He began: 'Norma, I don't know how to tell you this but how do I explain that I might have been the man responsible for killing the man I admired most in the world.'

Frank didn't mention the mine or talk about the explosion, just that he might have been the person who inadvertently killed her husband. He said how much he loved Skip and how much he valued him. He told Norma how sorry he was. A couple of weeks later, Norma wrote back, thanking Frank for the letter, inquiring as to his condition and telling him that he wasn't responsible, that it was something that happened in war.

While the letter helped, Frank began fretting, wondering about everything possible. Most of all, he wondered how his mates were going back in the jungles of Vietnam.

Chapter 23
HAPPY NEW YEAR, VIETNAM

The men had certainly enjoyed Christmas. There was plenty of food and even more grog. It was a time to forget what had happened, to not think about where they'd been and to let their hair down. Which they did. They were with their mates, that's all that counted. While in Vungers one bloke had swapped his watch in a bar for a bottle of rice whiskey, a rough brew, probably from an undercover VC. He'd hidden it away and Christmas was the ideal time to open it.

The break in Nui Dat didn't last too long. It appeared that any time the company came back to the Dat something else would quickly appear on the agenda. On 28 December they piled into trucks and headed out again, this time to the Horseshoe, a defensive position on an extinct volcano crater outside the village of Dat Do.

Before they left, the commanding officer, Major Belt, had approached the regimental sergeant major (RSM) with an unusual request: he wanted a transfer for one of the soldiers: Leigh Floyd. Someone had said that Floyd was the only remaining member of

the original 3 Platoon soldiers who had left Townsville together.
That the others had all been killed or wounded or, if they recovered, had been transferred to other duties away from infantry.
Belt considered the odds of being killed or wounded against
Floyd were too great and that he needed not only a change, but
a chance. The RSM agreed and made Floyd the RSM's batman.
When Floyd left the platoon it was believed, incorrectly, that no
one remained from the mob that had left Australia together and
spent those first few weeks in Nui Dat. From 27 men, Floyd was
the only one who had not suffered from a mine or a bullet or
some other misfortune.

Mick was upbeat when he wrote on 30 December:

Another short note. We came in on the 24th and the card
stayed in my pack and I didn't mail it. Still, it goes now.
Thanks for all the presents and goodies. It was really great
everyone coming back and opening their parcels. Litter
everywhere. Very strange some of the tinned food I received.
Olives? Asparagus? Lamb's tongue? Must have been away
from home too long; my tastes have been forgotten! We
had a traditional Christmas lunch where the officers waited
on us, boy did they get a hard time. We got to the beach
at the Badcoe for a day trip as there is no R&C for the
Battalions at present. Arrived at The Horseshoe two days
ago and have been running around ever since. The rest of
CHQ arrived today and 3 Platoon has gone out on land
clearing as protection force. Hope you enjoyed Christmas
and New Year. Only 4 ½ months to go at the maximum . . .

*

The Horseshoe was a fire support base on the rim of an extinct volcano some 8 kilometres from Nui Dat. Named for its shape, the Horseshoe dominated the approaches to the village of Dat Do. Stationed there was a unit of soldiers from the Army of the Republic of Vietnam (ARN) that CHQ was to train. It was also a haven for VC infiltrators. This was the starting point for many operations that gave protection to the local villages. It also marked the beginning of the infamous barrier minefield that caused so many the problems for the men patrolling in the area.

One night after the company had settled in, it was mortared by VC hidden in the huts and surrounds of the village. Several of the mortar rounds fell between two sandbagged 6-man tents occupied by 2 Platoon. Shrapnel holes through the tents left them looking like colanders and a corrugated iron shower was left fully ventilated. Luckily, there were only very light wounds among the men.

During A Company's patrols from the Horseshoe, 3 Platoon ran into more mine trouble, with two engineers killed and other soldiers wounded. More reinforcements were needed.

One of the things men noticed during their time at the Horseshoe was the sound of explosions as engineers detonated mines in the minefield. Under orders to scrap the minefield, heavy rollers and APCs with strengthened undercarriages of steel were being used to drive along the rows where mines had been laid, detonating them as they went. The method was noisy but effective, although it would be a long time before the danger was eliminated. To anyone who had been in a mine explosion, the sound was chilling.

*

The battalion had been out for six weeks and a 36-hour leave in Vung Tau was most welcome. That and another couple of days in Nui Dat was all the time that was spent in relative safety. The end of the tour was in sight and there had been much speculation and rumour about what would happen when 6 RAR's time was up. Information was confirmed that they would be flying to Australia on 15 May and marching through Townsville on 20 May. Then they'd be sent home by train. Each man looked forward to departure day but it didn't distract them from the job at hand.

Before that, work had to be done and there was plenty of danger to face. They had come so far, this was no time for upsets. The men were reinserted by helicopter towards the end of February. A Company was headed to confront two VC Companies who were located near a river junction called Suoi Giau. They had a 'hot' insertion, meaning the landing area was bombarded by artillery – brassing up, they called it – before they landed, setting the position afire. From there they set off on a 20-kilometre walk to the area where they were told that a large VC force, part of one of the companies targeted, was hiding in a bunker system. The platoons were ordered to move in from different sides of a creek, with 3 Platoon at the front. CHQ was by itself on one side of the creek. The men were operating in dense jungle and, while moving carefully, the two forward scouts ran into a VC sentry who fired from close quarters, severely wounding both of them. From about 20 metres away, the rest of the VC opened fire with everything they had: machine guns, AK47s, small arms, grenades and RPGs. 2 Platoon was pinned down by machine gun fire and could do little, while 1 Platoon had travelled much further down the creek. The close-range firing left 3 Platoon once again reeling from casualties. In all, the platoon suffered 12 wounded in a matter of minutes, including the new Platoon Commander Lieutenant Thornton and three NCOs. An urgent dust-off was called in.

Men were being hauled out of the firefight the simplest and easiest way they could be. There was no time for niceties; they just had to be dragged away from any more danger. Tony Muir was going to the wounded as fast as he could, treating the worst first, reassuring them and telling them a dust-off was almost there. The VC remained in the bunker system and withdrew during the night. Finally the shooting stopped, hearts slowed and the men were dusted off. There were more wounded than there were fit men left.

Mick wrote an undated letter home shortly after the contact:

Sorry for not writing for a while but the last couple of resupps have been a bit rushed. The Company had a big contact with a VC Battalion . . . 3 Platoon came in heavy contact with sentries and then continuing a sweep ran into a major bunker system and had 12 men wounded. Next day the Company went into the system but the VC had left during the night. Spent the next few days collecting documents, information and destroying the bunkers. 3 Platoon found another small bunker and we destroyed that too. Since then we have been moving south following the VC escape route which is only about 4 miles from Nui Dat. The Op finishes tomorrow March 10th and first night back will be the usual Company barbecue, then 36 hours in Vungers. . . .

*

The more the time passed, the more the men started thinking of home. As it went on, 'We Gotta Get Out Of This Place' became more real and more applicable. 'Leaving on a Jet Plane' was something in the back of their minds all the time. In typical army fashion, though, departure dates, times and routes changed with regularity. From going home by plane and train and marching through Townsville, there were various permutations, including flying in to Mascot Airport in Sydney and then being flown to each state. Whichever way they finally made it home, there was just one operation to go, which would last about a month, and then they'd be off.

On 24 March, A Company went by chopper to the northeastern boundary of Phuoc Tuy province near the May Tao Mountains, an area they were quite familiar with. CHQ was patrolling with 1 Platoon when they came across a bunker system which they checked out for a day and blew up the next. There was no enemy action, so after cutting a helipad by hand and with explosives the men were choppered out to a position north of the May Taos. CHQ dug themselves in and were to stay for three days, which Mick thought was pretty good. He'd had a bit to do for the last few days during which he and Company Medic Rob Laurent had to lug a big crate containing high explosives wherever they went. The men still had all their usual gear and pack but now had a pole slung between them with the crate swinging on it. The company had flown in too much explosive that day and it couldn't be left behind.

A few days later a resupply was scheduled and Mick dashed off a note home:

Only 24 days to go before this Op is over. Received your card on the last resupp. Wasn't too sure when Easter was but hope you had a good one. This time last year I was on pre-embarkation leave so it's been a pretty quick year. . . . Not much time left as the resupp is coming in soon. Tomorrow we are inserting into a new area as things are pretty quiet where we are . . . must finish. Hope everyone is ok at home . . .

Mick wasn't aware of where they were headed when he wrote the letter. He knew that other orders would be arriving and that A Company would be moving in a different direction. That night they were told they were going back to the area near the Long Hais, back to the Light Green. Sleep did not come easily.

Chapter 24
ONE LAST TRAGEDY

Thankfully, the last operation proved to be relatively quiet, at least compared to other operations that A Company had carried out. The end, not only of the operation but of 6 RAR's tour, was drawing near. While patrols discovered many bunkers and had a few contacts, no further casualties were suffered. The weeks were going quickly; the month in the bush had now dwindled to days. And then suddenly, it seemed, there was just one day left. The next morning would bring trucks and relief, Nui Dat then home. Tomorrow would arrive quickly but, for now, there was one day to get through.

A Company was searching through the scrub with the three platoons dispersed over various areas. 3 Platoon and CHQ were some distance apart but following the same track when the track split into two. 3 Platoon went one way and CHQ the other. The forward scout of CHQ didn't notice a mine marker – a stick sharpened at both ends left on the track by the VC to tell their own men what was underfoot. He walked over it. The company commander, Major Belt, picked up the stick and told everyone to stop, which they did. A few metres further on, the track widened slightly into a patch of sandy ground.

Those members of CHQ who had passed the stick were told to break track left, one of the methods employed in this type of situation to try and minimise the risk if a mine exploded. Each man had to walk to the point where the lead scout had stopped and turn at right angles and move off the track to a safe distance. Those forward followed this procedure, but there was still a risk.

As the forward observation officer, Lieutenant Bernard Garland, moved down the track he stepped on a mine and was killed.

The company medic, Rob Laurent, rushed forward and tried to keep Garland alive. Garland had lost most of his blood when Laurent reached him, but still Laurent told him everything was going to be OK, that a dust-off was coming. It was too late, Garland had already died. He had only a few days left in country before his tour would have been over and he would have been on his way home. Five others were wounded, including two radio operators and the CSM, Jim 'Smiler' Myles.

Dust-off choppers arrived and hovered above the area, the rotors sending sand billowing into the faces of those on the ground, stinging and making it extremely difficult to see. Laurent helped load Garland's body, wrapped in his hootchie, into the chopper. After the chopper left, Laurent shut his eyes, blocking out the thoughts and the vision, and violently stabbed the ground with his bayonet in frustration.

The operation was called off immediately the choppers took off. CHQ linked up with 3 Platoon and commandeered a couple of its men to carry the signal sets for them. The men who were left walked in patrol mode, slowly and carefully, out to a dirt road where they were picked up by trucks. The weeks left before heading back to Australia would be spent in Nui Dat, winding down and waiting for the plane to take them home. Trying to make sense of it all was verging on impossible. This was the last day but one of the battalion's operational commitments in Vietnam. One day – 24 hours – and it would have all been over.

*

Back in Nui Dat a day or so later, the men all packed up quietly. A Company was due to leave on 12 May 1970. There were no outrageous shows of emotion, although they were relieved and happy. Once everyone had left Vietnam, the battalion was to return to Townsville and then do a tour in Singapore. Talk circulated among the men about signing on for a year to go with it. The thoughts were only fleeting, though, something to talk about to occupy their minds. Really, they all craved the safety of home. The battalion held a farewell parade in Nui Dat on 15 May 1970 and was told by Brigadier Weir, the officer in charge of the Australian contingent in Vietnam, that they were the finest infantry battalion he had seen.

The men hoped to leave all together as a battalion and to have ten days or so at sea on HMAS *Sydney* to unwind. It wasn't to be. Back in Australia, it was the height of the moratorium marches and the *Sydney* was undergoing a few maintenance issues anyway, so the men were flown back piecemeal. Had they come back on the *Sydney* and disembarked at Townsville, there would have been a parade through the streets with people clapping and cheering them. For all but a couple of the last battalions to return on the *Sydney* a welcome march was held, but not for these men. Towards the end of Australia's commitment in Vietnam, a couple of parades were cancelled. In the years when there were parades, there was a distinct mixture of welcome and thanks combined with a portion of derision and abuse. After the marches broke up and the pubs around the city filled up with the servicemen, there were fights and arguments about Australia's involvement. Soldiers and sailors defended their honour proudly – if at times aggressively.

After piling into Chinooks early one May morning, the same way they had arrived in Nui Dat, Mick and the others, quietly lost in their own thoughts and memories, headed off to Saigon's Tan Son Nhut airport, where they caught a chartered Qantas flight back to Sydney. They touched down about 10 pm that night. Flights out were scheduled for various times in the morning, so the men had to settle in for the night. The canteens and cafes closed about midnight and while airport authorities would have been happier if no one was around, there wasn't much they could do about these soldiers waiting to go home. Most of the men stayed in the airport, although some went to local pubs or caught taxis to Kings Cross, returning in various states of disrepair.

Mick and a few others from 3 Platoon sat around a table – this was the last time for years they would be together – talking about simple things: family, friends, home towns and about being glad to be back. There were no stories spun about what they had been through; they all knew that and, besides, it was better left unsaid. Even Major Belt came along and had a few beers. Belt had tried to speak to the men on the plane and had been howled down. He started trying to say, 'Thanks to you all for your contribution,' but was interrupted by the murmuring chatter of the soldiers. Belt, a hard taskmaster and not overly popular with the men, gave up and returned to his seat. Now he was listened to politely.

The soldiers slept on the rows of seats or on the floors of the airport's lounges, bodies strewn around everywhere. The next day they headed for the departure gates when their flights were called. Some went to Queensland, others to Perth and Melbourne. A few went to Adelaide with Mick. When they landed, some would catch trains or buses to their homes in the country after landing in the capital cities, others would be picked up. All of them flew away to the rest of their lives. In the majority of cases, these men who had fought alongside each other and had seen many of their mates killed or wounded would not set eyes upon each other for more than 15 years.

It was said those soldiers who returned by air in the middle of the night had more trouble readjusting to life than those who came back on the *Sydney*. The military appeared indifferent to them, there were no crowds, no parade, just a cold airport lounge where they waited by themselves. It was an inglorious end.

Chapter 25
MAKING PROGRESS

When Frank was moved back to the Bay of Angels after his skin graft repair, he'd been in hospital for over 12 months. There were a different lot of wounded men in residence by this time but the feeling was much the same; they relied on each other and all had similar concerns.

Each morning the nurses would arrive, cheerful, most of them.

'How are you feeling today, Frankie, any problems, anything you need?'

'Well, now you mention it, yes,' Frank would reply, a mischievous glint in his eye.

'Behave yourself!' The retort was always the same.

Many an hour, especially at night when sleep was not to be found, when fear took hold, when loneliness made his mind wander and his skin ache, and when the pain became either real or imagined, would be spent talking to the nurses. They'd talk about their problems, Frank would talk about his. They'd chat about the world and what was happening in Vietnam. All the talk would help – both the nurses and Frank.

One special nurse was Mary Kelly, who spent time with Frank talking about life in the country, a shared loved. Mary understood what Frank felt when he talked of the Mallee and the open spaces of the countryside. She was a few years older than Frank, engaged, and looking forward to her wedding. Frank talked about his plans to be wed and later, when the silence between them came, as it inevitably did when he drifted off to sleep, Mary Kelly would steal away, her job done as much as it could be.

*

Frank didn't have a lot of visitors. His twin Bryan visited a few times a week. His cousins Veronica and Maree visited each Sunday if Frank was well enough. His mum came the first time and then his dad twice when they were called in because Frank was not expected to live much longer. Maurie came both times but Eileen couldn't face it. Frank said he understood. Two of Frank's uncles visited a couple of times, dressed up and wearing hats the way country men did when visiting the city. They would tip their hats to the nurses, always with a smile. The nurses loved it and told Frank that gentlemanly conduct was alive and well in Birchip.

Even though all visitors were appreciated, there was one that was special – the girl he'd met before he left Townsville and who had written to him almost every day while he was away. Her letters were the kind that soldiers waited for and read several times; letters that reminded them of home and kept them going through extraordinary times.

Constance and Frank had become engaged before he left, only a few weeks after meeting. Now she had turned 18, she had moved to Melbourne, managed to find a job in retail and was waiting for Frank to leave hospital so they could be married. It would be a long wait. Eventually it would take place, although it wouldn't become the 'happy ever after' story they had both hoped it might be.

First, though, was Frank's rehabilitation. It had been 13 long, arduous months since he had been on his feet. For all that time he had lain in bed with plaster on his left leg from his hip to his toes, save for the trips to the operating theatres when they cut it off and replaced it later. His weight had dropped to under 50 kilos. One morning the head physiotherapist and two assistants appeared at his bedside, smiling. After a few pleasantries, they got down to the business at hand.

'We're going to stand you up,' the physio said. 'And you probably won't last more than 10 seconds.'

Frank was concerned. 'Will I get dizzy?'

'A bit maybe, but there will be the pain of the blood going through your leg. It hasn't been there for over a year, so be ready for it.'

The physios helped Frank, still in plaster, gingerly out of bed. The idea was to stand him up and hold him so there was no pressure on the leg at all. They steadied him as they lifted and held him as he stood up. The pain was worse than anything he had experienced so far, including the mine, the shrapnel, and the stretcher with Johnny Needs. He cried out and the tears ran down his face involuntarily. He didn't realise he was crying.

They wanted Frank to lie down again but he was determined to last longer than they thought he would. He did, but only by three seconds. He lay down again after 13 seconds and took quite some time to recover, his leg throbbing, his head ready to explode and the pain throughout his body lashing at every nerve. In some small way, standing up was a victory.

Each time Frank had undergone an operation the plaster was cut off with a saw. Underneath, his skin would be black and dead. The nurses and doctors would peel the stinking skin off. The stench was unbelievable, abattoir-like. Frank had been given a bottle of deodorising drops of some kind that he would drip onto the plaster. The liquid would seep through the plaster and curtail the smell coming through and into the ward. The skin would then grow back under the new plaster before dying again. After the next operation, it would be the same. Sometimes people would come into the room and talk about the stink and Frank would ask for more drops.

Over the next month, the exercise of standing up was repeated regularly. Gradually Frank learnt how to walk again, to put one foot painfully, carefully in front of the other. He fought the pain and overcame it to the extent that he could move around on crutches, but still in full-leg plaster. It felt like freedom. He thought he'd be out of hospital and away in a couple of weeks. After over a year on his back, the thought of being upright was better than anything else he could imagine.

The physios placed Frank in what they called a Canadian Bucket, an elevated shoe with calipers that had plaster over it to the knee. This would support his foot but would give the rest of the leg freedom. It would allow the weight to be distributed on his knee and above but would allow his thigh, which had wasted away to almost nothing, to redevelop with physiotherapy.

The boot and plaster worked and Frank's rehabilitation progressed smoothly enough so that he spent more time out of bed than in it.

*

By mid-1970 protests against the war had increased across the country. Newspapers reported on protest marches regularly.

The papers were all available in the Repat and were read by the soldiers, upsetting them. Frank was beginning to turn away from his philosophical views on the reasons for fighting in Vietnam, even though he wasn't sure he was capable of thinking philosophically. His concern with the protesters was that none of them had been there. He'd been there, his mates were still there, and many more would go.

'These pricks don't understand, how the fuck would they know what was happening?' the men would say to each other. There was a significant disconnect between the public's perception of Vietnam and the soldiers' experience.

'I'd like 'em to see body bags with mates being put into Hueys. They might change their thinking,' Frank said to a nurse one night.

One morning soon after, Frank woke up and saw his brother Bryan with one of his mates. Bryan was a young man of the times: university arts student, long hair, bell-bottoms, political views, and different attitudes. Bryan told Frank he was involved with protest marches and was a member of the local moratorium committee. He had marched a few times in protest.

'We're not against the soldiers, Frank, only the war,' he said.

'Bryan,' sighed a disappointed Frank, 'I'm totally fuckin' sick of reading the papers and listening to reports about the protests. You people have no idea what's happening.'

The brothers argued about what was going on but, despite their opinions being polar opposites, they remained close. Bryan kept visiting. Frank told him that most of what was said and written about the war was to do with Americans: civilian casualties, drugs and so forth. None of it, he believed, was true of the blokes he knew. It was tiring and Frank tried not to think about the politics of the whole affair, only about his mates still over there.

The public mood had changed over the years since Australia had committed to fight in Vietnam. Most people supported the war in the early years, but as Frank had lain in hospital and his mates had battled on in the war-torn country, that had changed. Draft-dodgers, who were widely condemned in previous years, were now celebrated, with those against the war actively encouraging more to object to their call-up.

Television reports on the war were shocking. The everyday reports and things like the Tet Offensive, when the North Vietnamese launched a major surprise attack on the south with horrendous casualties, and the horrors of My Lai, a village whose civilian inhabitants were slaughtered by American Lieutenant William Calley and his men, made the public realise how terrible this war was.

Protests were very noisy and quite regularly turned violent when police tried to control the mob. In late 1969, the Vietnam Moratorium Campaign, or VMC, had been formed and they set a date for the first moratorium to take place in early May 1970. This mass demonstration brought about 100,000 people together on the streets of Melbourne. Across the whole of Australia, an estimated 200,000 people gathered to protest against the Vietnam War.

There were deep divisions in the community. What you thought about the war gave others an insight into your politics, or so some believed. The divisions weren't so prevalent or obvious in rural areas, but in the cities they were stark. The Vietnam War caused arguments everywhere. Families were at loggerheads, friendships were lost, relationships broke up and tensions ran high in workplaces. The feeling manifested itself in newspaper editorials, opinion pieces and letters to the editor. Young people vented their feelings through music, with protest songs becoming the big hits of the day.

Prime Minister John Gorton's Liberal government kept up its support for America while the Labor Party, under Gough

Whitlam, had made a promise to the Australian people to bring the troops home if he was elected. Whitlam narrowly missed out in late 1969, but three years later he would claim victory.

The confusing thing to the soldiers was that while most of them agreed with the right to protest, many of those objecting to the war actually supported the North Vietnamese. The soldiers could not understand why. The universities and the left-wing sections of society were prevalent among the more strident protests, but there were many other ordinary suburban folk who simply did not like the war and what it was doing to their young men. That was fair enough, most of the soldiers didn't like what it was doing either, but when accusations of rape and murder and the killing of women and children were spat at soldiers in uniform, it became too much. Clashes increased.

Frank experienced that attitude first-hand on a day's outing to see a movie in the city with some of the other hospitalised men in wheelchairs. A couple of passengers helped the nurses lift the chairs into a tram and then out again at their stop, but on the street they found trouble. Here in the middle of Melbourne a small protest happened to be passing as the veterans and nurses made their way along the footpath. One of the protesters stopped and abused the vets, who didn't say much although they wanted to.

After a minute or so Frank could not hold back: 'Piss off and find out what really fuckin' happened,' he yelled.

To that a young woman chanting slogans looked at Frank and came closer, rubbing her half-eaten pie in his face and hair.

Frank laughed as he cleaned it off. 'You forgot the fuckin' sauce.'

The nurses, who had tried to stop the protester, hurried their charges away before the incident became uglier than it already was.

*

The months went by slowly and painfully but in October 1970, Frank hobbled down the aisle at his wedding. The future looked brighter than it had for a long time. While it was a wonderful occasion, it again reinforced to Frank the limitations that had been placed on him by his wounds. To see others whirling away on the dance floor was difficult – after all, this was his wedding, he was supposed to be dancing. He decided to do something about it and took Constance onto the floor where he stood, leg in plaster, foot in the Canadian Bucket, and held her in his arms, swaying as much as he could without falling over. It wasn't much, but it was something.

Professor Hodge danced past and smiled at Frank, gently shaking his head at the sheer determination of his patient.

Chapter 26
ADAPTING TO LIFE

Frank was still in the army and even though he and Constance were renting a flat in East Kew, his trips there were few and far between. He was still a hospital patient for the vast majority of the time, the occasional weekend an exception. When he was able, Frank worked in the army cadre at the hospital, a section that did paperwork for the patients and visited those who had no one to see them. Frank would mostly go in a wheelchair, occasionally on crutches, sometimes hobbling in his Canadian Bucket. He would talk to the wounded men about their recovery. He tried all the while to be positive, telling his story and helping them understand that things could get better.

It wasn't only veterans from Vietnam that he spoke to. At the time the hospital was home to many World War II servicemen who valued the time he spent with them. Some had no families, nowhere else to go, and were entering the last years of their life. Frank was someone who listened, easing their burden with his presence. Not telling them what they should think but simply spending precious time with them.

While he was listening or offering the support that came naturally to him and was important for the men, Frank was comfortable, at peace in his mind. Afterwards he felt rewarded, pleased he had found a purpose in a place he felt at times had no purpose save for mending broken bodies. Broken minds also needed mending. He knew there were patients who were scared of being discharged, of being alone and uncared for. He found, in his own way, he could help.

While his treatment became easier and easier, Frank still spent most of his time in hospital until finally he was discharged on 27 February 1971, a few months short of the two years Professor Hodge had told him to expect. He had turned 21 a month earlier, but there was no big birthday party. Most twins would probably have had a joint party but Frank and Bryan didn't. Frank wasn't worried at all. He didn't think it was that important, so his 21st birthday came and went like any other day.

Frank was elated when he left hospital; at last, he thought, his battles were over. They weren't. With the hospital discharge came a discharge from the army. The army had asked him if he wanted to stay but Frank knew they were only half-serious. He knew that even if they kept him on he'd be behind a desk somewhere being looked at pityingly, and he didn't want pity. He loved the army, despite everything that had happened, but he couldn't be the soldier he wanted to be, so he left. Again, his mind was playing tricks. He wanted to believe that he loved the army, so he couldn't or wouldn't admit to himself that he was bitter about what he'd become.

When he limped out on crutches that last day, Frank felt totally and utterly lost. All the teamwork and mateship he'd felt and enjoyed for the last four years was gone. The people he'd known in his platoon, the blokes in recruit training and in Townsville, were all somewhere else. His family was a long way away, living their own lives. Those in the hospital who had surrounded him with care were all gone as well. He was a soldier, something that he knew he was good at but it had been taken brutally away from him. He was, apart from Constance, alone. Frank had been discharged with no counselling or even suggestions about what he should – or could – do. The army had basically said, 'Off you go, Frank, good luck.'

*

As much as he could, Frank pushed his feelings of sadness to the back of his mind. He was alive, after all. He was married, he needed to start again. A week later he made his way to the local Commonwealth Employment Service office to look for a job. He found it a difficult task: he caught a train and with his crutches had trouble making it up the steps from the platform of the railway station to the street. He decided to sit down and scramble his way up on his backside. There were not many passengers at the station, but enough to make Frank feel uncomfortable. His short hair and his jacket with the active service pin made it obvious he was a soldier, but no one came to his aid, they just stared and walked past him. Vietnam was a dirty word. One of them sneered at him.

'What are you fuckin' lookin' at?' Frank yelled at them. People simply ignored him, put their heads down and walked on, pretending he wasn't there at all.

He managed to make his way across the street and into the building, where a sympathetic CES staffer took his details.

'If anything comes up, I'll send you a telegram,' he told Frank, who didn't hold out any real hope of being contacted. If nothing happened, what was he to do? He had the rest of his life to think about and hopefully a family to look after. How could he do it in this condition?

When he arrived back at his flat after a few hours in a local pub, a telegram was waiting telling him to report for an interview a couple of days later for a position as a clerk. Frank turned up and was given the job. He worked there for a few months but found himself in the pub more often than he knew he should have been. He was an angry man. Angry that he had lost what he thought he might have had – his farming opportunities, his army career, his health and his future. Angry at what had happened to him and the way he could see that his disabilities meant life would never be simple for him. He was angry at the world. What was he going to end up like?

When he got on the tram in the morning, the conductor would help him on. He had to stand at the front bag section because he couldn't bend his leg enough to sit down and, besides, it would be in the way of other passengers. Each night he'd get off the tram near his flat and instead of going home to Constance, he'd go to the pub, where he met up with a couple of other veterans. They'd drink and talk and argue with other people in the pub. He thought the anger would dissipate with drink, but it didn't. Sometimes it would mask his feelings, but then they'd reappear. Nothing seemed easy. Eventually he'd go home but was scared of going to sleep, for when he slept everything came back to him.

The jungle was real in his dreams. He'd dream of falling into a punji pit but he would float and never hit the spikes that he could see. Everything would be black and faces would swirl around in his head like ghosts. In the dark of the jungle he'd feel his Armalite in his hand but when he looked down there'd only be a stick and he'd panic about what he'd do if a contact came. Always in the background was the constant metallic cough of an M16 or an SLR and the crackle of radio messages that made no sense at all, even if he could hear the words. His mind would remember the mine explosion and he'd be back on the ground waiting for relief with the sounds of the dust-off helicopters just over the rubber trees. The sound would grow louder and louder but the choppers never came into view. He'd feel his shattered leg, feel the blood soaking him, but when, he woke with a start, it wasn't blood, just pools of sweat. Then he'd lie awake until his pounding heart became calm.

The next day he'd do it all again: struggling at work, drinking on the way home and, many times, the nightmares. Life was becoming a problem. He'd only been in his new job for three months and he knew he could not go on like that. He had enough presence of mind to know that he had to look for options.

A family friend had moved to the small country town of Bega on the far south coast of New South Wales to work for a local car dealer. He rang Frank one day a few weeks after he'd arrived.

'How'd you like a job as a credit manager up here?' he asked Frank.

'Shit, I've got no idea about any of that but I'll be happy to have a chat. Sounds like a good challenge.'

Frank thought the move could help, so he and Constance left Melbourne, bought a housing commission house with a war service loan and settled in to life in the country. The job was good, the couple welcomed a daughter and Frank joined the RSL where he found some solace. His life was back on track. Or so he thought. It wasn't long before he was spending a lot of time in hospital. During his extended recovery in the Repat, it was not only Frank's leg that caused him problems. While his wounds were healing, the rest of his body was breaking down. The weight of the plaster had caused complications with his hips, his other joints and, worst of all, his back. His spinal muscular system had deteriorated badly. When he sat in a chair for an extended period, such as he needed to do at work, the pain was intense. He'd then go home and not be able to move. He had no other option than to work, although sooner or later the problems he faced with his body would overcome him and he'd go to hospital for a week or two at a time.

Frank slept on the floor at home, as it was the only way he could find relief. From time to time Frank considered going back to the strong medication he'd been on during his time in hospital, but he'd seen what drugs had done to some of his mates, the way they had come to rely on them, and he was determined to do things differently. His determination could have been construed as obstinacy but when he took potent drugs, as well as helping with the pain, they took away his sense of reality. Frank only allowed himself the strongest over-the-counter painkillers. He was 21 years old and he wanted to think that one day soon he'd be better. Surely it couldn't last much longer?

The pain was horrific at times. He was missing some three months a year from work. He needed to work for any number of reasons, sanity being one of them, money being another. Frank also tried hard to keep up with domestic duties, still mowing his own lawn, limping and stumbling behind the mower for hours. He'd tidy up the garden, weeding and cutting here and there, although he paid for it in pain later. Shattered bone and shrapnel moved constantly around his body, hitting nerve ends. Degeneration was present in his tendons, his bones, his nerves, his muscles – everything about his body was deteriorating. He became angry again. He began drinking again. His rehabilitated life wasn't working. He wasn't rehabilitated at all. 'Is this how it is always going to be?' Frank wondered.

Gough Whitlam had been elected in 1972 and had ended conscription and brought an end to Australia's involvement in Vietnam. This was a move welcomed by all. For Frank it was a bittersweet day. Just because the war was ending didn't mean the torment he and other veterans felt would also end. It didn't stop the nightmares, the sweats, the flashbacks. It didn't stop the problems with drinking or the fact that there were those who still harboured grudges against anyone who even mentioned the word Vietnam. He was still angry; still lost at times. He was still coming to terms with the way he limped and the pain he still felt.

*

In an ironic twist, Frank and Constance had become parents of triplets born on Long Tan Day – which would become Vietnam Veterans Day – in 1973. There were now four children under three in the house. Problems abounded – Frank's problems, the problems associated with young children, the problems of providing for them and the problems between husband and wife.

Frank's drinking again became very heavy, not helped by the fact he was now a board member in the local RSL. Frank again had found something that he liked and he thought he was good at. While there were a few who were against the war, most members of the RSL were pro the Vietnam War. By and large, that was the way things were in the country regions. It was mainly the metropolitan, suburban and inner-city types that were against it. In the country, conservatism reigned and if the government said the war was OK then it was OK.

The occasional dissenting voice was heard but mostly Frank was welcomed, as were other Vietnam veterans who found their way to smaller rural areas. These men would sit around the bar and talk to other members, drinking themselves into oblivion and finding comfort in like-minded souls. Or they would just stay home and drink by themselves, feeling rejected by the world. Frank's friends formed a local branch of the Vietnam Veterans Association and Frank took on the role of president. It was another activity that would keep his mind from drifting off to unpleasant places.

None of it helped at home, though, and it didn't help with the pain or the time he spent in hospital. And his mind always played tricks. Frank was twice found in the back garden behind the bushes: he thought he was back in the Jay, back in the front of the platoon, checking out the way for his mates and looking for enemy contacts. When Constance found him, he said, 'Shh, don't let them hear you. I'll look after you.'

On another occasion, after a few post-work beers at the RSL, he disappeared and was found later the following day weeping in a car 100 kilometres away. He had travelled over 400 kilometres and must have driven round and round, having bought, or stolen, petrol somewhere. A friend who had once been a psychiatric nurse found him. Frank was stunned. He had no idea how or why it had happened.

Work continued, though, along with some degree of normality. Frank wouldn't give up. He'd work extra time to make up the hours he missed. He obtained a private agent's licence, which he needed to progress in his job, part of which involved repossessing goods when someone lapsed on the payment contract. At times he was torn with his job, believing that everyone was entitled to a second chance. To that end, in the majority of cases he'd renegotiate the contract and everyone was happy.

There were times, though, when things didn't go well. Frank always needed someone to go with him, to help with driving.

Sometimes he needed protection. One day he had to talk to a man about payments on a chainsaw. The man, tall and strong with a fierce demeanour, wasn't impressed at all and threatened to throw a small generator at Frank, after which he started the chainsaw and said he would 'Cut your fuckin' legs off'. Being only as tall as Frank, Frank's driver, positioned behind the car, stood on a can and waved a shovel around, saying he'd do some damage. The man with the saw eventually relented and they came to an arrangement, but when he saw how short Frank and his mate were, his anger reignited. But it was too late. Frank and his driver had sped off, laughing at the absurdity of it all.

In the middle of winter one year, Frank and his driver had to put a repossession notice on a small fishing trawler in the coastal town of Eden. As he was doing so, the owners started to run down the wharf screaming abuse and waving implements of varying sizes and danger. There was nowhere for Frank to go, so he jumped in the water and began swimming as best he could the short distance to the other side of the wharf where his car was. The fishermen had to run back down the wharf and around to the other side. Frank watched them closely and had nearly made his escape when one of the miscreants grabbed at his leg, ripping off his calipered, raised shoe. Again, his driver helped by keeping them at bay while Frank made it into the car, his boot following quickly as it was hurled towards him with force. Frank leaned from the open door to pick up his boot as the car took off. The two men laughed for a while, until the pain began and Frank's leg started throbbing almost unbearably.

There were many such episodes, most of which were resolved peacefully and, more often than not, humorously. Then, sometimes, all Frank's problems would surface again and he'd go away by himself, turning up again a few days later.

One day another Vietnam veteran who lived in town, Warwick Butler, rang Frank about a fellow soldier who was in strife. Butler had become a close friend of Frank's, helping him whenever he could. He became godfather to Frank's children and someone to whom Frank could turn when he needed help, which was often.

Frank had been helping other vets fill in forms and chatting to them at the RSL and was becoming a friend to many of them. The parents of the man Butler wanted Frank's help with had written to the local RSL from Tasmania saying they thought their son was up on the coast but they had no real idea as they hadn't been in contact with him for some time. They were worried for him and knew he needed help. Butler and Frank found out through the Department of Veterans Affairs that the man was hidden away in the hills surrounding Bega. When Frank contacted him, the man said his house was floating away. He thought he would lose everything he had. He was desperate and losing his mind with anxiety. Frank investigated what was happening, finding a water spring close by that had caused some flooding. He assured the man that nothing bad would eventuate, and left him calmer and happier than he had been for some time, even writing to his parents.

Frank began talking more to other veterans, many of whom had shunned city life for the country, attempting to lock themselves away from the world. If the local police found a veteran with a problem, they would call him. The vets didn't trust authority, but they trusted Frank. He was one of them.

Many times he visited veterans who had fallen foul of the law and were in prison. Some were hard men, ruined by their time in Vietnam, while others had just been stupid. Frank worked tirelessly with each of them, listening when they spoke, talking when it was needed. The veterans were happy and calm when

Frank left and the prison officers said they looked forward to a return visit.

The more the contact Frank had with veterans the more it led him to believe it might be something he could do more often. More people spoke to him and when he went to other RSL meetings and Vietnam Veterans Association meetings, his network became wider and before too long quite a number of people with problems were told to 'talk to Frank at Bega'.

Over the months many of Frank's problems were lessened. With his drinking reduced to more normal levels, he was more approachable and communicative. His pain remained and trips to hospital were still regular and he still rejected drugs, yet there was a distinct change in him. He could feel it. He had a purpose again. Even though there were still two distinct parts to him and every now and again he'd fall off the edge of despair, for a lot of the time Frank was happy. For much of the time he used crutches to get around and he'd take them everywhere. On some occasions he'd need a wheelchair but mostly Frank could, and would, hobble his way from place to place until he became tired and sore.

At one stage he had to go to hospital in Sydney for three months. There he was placed in a palliative care ward for cancer patients, a confronting experience, with death a constant. Death had been a companion in Vietnam but this was not the same. He was there because the surgeons wanted to operate on his back, but Frank refused. He couldn't bear the thought of anything going wrong. They wanted to see if he had any tumours on his spine and what was causing all the pain in his spinal and pelvic area. He had tests each day, he was poked and prodded and had blood taken. They opened his leg for a look and stitched it up again. Frank felt he was going mad and he couldn't do anything about it. To keep busy, he helped the nurses doing what he could to assist with changing the bed linen when patients died and were taken away.

'I want to go home,' Frank pleaded one morning when he was feeling better. 'I want to go to my family. I've been away too long and I miss them.'

After a close examination, the doctors agreed and put him on a train to Nowra from where he'd meet a bus that was to take him to Bega. Whoever had organised the journey had got the timing all wrong and no bus arrived. Darkness was falling but Frank was determined, so he began to hitchhike, snagging a couple of lifts. When the lifts stopped, he walked. And walked. And walked. He walked, or rather, stumbled, until he bled. The stitches in his leg burst open, his feet were raw, his boot full of blood. It was late at night. He used his crutches to limp along the road. When his armpits became sore, he carried his crutches and hobbled.

In the black of night, no one picked him up, so he kept going, continually changing hands with his load, until finally he came to a farmhouse near the road. The farmers looked at him sympathetically, gave him a cup of tea and drove him into town to a motel that put him up for the night. In the morning, a travelling salesman took him home.

When he arrived, he was in a mess physically and emotionally. Frank was taken straight to hospital, stitched up by the doctor, bandaged and, after a week of rest and pain relief, went back to work. There was nothing else for it but to work, he decided. He couldn't stay at home and anyway, all there would be was more pain. And Frank was used to pain.

A few months later, when he recovered from another stint in hospital, Frank decided to retrace his steps. He drove up in his car and measured where he'd walked. Counting the couple of small lifts, it was 34 kilometres. He had not walked all of it. Indeed, it was mainly through lifts that he covered the distance, but he thought he'd walked 10 kilometres or more by himself. He'd temporarily lost his mind, but he hadn't realised it. At the time he was in a dream.

*

Help for veterans during those years was limited; nearly all were left to their own devices, to fend for themselves. There was precious little counselling, not many psychiatrists and veterans were simply told to get on with their lives. Many couldn't. They needed someone to help and Frank was becoming a man they wanted to talk to. As his involvement in the RSL became more widespread, if anyone had a problem Frank would help out. He would receive phone calls and letters from veterans, but also many from their parents or wives. He would chat to them and get in touch with the vets and, more often than not, stability would be restored. Vets didn't want psychs, they didn't want counsellors. After all, they thought there was nothing wrong with them. They only wanted to talk to someone who understood.

Some veterans who had been living shut off from society were having problems. Little things could set them off. One day a woman who lived on a small acreage rang Frank and said her husband had shot most of the animals and was wandering around waving the gun at her. Frank asked her to tell him the boss was on the phone.

'There's nothing out there, mate,' Frank told him when the man came on the line. 'Reos are coming in soon, so stand down until they come in with new orders.'

'Yes, boss,' the man answered crisply.

Two hours later, Frank arrived and found the veteran in the bush looking carefully around, still holding the gun. Frank spoke to him in a military fashion for a few minutes before the man came in and talked. He cried for two hours. He was talking about desperation, about frustration and the loss of men he loved; he was a mess. He'd been in severe battles in Vietnam, Long Tan among them, and was reliving it. When the flashbacks hit, he'd just leave his normal persona and retreat to a dark place that only he could inhabit. Frank took him to a doctor, who then organised a psychiatrist's appointment and treatment for the man.

The appeals were ongoing. Frank had not been taught how to counsel these men, he had never done a course. He was simply a good listener and could make them feel comfortable. He gave them options, found them help and took care of them as much as he could.

However, some encounters didn't work out well.

One day a deceased man was found in his car near the Victorian border. There was nothing to identify him but the police found Frank's name and phone number in his otherwise mostly empty wallet. They rang and asked Frank if he would come to identify the body. He drove down and met the police. The man had gassed himself and his body had been in the car for a week. Frank said he knew the man vaguely and could see who he was. He phoned around, found the vet's family and a small funeral was organised. The dead man had estranged kids and a wife who refused to attend. The only family member present was a brother who was also a Vietnam veteran. Frank handed him the medals he'd found in the car but the brother threw them into the grave in disgust.

Frank gently said, 'His kids might like them later on, y'know, when they think about their dad. Should we get 'em out?'

'Fuck 'em,' said the brother, storming off. 'Fuck them and fuck him.'

He was angry at his brother and himself and everything else it was possible to be angry at.

Two weeks later, Frank had a call from police in the mountain area near Bega. A veteran had shot and killed himself. Another few days went by and Frank was called to a town on the coast. There had been another shooting. A veteran had taken his own life, leaving a wife and two children. Frank found out later he'd planned to take the family with him. Luckily, they had gone shopping for the day but came home to find their lives in pieces.

This three-week period did nothing for Frank's state of mind.

*

Frank had by now given up his job in credit control. The business needed a full-time worker, not one who was absent much of the time. A year or so later, Frank managed to obtain a job as a clerk at the local council. Local government rules at the time were such that if two people were equal in qualifications for the job and one was a returned serviceman, then that person should be given the position. Frank was employed under those rules.

He was using crutches each day but managed to get his work done. However, when the pain came, it was without mercy. He was still spending a lot of time in hospital and off work. And, still, many a night he'd have to sleep on the floor at home. After about five years of torment for Frank, the council was sacked by the government and an administrator appointed. He offered Frank the option of working half a day each day, an offer that Frank accepted. He managed to keep that up for six months, but in the end the only answer was to cease work completely. The pain he could do nothing about. His body simply wouldn't work the way it was meant to.

Frank was nothing if not resilient. Although there were problems at home, what with his nightmares, his sleeping problems and with the needs of four young children to be met, he did what he could. He played some sort of cricket with the kids, managed to kick a soccer ball occasionally, went to the beach and did all the family things as much as possible. In fact, to add insult to injury, Frank broke the big toe on his good foot kicking a ball on the beach. His bad leg gave way and his toe became stuck in the sand. Over he went, in agony. He was put back into plaster again, only this time on the good leg. What was difficult before, now became even more so for a time.

Even though he wasn't working, Frank wasn't idle. He became involved with his children at school, helping when he could. He worked with other children as well and the teachers praised his work, enjoying a local parent in the classroom. The first thing he taught the children was marching. The kids would fall over themselves laughing and loving it when he yelled out, 'Left right left right left right!' at the top of his voice. What an adventure for them, a real soldier teaching them marching.

One thing Frank could do was speak well. He had been getting more and more invitations to speak to local groups about Vietnam. He spoke on Anzac Day around the district, swapping towns each year. On one occasion he and Warwick Butler were asked to be involved in a debate at an Apex Club. At one stage it became so heated with opposite points of view coming from the audience that Frank and Butler simply stopped talking and watched and listened in amazement.

The more he spoke, the more he realised he had a talent for it. So when he went to school for other matters he began talking to the kids, instilling confidence in children who had a stutter or were shy or didn't think they could speak well. Then he taught them about speaking out loud in public. This became so popular that eventually other schools became involved. They called it the Young Speakers Club. It gave Frank a purpose, made him forget about things some of the time. The pain and the sleeping problems were still there but at least his mind was occupied for a while.

*

When Frank had left hospital and the army, he had been granted a small disability pension. Not a great deal of money, but something to supplement his income. When he changed to part-time work he had asked for an increase and was refused. Finances at home were tight. Despite Constance working, the costs of bringing up four children with only one meagre wage and the pension, such as it was, meant the Hunt household could hardly manage. Eventually the government gave Frank a little bit more, but not a great deal. When he was employed, he was only allowed to earn a certain amount before the pension was reduced. He had stopped work, but there was still reluctance by the DVA to look favourably at his problems. Once a pension was set at a certain amount, it was extremely difficult to change.

The system was a concern for many veterans, most of them young. The DVA was reluctant to grant large pensions and men were encouraged to work to avoid the problem, it was thought, of young men sitting around idle for many years. What would they do? In Frank's case, that was not a concern as he was active in the community. His injuries meant he couldn't be in a paid position, because businesses wouldn't or couldn't have a person like him in their employ. Frank's work was voluntary and it helped the community, which was all well and good, but his family simply couldn't manage.

The local community was outraged and supported Frank in his battle with the DVA, which went on for quite some time. In the end Constance, who had worked tirelessly for Frank's case, wrote a letter explaining how her husband was in pain, had to sleep on the floor and was suffering like no one should suffer. Her letter to Veterans Affairs was accompanied by a petition conducted by the RSL that had gathered some 1300 signatures from locals supporting Frank's case. The result was that in 1982, Frank was made a TPI – a totally and permanently incapacitated veteran. Frank knew nothing of what was going on and was incredibly moved and grateful when the notice came informing him of the transformation of his pension.

PART FOUR

Chapter 27
AN ANTHEM IS CREATED

In 1975, a folk music band called Redgum was formed by John Schumann and three friends who were students at Flinders University in Adelaide. Schumann, who was undertaking a degree in politics and art, was the driving force and main songwriter of the group. The band quickly gained a following at the university as well as the pubs around Adelaide and in 1978 released their first album, *If You Don't Fight You Lose*. Other albums and more success followed then, in 1981, Mick Storen's sister Denise, or Denny as she was known, met Schumann at a dinner party. As the couple grew closer, they exchanged stories about their families and histories. Denny told Schumann her brother Mick was a Vietnam veteran.

As a younger man, Schumann, like most, had been exposed to the war through television reports and black and white footage of jungles, guns, soldiers, helicopters and firefights. And bodies, either in bags ready to come home or just lying in the scrub. Schumann began listening to and reading the arguments about the war and was intuitively opposed to what was happening, even at his young age. He didn't become engaged in any of the anti-war campaigns, mainly because of his age but also because he was distinctly uncomfortable with those who carried the North Vietnamese flag in marches and helped to raise money to be used in the fight against Australian troops. He didn't agree with that. He simply thought Australia should not be involved in the conflict and needed to bring the troops home.

By the time Schumann began his university studies, Gough Whitlam had been elected and the troops withdrawn. In some ways that was only the beginning of veterans' problems. Schumann began reading more and more about the trauma they suffered, about the lack of respect for them in Australian society and the disregard for their health issues. He saw the antipathy of the government and the RSL and his sympathy for the veterans increased. He imagined writing a song for these men, but not from media reports and what he imagined to be true. The only way to do it properly would be to talk to the veterans, which was a notoriously difficult task. Denny could help with that.

Schumann met Mick Storen on a number of occasions. He never broached the subject of Vietnam because Denny had told him her brother never spoke about the war. That remained the case until Christmas 1981 when, after a Redgum concert in suburban Adelaide, Mick, Schumann and a group of friends went out together. Schumann and Mick sat together, talking about music and songwriting and life in general. Schumann said he'd like to write a song about Vietnam and asked whether Mick would talk to him about it. Mick was a bit wary at first but said he would with a couple of conditions. The first was that Schumann wouldn't denigrate Vietnam veterans. The second was that any song written was to be played to him before anyone else.

If he didn't approve, the song wouldn't see the light of day. Both conditions were accepted by Schumann without hesitation.

A few months later, when Schumann returned to Adelaide after a Redgum tour, he met Mick at the house that Denny rented in the Adelaide Hills. The men settled in for a long night of talking. They looked at photos, drank and Schumann filled many cassette tapes with the story of Mick's army service from recruit training at Puckapunyal to Townsville to Vietnam and his return.

The stories solidified in Schumann's mind all he believed about the Vietnam War and its veterans. He wasn't a hardcore left-wing idealist, and was not interested in doing or saying anything to damage his country, as he was extremely loyal; he simply wanted to make his country see the error of its ways. A paragon of virtue he was not, but he had a sense of justice and injustice and instinctively knew what was right and wrong. Schumann was confident he had a sense of morality and of what was fair and unfair. What drove his wish to write the song and the eventual writing of it was much more than the politics, it was a reflection of everything he believed in.

Talking to Mick was the culmination of all the roads Schumann had walked leading to where he now stood. It offended him that the people who had done the jobs asked of them in good faith and who came back sick, confused and unwelcomed, were not receiving the help and respect they deserved.

The gestation of the song took a long time, but Schumann wasn't worried about writing it. He really wanted to but experience had told him that it would either come to him or it wouldn't. As he listened to the tapes, he became engrossed in the stories Mick told him. Many months later, one November morning in 1982, Schumann sat down in the backyard of his inner-suburban house in Melbourne, and out tumbled the song in about 15 minutes. While happy with the outcome, Schumann considered himself just a conduit, someone who had the ability to say things to the world on behalf of the men who couldn't or didn't want to say those things for themselves.

As he had promised, Schumann played the song to Mick at one of the Storen family gatherings that were a regular occurrence on Sunday evenings, when everyone got together for a meal. After dinner, Mick and Schumann went to a bedroom, where Schumann sat down with his guitar and played the song. When the last chords faded away, Mick just stared at his future brother-in-law, transfixed.

Schumann was stricken. 'What did Mick think? Why did I do this? What's the matter?' The seconds were measured in heartbeats. To Schumann the silence was confronting.

Mick was stunned. He was amazed. He couldn't speak. Was it too sad, he wondered? Was it depressing? Mick couldn't find the right emotion but he was incredibly moved. Mick didn't consider himself a poet or a musician or a writer, yet he knew Schumann had captured Vietnam like no one had ever done before or ever would again. He had painted a picture in words and music that would resonate with those who had no real idea of what had happened to the soldiers in Vietnam as well as those who had fought the war themselves. The imagery of the story encapsulated it all: there it was, all there. But it brought everything he'd seen and done flooding back to him. This was no general song about Vietnam; this was his story. He hadn't expected this. The hairs on the back of his neck stood up. The images were real. Mick was speechless.

To Schumann, it seemed like an eternity before Mick was composed enough to speak.

Schumann asked if it was OK.

'Yeah,' said Mick softly, 'it's OK.'

The only change he wanted was to one of the words. Schumann had written that 'Tommy kicked a mine'. Discussing the song afterwards, Mick told Schumann he thought the name 'Tommy' was a bit weak and didn't fit well. He hadn't known anyone called Tommy in the army and thought it too reminiscent of the name given to British soldiers of the First World War, who were called Tommies.

The two men began to throw around a few names that might fit into the song. Peter fitted but the person who actually kicked the mine was Lieutenant Peter Hines, whose wife and child back in Australia were now on their own. If the song did go out into the world, it would be a constant reminder to Hines' wife. Would it be too much? Even after all that time 3 Platoon was protective of its own, particularly of Skip, and that sensitivity and protection extended to his family. Mick remembered Frank Hunt had been badly wounded in the incident and suggested using the name 'Frankie', as Frank had been the closest to Skip. Frankie fitted beautifully, so Schumann agreed.

Now the song was complete, but Schumann still had one thing left to do. Mick had told him he'd better go and see Frank: his permission needed to be given.

A few weeks later, Redgum started a tour along the east coast. One of their shows was in Tathra, a small seaside town 18 kilometres from Bega. While there, Schumann found a phone book and rang Frank.

'My name's John Schumann and I'm a mate of Mick Storen,' he said when Frank answered.

Frank replied that if he was a mate of Mick, he needed no more introduction.

'I play in a band called Redgum and I've written a song I'd like to talk to you about. Can you come to see us after the gig tonight?'

Frank was going to a meeting, but arranged to meet Schumann the following morning at his motel.

Early the next day, Frank knocked on the door of the Tathra motel room and was greeted by Denny, who had travelled with the band. After an exchange of pleasantries and a few explanations, Schumann picked up his guitar. Schumann had already started playing the song at gigs after Mick agreed he could. Because of that, the previous night the band had played the song at the Tathra pub and Frank's phone rang hot all night with people calling to say they'd heard the song and wanted to talk about it.

Now, in the motel room, Schumann played the song to Frank, whose reaction was the same as Mick's. He was quiet and still, thinking of so many things as his mind raced. What seemed like several minutes went by before he could talk. Frank's eyes filled and he struggled with his emotions. This was confronting.

'Would you play it again?' Frank asked.

So Schumann played it again. Then again. And again. Eventually Schumann's fingers were sore, so he asked if he could play it into the cassette recorder Frank happened to have in his car. Each time Schumann played the opening chords it brought back memories to Frank. All the time he'd spent in hospital, all the hopelessness he felt lying in bed, all the agony he'd suffered from his injuries and all the pain he felt from the loss of his mates were consolidated in a few words and a few notes on a guitar. However, one thing puzzled him.

'But I didn't step on the mine,' he said quizzically.

Schumann explained what Mick had said about Skip's family and asked Frank if he agreed, at the same time offering him a beer. Even though it was only late morning by now, the men needed a drink. Four long-necks later, Frank walked across the road and onto the beach, where he hobbled up and down along the sand.

He cried and cried and cried. In some ways he was frightened. What would people think? Would his mates who knew what had happened with the mine accept the song? Why did Schumann say it was him when it wasn't? How could he or Schumann justify that? He took the tape home and played it to his family. He had listened to what Schumann had said about wanting to protect Skip's family, so he rang Mick. He needed to talk.

'How do I do this, how can I do it?' Frank asked.

Mick told Frank why he suggested his name – that he was so close to Skip and that it fitted so well.

Frank said he still wasn't sure about the song claiming he'd stepped on the mine. He hadn't.

Mick told him that there were some in the platoon who thought it might have been Frank anyway. The men chatted about old times, laughed a bit, cried a lot, and agreed that other vets would have the same response and would like the song as much as they did. Frank went back to the motel and told Schumann it would all be alright.

After it sank in, Frank knew he was doing the right thing. He loved his Skip and if he could help, he would, no matter the personal cost. He was glad that, if the song was successful, Hines' family would be protected from the media and left alone. That it would not be a constant reminder of their loss. Frank could handle it, but they might not be able to. Once again, his life was about to change.

*

Schumann started playing the song to a few audiences as a precursor to a hopeful release. Redgum had released a couple of singles previously which hadn't really sold well. The band had sold LPs and pulled big crowds at gigs but was, Schumann thought, 'dancing on the edge of the firelight'. They were an uncompromising, political unit with a lead singer, Schumann, who sounded, by his own admission, unlike any other on the airwaves, so it was always extremely difficult for them to get any radio airplay. Yet Schumann had high hopes for his new song.

Redgum's other members had told him they didn't want to record the song as a single. In fact they didn't want anything to do with it because they didn't think it would be popular, but Schumann believed in the song and something told him it would be well received.

'I Was Only 19' was recorded by Schumann with one other member of the band, Hugh McDonald, and released in Melbourne in March 1983, just over a month before Anzac Day. His recording company, CBS Records, threw its support and resources behind it, even to the extent of delaying the release of a Billy Joel song about Vietnam so that 'I Was Only 19' could have clear exposure.

After a gig in Melbourne where the band played the song to a receptive, hushed audience, Keith Fowler, the music director at 3XY, the unchallenged leading radio station in Melbourne that drove the trends in music, poked his head into the dressing room. He was met by a belligerent Schumann, who had just come off stage and was hot, sweaty and grumpy.

'Yeah, I know,' said Fowler, sensing Schumann's question.

'We don't play your records and we should. But I have to tell you I have been to six major gigs tonight, sticking my head in and watching the atmosphere, and I can tell you that you had the biggest and the most attentive crowd. None of the others had the attention of the room like you did when you played that song. If we are not playing your records and that song, it is our fault not yours.'

Fowler went back to the station the next day, found the single that had been delivered a few weeks earlier and ignored, and put it on the list to be played at high rotation. Once 3XY started playing the song, all the other stations did as well. People were ringing up radio stations across the country asking for them to play the song, and they in turn did as they were asked. Rock stations, country music stations, even the more conservative ABC, were overrun with requests. The response was astounding and word moved fast. Schumann had even heard it on some obscure country station in the middle of the night as he drove across the inland to a gig. As Anzac Day approached, the song gained more and more airplay and sales around the country boomed.

Schumann was in Sydney a couple of weeks later and one morning there was a knock on his motel door. Three burly, confronting figures stood there. One was Phil Thompson, president of the Vietnam Veterans Association of Australia (VVAA). Someone had rung him about the song and he'd come to talk about it. With him were two other members, Terry Loftus and Tim McCombe. These were men who didn't mince words or muck around – they had seen and done things that meant they didn't need to.

'I hear you've written a song,' said an unsmiling Thompson in a way that could have been construed as an accusation more than a statement. 'I'd like to have a chat about it.'

As leaders in the VVAA, the men were protective of their own and wanted to make sure that Schumann was above board and that the song didn't defame or misrepresent veterans. There had been too much of that for too long. Now the vets were fighting back.

Schumann picked up his guitar and played the song. As with Frank and Mick, he played it a few more times and, again as had happened with Frank and Mick, the silence in the room was filled with memories.

A composed Thompson told Schumann, 'It would be good if you came down to headquarters with your guitar and met a few of the boys.'

Like many, Schumann had always associated Vietnam veterans with the RSL, with big clubs, money, prestige, resources and all the other trappings that come with being a returned war veteran. It was a natural assumption to make, he thought. The reality was quite different, a shock. 'Headquarters' was a small fibro hut out the back of the Granville RSL, not a flash club itself at the time. The vets were not even in an office in the main building. Outside were a few veterans with nail bags on and hammers and paint brushes in their hands, working to get the place into a half-reasonable condition. Inside, Schumann looked around and noticed a couple of old wooden office desks, a Bakelite phone or two, an 'in' and 'out' basket, a typewriter with a few keys that appeared as though they wouldn't work properly, bare floors and very little else. Here the association was running its national affairs, campaigning for better conditions for veterans, with very little success.

Schumann was made welcome, played the song a few times, getting the same response he had from the other vets, and then spent a couple of hours talking about the association and what it had set out to do, and where it had got to – which was mainly into a brick wall. One of the association's major concerns was the battle for recognition of the effect Agent Orange had had on veterans. The VVAA had published a list of symptoms for veterans to look for and eventually, after much difficult and intense lobbying, a Royal Commission was established.

Schumann was concerned about the VVAA and wanted to do something for it. Mick was one of them, Frank too, and if Schumann could help, he would. The association had no money and was trying to take action for veterans without anything in the coffers – not to mention they were up against the might of the multi-national chemical company Monsanto, who manufactured Agent Orange. In 1985 the findings handed down by the Royal Commission recognised that veterans had health problems but found no link to Agent Orange. It wasn't until many years later that the Department of Veterans Affairs actually admitted there might have been a connection and allowed claims from veterans, mainly for cancer, as being war-related.

Schumann's mind began working overtime, and he decided to donate all the song's artist royalties to the VVAA. Over the years this added tens of thousands of dollars to the association's funds, for which the vets were extraordinarily grateful.

Chapter 28
EFFECTS OF A SONG

'I Was Only 19' had captured the imagination of the country. Radio, television, newspapers, magazines – it seemed everyone everywhere wanted to talk to Schumann and 'Frankie', and requests for interviews were constant and unrelenting. There were a few Vietnam veterans, but many more sympathisers, sprinkled through the arts and media world. A video of the song was made with the help of Dave Allen from Channel Seven, who sourced footage as background vision to the song.

The song's popularity created an issue as the stories the song was based on were Mick Storen's, not Frank's, but Mick didn't want the publicity. He told Schumann he wished to remain anonymous and had no interest in being interviewed. While he was happy to have told his story and was content with the result, he would have preferred the song to be about all Australian soldiers. As it was personalised, he thought that if he remained anonymous that might have the same effect – veterans could identify their own experiences in the song. He just wanted to stay in the background. He didn't even go with his closest mates to Schumann's concerts to hear the song. He didn't want the spotlight.

This was a very personal story for Mick. He didn't promote it at work; he didn't tell anyone it was about him. He bought a few copies and gave them to three or four of his closest mates and the family, but he had a few reservations. What if it affected other veterans in a bad way, bringing back unwanted memories? What if they couldn't handle it? What if it all came rushing back to them and they suffered?

Mick was torn. While he didn't wish that the song had never happened, he had such an emotional tie to it that sometimes he found it difficult to contend with the conflicting feelings he experienced. He didn't want to be constantly reminded of what had happened to him every time it was played. Even though he had been home a long time, on each occasion he heard the song it reminded him of the death of his mates. In his own mind he could bury all that and dismiss it, but when it came out of the radio, there it was again, raw and emotional each time he heard the opening chords.

Mick was proud of the song, but he'd managed to get through the last 10 or so years without being plagued with bad memories and now, all of a sudden, here was a song that made him feel he was being confronted again. Everything had been going along quite well, work and family were fine, life had been good, and that's the way he wanted it to stay.

*

Schumann had spoken to Frank and his family about Frank promoting the song. Frank was a bit reluctant at the start, but after Schumann talked to him about it and convinced the family to let him go on the publicity tour, Frank agreed. If the song was to be successful, Frank had to maintain the idea that he had 'kicked the mine'. There was really no choice.

At the song's official release, over 3000 people, many of them veterans and their families, packed into Sydney Town Hall. The audience was stunned into emotional silence when Schumann touched the strings of his guitar, but that emotion was nothing compared to what was happening in the wings. Mick wasn't completely sure he wanted to attend, but had been convinced and was flown over courtesy of the VVAA. From the side of the stage, he and Frank watched Schumann perform. Frank broke down and so did Mick, the two mates arm in arm in tears, everything flashing in and out of their minds like strobe lighting. They were overwhelmed, and could not feel anything other than astonishment. They clutched at their feelings, which coursed through their bodies. The two men's emotions were laid bare with 3000 or so people close at hand.

The next day Mick flew back to Adelaide, while Frank and Schumann began to travel all over the country, conducting interviews and listening to audiences praise the song. The feedback about the song was extraordinary. They sat in hotel rooms and bars and smoked and drank and talked. They worked hard at their task, which while onerous was enjoyable and satisfying.

Among the many places they visited was the psych ward at Concord Rehabilitation Hospital in Sydney. When Schumann hit the first chords, Frank looked around at the ruined minds and bodies and, almost breaking down, told them: 'This is for you blokes; this is your song.' The response this time was not complete silence; this time it was cut through by the sound of tears.

Frank was a born raconteur with a way of expressing himself that interviewers loved. When he wasn't in a car or a plane, he was back in Bega on the telephone. All the major television and radio shows with all the major stars of the day were lined up wanting to talk to this bloke 'Frankie' who had 'kicked the mine'.

At times, Frank didn't recognise the man being interviewed. The person they were talking about wasn't him. It couldn't be him. He was only a bloke from the Mallee. He wasn't the wartime 'hero' they were trying to make him out to be. He didn't want to be a symbol. Yes, at times the publicity created a boost to his ego but when the pain kicked in again, when he had to lie on the hotel room floor because he couldn't sleep, when he had flash-backs of those days in the jungle, it didn't matter where he was, it was still the same: there was no escape.

While taxing, the publicity was also enjoyable. Frank met people in high places, and gained contacts he could use to help other veterans when the time came or if the opportunity presented itself. As well as helping to heal others, everything he was doing was helping Frank to heal as well. Each time the song was played, Schumann and Frank made sure they conveyed to the audience that it was a song for all veterans, that if the audience had one in the family or even knew a vet down the street, to let them know they were being thought about and that they were all part of this story. In each interview, both Frank and Schumann emphasised the treatment of Vietnam veterans and what the government should be doing to help.

It was an intense period and the pressure on Frank mounted. He'd become the face of the song. The more the song was played and the more questions were asked of him, the more he began to think that maybe he did step on the mine. He remembered the letter he'd written to Norma Hines. He was confused. Was the letter true after all? Why didn't anyone tell him? His mind was in a bad way trying to cope with the pain but now even that was overwhelmed by concern and angst. Was he responsible for everything that had happened? Should he have been aware, should he have been in Skip's place? The survivor mentality had kicked in: the guilt. Not constantly but at those times when he could stop and think and go over and over the incident in his mind. Where was he? Where was Skip? Shrugging the thoughts away was difficult and even when he thought he had, they appeared again from time to time. But life had to continue and it did.

*

When 'I Was Only 19' was released and became a hit, there was a bit of angst among the men of 3 Platoon. While Mick and Frank had agreed with John Schumann about the need to protect Lieutenant Hines' widow and child from publicity, there were others who hadn't been told. A few were irritated that they hadn't been informed about the reasons for Frankie's name being used. They all knew that he hadn't stepped on the mine. Constantly hearing the song and the publicity surrounding it became a bit too much for some of the men involved.

Graeme Davis couldn't understand it. He became upset and couldn't listen to the song for a time. He didn't understand why anyone would say Frank had stood on the mine when it was Skip. Alf Lamb was another who was concerned. He said that at the time the song came out he was busy drinking himself to death and he had not spoken to anyone, either about Vietnam or about the song. He heard it and was annoyed. The other men involved in the mine incident each had their own lives to live, bringing up their families, some making new starts. While most knew to some extent where the others lived, they had no contact. When the song was released, it came as a bit of a shock. The phones rang in many households once they worked out what the story was about.

Over the next few months, these men were confronted by the image of Frank in the publicity. It took a while before they changed their opinions. Frank seemed to have taken ownership of the incident in some ways. It wasn't his story, yet all the articles were basically about how he stepped on the mine. It was a difficult situation. Frankie couldn't contradict the song by telling everyone that he hadn't in fact stepped on the mine. The story needed to be consistent.

The majority of 3 Platoon were not worried at all and eventually things settled down. The men who were upset mellowed. They might not have agreed with what was done but they understood the reasons. Despite knowing the truth behind the song, they recognised that the changes to the story were made out of respect and that Schumann, Frank and Mick had thought it was the right thing to do.

The one person whose opinion really mattered and who wasn't affected was Norma Hines. She felt for Frank, who at one time believed he had been the cause of her husband's death. She'd kept the letter he wrote to her from hospital and had been comforted by it. Norma understood why some of the men objected to the lyrics, indeed they told her so, but she also understood – and was grateful – for why it was done that way. She knew all the men in the platoon from the time in Townsville; many had been in her home. They were close to her as well as Skip. She later said they were such a close-knit platoon that, to her, it really didn't matter who had stepped on the mine.

*

The song soon went to number one on the music charts. The lyrics had spoken to veterans in a way no one had ever done before. It was a simple song that wasn't simple; complicated but also clear. It was, Schumann believed, a song that spoke an undeniable truth. He told interviewers that the song spoke the language of the men and women in the street so those who didn't understand veterans and their problems would be helped to understand. As for veterans, the song told a story about two blokes that all vets could relate to.

People were talking about the song, saying how it 'grabbed me', 'put the hairs up on the back of my neck'. The song wasn't sad but it was sad. It wasn't difficult to hear the words, but they were difficult to listen to. And quite simply, critics said and Schumann believed, it was a good song. It was honest, it was accessible, it was a way of seeing what was happening to veterans in the street. It didn't have trumpets or violins or background choruses; it didn't need them and, anyway, they'd have been out of place.

'I Was Only 19' had a context. There was an inquiry going on, a battle for veterans and their health issues. The country had some collective shame about Vietnam, about the struggle for the Royal Commission into the effects of Agent Orange on veterans. Schumann said later that the song 'worked because Australians were waiting for someone to talk to them and tell them they had fucked this up and we need to do something about it.'

This was the first time that anyone had managed to capture the Vietnam experience in a simple way, the first time anything meaningful had been done that veterans could relate to. Plenty of articles had been written about what they should do, and a lot of self-help ideas floated for them. Prescription drugs were handed out, there were psychiatrists and counsellors now, and everything else that went with being a veteran, but this was just a bloke with a guitar who said things that they could relate to and which meant something to them.

There was a degree of sadness in the song and some of the wives and girlfriends of veterans thought it was too sad, too close to the bone, too upsetting, too depressing. Most veterans didn't think so, and when the women talked to their men about it, those thoughts – fears in some cases – were mostly allayed.

There were those who found philosophy in the words, understanding that some things in life don't have a happy ending. The song didn't have a happy ending; veterans in a lot of circumstances didn't have a happy ending. While some veterans thought about the song and became worried like their wives, many recognised their own problems and did something about them. They also knew that someone was thinking about them, that someone understood.

And it all happened on a disc of vinyl in four minutes and 19 seconds.

Chapter 29
A NEW LIFE

Frank had never wanted to be a politician, but was very interested in politics. He joined the local branch of the Australian Labor Party, the party he thought best reflected his belief in equality, helping others and contributing. It didn't hurt that it was also the party that stopped conscription and the country's involvement in Vietnam. It brought a bit of criticism from some in the RSL, who were, by and large, conservative, but Frank and his views on the futility of war in general, and Vietnam in particular, were not swayed. Frank was always his own man, despite all his problems. He was soon elected president of the branch.

The Bega Valley had become home to people who were quite like hippies, seeking an alternative, simpler life in the hinterlands among the forests. It was a contrast to this typical Australian country town and the locals who lived there, but the majority accepted the newcomers. An organisation called People for Peace and Nuclear Disarmament was formed and Frank joined up. He had a profile and when the local council reluctantly agreed to a referendum on whether the Valley should become nuclear-free, there was some objection from the locals who had lived in the Valley for generations. People for Peace and Nuclear Disarmament organised a march in favour of the referendum and its aim, and when people saw Frank Hunt, 'Frankie from the song', marching, or more correctly, stumbling along for a while, at the head of the small group, they were astounded. He was criticised by some right-wingers in the RSL, but at the referendum 65 percent of people voted in favour of the proposal. It was proof to Frank of the influence he could wield. Not because he was Frank Hunt, but because he was 'Frankie'.

Frank's life swung between complete normality and abject despair. Despite the diversion of the publicity for the song and being upgraded to a TPI pension, Frank's problems didn't go away. There was now relief as far as money was concerned, yet money didn't take away the pain, the problems with mobility, the sleep deprivation, the nightmares, the anxiety. None of that disappeared. Nor did the problems at home.

Frank had started going to a counsellor as well as a psychiatrist on occasions. His pain and anxiety were exacerbating what was happening at home. He was now drinking again, even more than before. He was spending more time in the community and less at home, with arguments becoming more regular. His marriage was in trouble. He opened up to his counsellor in ways he never had before, so that was at least something, he thought. His nightmares had reduced because he was so busy and he could even sleep for a few hours in the bed, due in part to the painkillers he now allowed himself to take.

His work in the community had caused Frank to ignore the other concerns in his life. He was subconsciously covering them all up. If something did come up, he'd ignore it. Even though he thought everything was going well, it wasn't. His pain was still extreme and exhausting him. He was becoming intolerant when he was home and difficult to live with. His priorities were all out of kilter. He was paying more attention to veterans and the RSL than to home. He liked the work he was doing; it kept him active and he was creating an environment for himself that he could handle and where he felt comfortable. Work was a distraction. He didn't have to think about anything apart from his pain. But when he got away from that, his other problems came to the fore and became worse than they would have been had they been handled differently. Communication stopped at home.

The counsellor gave him tools to act on and Frank tried to adhere to them, although it didn't always work. He was still putting everything first before his family, although he still was involved with his children at school. Under those conditions, the marriage couldn't last and it didn't.

One day in the middle of 1986, Constance told Frank his drinking and the problems the couple faced were too much and that she was leaving. He reluctantly and sadly agreed and the marriage ended. The children, who were just entering their teenage years, stayed with Frank.

There were now new and extremely difficult challenges for Frank. It took quite some time to accept what had happened to his marriage and in his condition he found it difficult to come to terms with what it meant to have to care for his children. He immediately put in place some rules for the house and together he and the children started a new life. Frank felt guilty about the situation he and his children found themselves in, but he stayed involved in his community work, all the while never losing sight of his children and their needs. The washing and ironing were always done, the housework was shared on a roster system and there was always a cooked meal on the table at night. He talked to them about anything and everything; he wanted them to know they were loved unconditionally, wanted them to know about the world and about life. He wanted them to know about the war and why, whatever had happened to their father, they should not hate anyone especially the Vietnamese people. That his situation was just one of the things that happened as a result of war.

While family life, such as it was, continued, Frank explored options for his pain, trying to find a solution that didn't involve harsh and powerful drugs. It was even more important now that he was alert and his mind clear of anything that might cloud it. One answer for his pain was to embrace alternative health remedies: meditation, acupuncture, acupressure, as well as a lot of physiotherapy. It worked for a while, but not always and never consistently.

When he was busy he was OK, but when whatever he was doing stopped, he stopped as well. Some things were too deep, too ingrained, for them to disappear. When he closed his bedroom door, he thought the kids didn't know what was going on. But later they told him they had always heard him crying, heard him calling out in the night when he went back to some dark place where he could hear explosions and guns and the sounds of the jungle. When he dreamed about Needsy and Skip. The children knew.

*

Frank had gained a degree of notoriety as the 'man in the song' and with that came a range of pressures that were building up. While the publicity for the song had reduced considerably, Frank was now asked to speak about his experiences for more people in more places. Before the song, he was simply Frank Hunt,

Vietnam veteran and a father who was interested in his kids and their friends; someone who would do what he could to help. What Frank contributed with his time to the benefit of veterans was done willingly because he could. For that reason alone, he thought he should. Now, he was Frank Hunt, 'Frankie' from the song. He was somewhat famous and as such he had many more demands placed on him. Relinquishing the presidency of the local VVAA relieved some of the pressure at home, but not much.

As many veterans had returned in small groups and had not received any sort of welcome, it was decided to emulate the Americans, who had a welcome home parade in 1984. The VVAA organised a march to be held in Sydney on 3 October 1987. The full, formal title for the event was the National Reunion and Welcome Home Parade. When it came time to think about attending the parade, Frank was reluctant. He thought he was not up to it. He decided he wouldn't go. His children had other plans and convinced him to attend after hearing that a bus had been arranged for the veterans from the south coast area. Frank spoke to his doctor, who told him he agreed with him going as long as he was careful, and if he participated in the parade itself, he had to use a wheelchair.

'I want to march,' Frank told him. 'There'll be blokes there that will get along somehow. I'd like to do that too.'

'Well, Frank,' the doctor said, 'you can do that if you like but don't blame me when you can't walk for weeks afterwards or when the pain is so intense you can't do anything to stop it. And, you might break a hip or something too.'

Frank knew it was a brutal but accurate assessment of his mobility and took the advice about using a wheelchair. Early one morning he and the children boarded the bus for Sydney with other veterans, Frank's wheelchair stashed under the bus with the luggage.

*

Sydney had never seen anything like it. They came from everywhere in the country and by every means possible: planes, cars, trucks, trains, motorbikes. All across the city, accommodation was booked out and many ordinary citizens opened their doors to veterans who could not find anywhere to stay. Frank and the children stayed in a motel in Kings Cross. Throughout the city, emotion flowed through the streets like a flood.

The weekend began with Friday night get-togethers of men who hadn't seen each other for years. Pubs overflowed with tall tales, emotional reunions and lakes of beer. Frank saw men he hadn't seen since he had been dusted off all those years ago. He saw men he heard had been killed. Music blared from what seemed to be every corner of every building and some parties continued until the dawn service at the Cenotaph in Martin Place. There the mood had changed. It was a sombre reminder of what the men had been through. 'The Last Post' and 'The Ode' sliced through the morning stillness as men were lost in their own memories.

Later, they all moved to the Domain, where they formed up for the parade. Over 25,000 veterans marched, with an estimated 400,000 lining the streets cheering, clapping and shouting out to them. At the front were the next-of-kin of those killed in action, each with an Australian flag to commemorate those men who hadn't made it home. It had been 15 years since the country had pulled out of Vietnam and many of the vets had never identified themselves as Vietnam veterans before. Many had never marched on Anzac Day or joined the RSL, the organisation that in many cases, had rejected the men because the older veterans didn't consider Vietnam to be a 'real war' and Vietnam vets to be 'real' vets like those who had fought in the two world wars.

There were men who limped, some who hobbled along on crutches, and others who were pushed in wheelchairs, one of whom was an emotional Frank Hunt, being pushed along by his old platoon sergeant, Gerry Newbury.

Frank's children were in the crowd and watched as a young Vietnamese girl, only about 12 years old, rushed from the barriers and placed a small, hand-picked bunch of flowers into Frank's hand. 'Thank you, thank you,' said the girl as she nodded her head and backed into the crowd.

As the parade headed down George Street to the Town Hall, Prime Minister Bob Hawke was taking the salute. Many didn't bother saluting; they instead remembered him as the trade union leader during the waterfront strikes and someone who advocated against sending supplies to Vietnam. Hawke made a political speech about differences of opinion, but it didn't wash with a lot of the men, Frank being one of them.

'Jesus, Hawkey,' he said nodding to Newbury, 'yer full of shit.'

After the march, Frank went back to his hotel, where Newbury carried him up two flights of stairs and laid him down on the bed. Frank slept for a short time while the children watched over him, then headed out again.

Day flowed into night and flowed back into day. Sunday was concert day, and thousands gathered again in the Domain to hear Normie Rowe (a veteran himself), Lorrae Desmond, Little Pattie, Col Joye and a few others performing as they had in the Luscombe Bowl during the war. Children of veterans had never seen or heard their fathers sing along like this, especially to songs they'd seldom – or never – heard. The parkland reverberated to 'We Gotta Get Out Of This Place' and then 'Leaving on a Jet Plane'.

The mood changed slightly when another performer took to the stage. John Schumann sang what had now become the Vietnam veterans' anthem. While some sang along, many more listened quietly and thought about things that no one else was privy to. At one stage, the crowd lifted Frank, in his wheelchair, onto the stage. The children followed.

While thousands attended, others could not. There were many suffering hardship, many lost souls and others who were no longer living. One in particular was Phil Thompson, who had become a close friend of Schumann and who had taken his own life some 12 months earlier, at the age of 42.

There were many veterans who followed that tragic path, but when the national president of the VVAA did the same, it high-lighted everything that the association faced. Thompson had been a tireless advocate for veterans, even though he had suffered from cancer for many years. There were many who had Thompson on their minds during the weekend. Schumann wrote a song for Thompson: 'Safe Behind the Wire'.

Mick Storen and his family drove to Sydney for the welcome home parade. They stayed in the suburbs with his sister and brother-in-law and their family and caught the train to the city for the functions.

Seeing the men again was everything he had hoped it would be. To be reunited with the blokes he'd shared so much with was both affirming and challenging. The men had changed, yet they hadn't. Physically they were different but inside they were the same. They could all be seen through the prism of reflection. Time and time again Mick would say to his mates how fantastic it was to see them. They talked about things only they could talk about. They hugged, they laughed – and they remembered. While for most of them it had been 17 years since they had seen each other, they were quickly back behind the wire at Nui Dat and in the jungle and the scrub. It was there they were together. It was there they could trust, and it was there the truths they had never talked about were evident.

At one of the functions, the devastation of 3 Platoon became clear. Mick reflected that it was funny how life demonstrates things to you sometimes. Most of the original 25 or so who had left Townsville together were in attendance. But because of casualties there had been reinforcements added several times during their tour of duty. Some of these men had never met each other. Those who had returned to Australia wounded only knew the blokes they went over with. Reos filled the other spaces and when they were wounded, which many were, their replacements didn't really know those they were replacing. There were so many of them at the function, nearly 60.

Mick marched in the parade. He looked into the crowd, wondering what it would have been like in 1970 had he returned on HMAS *Sydney* and marched through the streets of Townsville again, or Sydney, or wherever the ship might have taken him. He remembered the cold airport lounge at midnight. He smiled at the cheering and clapping now washing over him and his mates.

Mick didn't go to the Sunday concert. Schumann had told him that there was a plan to drag him and Frank onto the stage when he played the song. He didn't want that; he was comfortable in the march. Even though he knew that most in the crowd knew the song, he was anonymous among the throng and that was good. The Domain stage was too much hype for him and he wasn't about to lose his anonymity. It would have been like the emotion he felt at the official release of the song at the Sydney

Town Hall all over again. Instead, Mick and his family stayed away. He and Anne and the kids played tennis on a local court with his sister, brother-in-law and family. It was an enjoyable family day, away from all the fuss and celebrations.

*

Frank, as he had expected, experienced a letdown when he returned to Bega. The weekend had taken its toll. He thought about his life. Everything he was doing was because he felt he needed to serve the community. While he had been brought up in a religious household, that religion had been lost somewhere along the way, either in the jungles of Vietnam or in the hospital. But he still felt some sense of obligation. Where it came from, Frank wasn't sure. Was it that he hadn't completed his time in the army and so hadn't carried out the role which was entrusted to him? Whatever it might have been, it was constantly niggling away in his mind.

'I Was Only 19' had opened doors previously as impenetrable as castle walls. Frank spoke as an Australia Day Ambassador, as well as being in demand as a guest speaker on Anzac Day, Vietnam Veterans Day and at various groups around the country. The interview requests never seemed to stop and Frank couldn't say no. He spoke about overcoming adversity, about teamwork and about never giving up. He was an inspiration to many who came up after his speeches and contacted him later, saying they had a different view on life after seeing him and hearing his story.

Frank was recognised for his services to the community with an Order of Australia medal in 1988. He was humbled by the award and vowed to keep working as long as he could. But at home the requests for him to become involved in things was becoming onerous. By this time he had relented and started to take more potent drugs. He had been involved in the formation of the Sapphire Coast Australian Rules football league, he helped out at school history lessons, talking about the North Vietnamese and the war from all sides, and he continued his involvement with the Young Speakers Club. The involvement with young people kept his sanity. He loved being there and the feeling was reciprocated. He spent hours at St Patrick's and Bega West primary schools, talking to the students. Some members of the Young Speakers Club won national awards for public speaking, all under Frank's guidance.

The police and the courts had asked him to help out with troubled youth and those who were in constant strife. He talked to sporting groups and Aboriginal youth. He was also asked by the courts to provide care and counselling for young people who had fallen foul of the law. He would talk about respect for the community and the law, and other people, and the dangers of drugs and alcohol. And he'd talk about how, no matter how dark the world seemed, there was always a way out – they could overcome their difficulties.

It was a circle. Frank would also talk to the wives and families of veterans then, as people do, they would talk to each other at school or somewhere else, after which Frank would get another phone call. It had a snowballing effect. Frank insisted he was nothing special but, unlike many others, he was someone who simply listened and didn't tell people what to do or say. That's all many of them wanted.

With everything, the children came first in every respect. That was the way it was for the next decade, but when the children left home and ventured out into the world in the 1990s, Frank was lonely again. His pain was increasing and he allowed himself to take more potent drugs. He'd been taking more effective painkillers for the previous five years, but now he needed more. Morphine patches were just one of them. But even those caused problems. If he used the lighter dosage they wouldn't work, yet if he used those that did work he would be almost stupefied.

To overcome the loneliness, Frank decided he could do more in the community, and he did. He increased his involvement with Legacy and Family Day Care. He spoke to all the groups he had worked with for 30 years or more. His involvement was something to keep his mind active, and the concentration required provided a distraction. He was very good at what he did, but it took its toll. Gradually, as the years rolled past, Frank needed to give things up. While he was always upbeat and positive in public, no one saw the man who went home at night. When it came, the pain had to be handled the best way he knew how.

Frank made a decision about anyone who wanted to interview him. He had a rule that he did it all from home. Anyone who wanted to talk to him had either to visit or to telephone. They were the rules. It meant that he did less community work, and during the late 1990s without the distraction of community work, all his other problems returned. His counselling sessions morphed gradually into more regular visits to a psychiatrist who diagnosed Frank with Post Traumatic Stress Disorder, the dreaded PTSD that many veterans suffered. The psychiatrist said that he'd always suffered from it but Frank had always denied he had it, he always thought he was too strong. Like many others, for years he refused to accept he might have it and pushed it to the back of his mind, packaged away somewhere safe, he thought. However, it had been wandering around in him for years and when he'd had other things on his mind, he could handle it. That was no longer the case.

Now that he was doing less, his mind wandered. The song started to affect him. Not that he hadn't been touched by it before, he had. It was just that he had so much else to do that his mind had had to move on and not think too deeply. Each time he heard the song now, he started thinking, remembering. In his mind he would revisit the Grand Hotel in Vung Tau where he would drink tinnies. He would remember lying, screaming in the jungle and then the excruciating ride in the stretcher as it rose to the dust-off chopper. He heard helicopter ambulances flying over his house towards the hospital and was taken back to the incident, back to Schumann's lines in the song: '. . . and why the Channel Seven chopper chills me to my feet'.

Then, a couple of years after the dawn of the new century, Frank withdrew more and more from community life. He said that he was 'Vietnamed out'. During those years, awards kept coming. Along with the OAM he had received in 1988, Frank was the 2001 Bega Valley Citizen of the Year, received a Federation Peoplescape Award the same year and the Centenary Medal in 2002.

Frank's anxiety levels increased profoundly. He thought one day he'd had a heart attack but it was an anxiety attack that grabbed at his heart and wouldn't let go. He had dropped to the floor in agony, thinking his time was up. He now recognised all the things he had previously put aside. It was time to slow down, to retreat into whatever comfort he could find.

Chapter 30
AFTERMATH

Whatever the real story and whatever the variations in opinions about what should have been done, the reality was that 'I Was Only 19' resonated with people everywhere and from all walks of life and of all ages. Frank spoke well and the success of the song was, Schumann admitted, in no small way due to the hard work of Frank, who was also combating his own demons during that time. Without any of that, there wouldn't have been the thousands of dollars for the VVAA and Frank would not have had such an effect on so many lives through his ability to talk to veterans and their families.

The song was also credited with dramatically increasing the numbers at the National Reunion and Welcome Home Parade, numbers that would not have been there if not for the song. And it had a huge impact on the VVAA's case in the investigation of the effects of Agent Orange in the Royal Commission that was conducted from 1983 to 1985.

The men of 3 Platoon who once were worried about the song came to love it. Graeme Davis began telling people what it was all about and for many years told anyone who asked that he was involved.

'It was a bit of history that day,' he'd say. 'Man landing on the moon and us landing on that mine. And I'm a little bit of that history.'

Alfie Lamb eventually became proud as well. His children and his grandchildren know he was in the song.

*

The men of 3 Platoon met many times at reunions, renewing old friendships, although Frank, wary of the way he would be received, went to only a couple. Mick, who had a happy family life in Adelaide, went along, safe in his anonymity. He even helped organise the first reunion in Adelaide. As the years rolled by, more people understood the song was based on Mick's story; every line was about him. Gradually he let others in. There were newspaper articles, a radio interview, and a special segment on an ABC TV program played after the 2010 Anzac Day march in Adelaide.

Leigh Floyd now lives a quiet life in Adelaide, catching up regularly with Mick at the local gym.

Graeme Davis went back to Vietnam with Alfie Lamb and found the exact spot of the incident by means of GPS co-ordinates. They could see exactly where everyone had stood on that day. The signs indicating the minefield were still there. They dug a hole and buried a time capsule.

Phil Baxter received the Military Medal for his bravery during the incident, reflecting his actions in clearing paths to the wounded as well as treating other men's wounds while being wounded himself. Lamb's father wrote to the Veterans Affairs Department wondering why John Needs wasn't simi-larly rewarded for his bravery. The answer was that the quotas for bravery awards in that company had been filled. A Company Commander Major Belt said later that Needs would have been decorated had he survived. Lamb thought it was clear he could have received that honour posthumously.

On 21 July 2004, members of 3 Platoon organised a memorial service for Peter Hines in his home town of Wangi Wangi, New South Wales. Norma and their son Shane attended.

*

John Schumann toured constantly with his new group, The Vagabond Crew, formed after Redgum disbanded. He played 'I Was Only 19' for soldiers in Afghanistan, where he received a rapturous welcome from 800 or so soldiers. He played it in small gatherings and at large festivals, in intimate rooms and larger concert halls, inside and in the open, for the old and for the young. The song resonated with everyone. It evoked such an emotional response that it was taught in schools and, more importantly, understood.

The song won almost every award the Australian music industry had and was named on all song lists of note. It was recognised as one of the top 25 Australian Songs of All Time in Q Magazine's special edition January 2003 issue and, in America, was listed as one of the 100 Songs That Changed The World. It has been described as an anti-Vietnam War anthem, which Schumann considered strange as it was written 10 years after the war ended. But it is an anti-war song. Not deliberately so, although it made people stop and think about the cost of war and how it inflicts damage on ordinary men and women. It means so much to so many people and is treated with reverence because they think it is important.

Schumann has played 'I Was Only 19' thousands and thousands of times and only on a couple of occasions was the room not completely hushed. One of them was in Newman, a tough Western Australian mining town where about 600 people had turned up to hear the band. As was the case at each gig, 'I Was Only 19' was last on the set list. About 30 percent of the audience knew who Schumann and The Vagabond Crew were and listened intently. The rest were stacked against the bar drinking, laughing, talking and not taking much notice at all. Schumann was annoyed and said to the others in the band that he wasn't doing the song. After a minute of fulminating, he walked to the microphone.

'We're happy to play all our songs and whether you listen to them is up to you, but if you want us to play "I Was Only 19" then you'll fuckin' listen! Not for us, but out of respect for the men that it is about and you'll not fuckin' talk over it!'

The room was dead silent as Schumann hit the first chords.

Schumann has always been proud and thankful for what came to him. The song changed his life and allowed him to go to many amazing places and meet many amazing people for which he will be eternally grateful. He will never be able to convey the depth of his gratitude and appreciation for the bravery that Mick and Frank displayed in allowing the song to be written. He knows that whatever happens to him, he'll always be the bloke who wrote 'I Was Only 19'.

*

The welcome home parade created a desire among the organisers for a memorial to commemorate Vietnam veterans. When the site was selected, a wooden cross was placed in position and, even though construction would not start for four years, people began to come and visit. The memorial became a reality in October 1992, five years to the day from the welcome home march, when the Australian Vietnam Forces National Memorial was constructed in Anzac Parade, that leads to the National War Memorial in Canberra. An estimated 15,000 marched, while a similar number watched. As well as the names of those who died, a series of quotations are inscribed on the walls. Among them is:

> ... Then someone yelled out 'contact' and the bloke behind me swore. We hooked in there for hours then a god-almighty roar. Frankie kicked a mine the day that mankind kicked the moon. God help me, he was going home in June.

When the memorial was opened, it was a humbling and immensely proud moment for John Schumann, as it was for Frank and Mick. To reconcile their lives with such an event was difficult, confusing almost. These two middle-aged men who had once been naive young blokes, and whose lives were thrown together, would now be remembered forever.

*

Frank's life has become a struggle. At times he is desperately lonely, but that is the way he chose it to be. He knows that his dark times affect others and he doesn't want that to happen anymore. He attempted to start another relationship, but with his PTSD and his pain it was impossible. His house is now mostly quiet with only the occasional visitor, where once it was full of children and visiting veterans. Colin and Robyn Beveridge, his neighbours of 40 years, check on him most days to see if he is OK and when he's finding the world trying, Robyn is always there with a meal for him.

At home by himself, everything that happened to him seems to be so much bigger. By 2014, he has been involved with Vietnam in one way or another for more than 40 years.

'And in that time I can remember clearly that I have had only two days where I didn't feel any pain,' he told his counsellor.

His mobility has deteriorated to such an extent that where once he spent three days a week in bed and four up and about, it is now reversed. Day after day, sometimes week after week, is spent in bed and limping to and from the kitchen or the toilet. That in turn has led to more falls, which means more pain and more medication. He has a walking frame and a special structure above his bed to help him get in and out without falling over.

He makes the occasional trip to the shops, to his regular medical appointments or, when he is able, to some meeting or other; and there are times when he feels and looks on top of the world. He manages to travel sometimes to visit his children, who have all made their mark on the world and of whom he is extremely proud. Of the triplets, Brett is a highly success-ful international singer-songwriter, Pamela is part of the senior management team in a major multi-national insurance company and James runs a successful hardware business in country New South Wales. Frank's first-born, Kerry, is a senior manager in a major regional council. Frank loves seeing them and his nine grandchildren; and even though the price for that is extreme, physically and emotionally, he vows he will never stop trying. He knows what will happen to his body when he travels but also knows that, if he doesn't go, he doesn't dare think about the alternative.

'I Was Only 19' was a burden and a blessing for Frank. It gave him more opportunities and exposure to dramatically increase his work with veterans, but it took a toll on his body and his mind.

Sometimes, in bed in the home he moved into in 1972, Frank contemplates his life. He knows that, whichever way he moves, some of the 30-odd pieces of shrapnel, or one of the uncountable bone fragments, might also move around his body a little and rub against a nerve. His hips have deteriorated to a large extent, and his bones are weak from the years of torturous movement and the degeneration caused by the medication. His joints lock up constantly and arthritis has become rampant throughout his body. Scans have indicated that most of his joints are simply bone on bone. Any imperfect movement causes pain like a stake being thrust through his foot and up to his head. His back, through spinal degradation, aches constantly. At times, when the dark thoughts gather and he doubts if he can go on, he still wonders if he would have been better off without his legs.

For days at a time he locks the front door, placing a note on it that asks people not to knock. Much of the time he is in pain, depressed and anxious, yet he knows he is better off than some.

He has never felt sorry for himself; he never considers his has been a 'poor me' life. That would never enter his thinking. It hasn't been. He admits there are things he wished had turned out differently, but that's the way it is. One of his mates told him that 'life is about what happens, not what might have happened'.

His experience has taught him much about life and the effect that Vietnam had on so many in so many different ways. He has learnt about good and evil, about life and death and the intangible bond between men in those circumstances.

He lives by the same mantra he passed on to children and veterans and anyone else who was in trouble and needed guidance or inspiration: 'Strong people don't give up, and if you think you're not strong, you are. Setbacks can make you stronger;

believe in yourself and things can get better.' He is happy that he's helped people of many ages and that he never gave in.

Sometimes, lying alone in the quiet, he wonders if it was all worthwhile, if there was a point to it all. Then he thinks about his family, his mates, and reflects on his life. He remembers the contribution he has made, the places he has been, the people he has helped, and is satisfied.

ACKNOWLEDGEMENTS

There are many people to thank for their help during this book's long journey.

First and foremost I will always be indebted to Frank Hunt for his trust and bravery in telling his inspirational story. To contribute to the world the way he has done while suffering the physical pain and mental anguish that he has over more than 45 years is testament to his character. His friendship is beyond value.

Mick Storen was patient and particular – two virtues which helped correctly tell the parts of his story that he was prepared to share. As with Frank, Mick's bravery in talking about the darkness in his life is remarkable.

John Schumann, whose amazing song was the catalyst for telling Frank's story, was extraordinarily open, friendly and giving. I will always be in his debt.

The other soldiers of 3 Platoon I spoke with were Leigh Floyd, Tony Muir, Graeme Davis, Alf Lamb and Jim Kelly. I am grateful to all these men for their patience and for giving me the time they did.

Sapper Phil Baxter was very helpful as was A Company Medic Rob Laurent.

Colonel David Butler gave me time on the telephone to explain some of his decisions. I am also enormously grateful to Norma Hines for her compassion and insightfulness.

I received help from a range of veterans including Frank Cunningham, Chris Schaper, Tack Riether, Les Fuller and many others.

My extraordinary son, Zac, asked me hard but relevant questions at the difficult times but always encouraged me. His love and support gave me succour.

The late Eileen Hunt, Frank's mother, spoke with loving care and a certain amount of guilt about her son. Frank's brothers Bryan and Kieran were also helpful.

Doogle and Scally are a mother and son who keep me sane with unconditional love.

My immense gratitude must also go to Claire Craig and Sam Sainsbury from Pan Macmillan whose encouragement through the whole process has been unwavering. Sam's eye for detail and patient questioning have been invaluable.

If I have missed thanking anyone, then I am truly sorry. It would only be inadvertently so please accept this as my personal thanks. Finally, words can't describe the debt I owe to my hero, the incredible Pammy, whose tolerance, love and kindness are what makes everything worthwhile.

REFERENCES

I gained information from a range of books including Paul Ham's definitive *Vietnam: The Australian War* (Harper Collins, 2007). Paul's documentary 'All The Way' (ABC and Screen Australia, 2010) was a big help as well. Paul was very helpful to me with the history chapters and I am very grateful to him.

Also of great help were: *The Minefield, An Australian Tragedy in Vietnam* by Greg Lockhart (Allen & Unwin, 2008); *The Vietnam Years* by Michael Caulfield (Hachette, 2008); *We too were Anzacs-6RAR in Vietnam 1969/70* by Brian Avery (2004).

Rob Laurent's terrific book, *With Anzacs in Vietnam*, (Blue Flyer Publishing, 2011) was written from the inside and gave many insights. Rob kindly gave permission to use some of his photos, as did Peter Wallbridge.

The Australian War Memorial website was extremely helpful, as were many other websites too numerous to mention.

Information was also gathered from newspapers including *The Age*, *The Sydney Morning Herald*, *The Daily Telegraph*, *The Sun* (now the *Herald Sun*), *The Adelaide Advertiser*, *The Australian*, *The Bega District News*, *The Birchip Times*.

INDEX

family history 16–19
first ambush 102–7
helping troubled youth 274
helping veterans 225, 231–9,
    274
helping Vietnamese villagers 118
hospital xvi, 148, 157–76,
    198–204, 217–26, 235–7
'I Was Only 19' and 250–1, 254,
    257–61, 267, 272–7, 280, 282
injuries 160, 173–5, 230, 283
joining 6 RAR 52–67
joining army 28–30
Kapooka 31–41, 49, 52, 62, 130
Last Rites given to xvi, 159,
    171, 173
leaving for Vietnam 69–72
letters home 31, 70, 76, 119,
    126, 209
mine explosion 133–9
nightmares 228–9, 231, 240, 265
Nui Dat 86–8
Order of Australia 273, 276
pain 230, 232, 236, 239, 241,
    265–7, 274, 281, 283
post traumatic stress disorder
    275, 281
promoting 'I Was Only 19'
    257–61
psychiatric problems 232, 265,
    275–6
public speaking 240–1, 258–9,
    273
R&R in Vung Tau 114–16
rehabilitation 219–26
RSL board member 231, 237
Schumann and 249–50, 257–61
scout 92, 96, 100–1, 118, 125
signalman 125–30
triplets 231, 282
wedding 224
working after Vietnam 228–33,
    239
working on family farm 24–8

Hunt, James 282
Hunt, Keiran 20, 21, 286
Hunt, Kerry 282
Hunt, Maurie 15, 18–25, 28, 30, 71,
    166–7, 171–2, 218
Hunt, Michael 20, 21
Hunt, Pamela 282
Hunt, William 17–18
Hy Hom Secret Zones 123

'I Was Only 19' xiii, xv, 246–63,
    267–8, 272–81
    3 Platoon men's reaction 260–1,
        277
    awards 279
    effect of 256–63, 277
    Frank and 250–1, 254, 257–60,
        267–8, 272–7, 280, 282
    Mick and 248–9, 254, 256–7,
        272, 278, 280
    number one 261
    public reaction to 256, 258, 261,
        279–80
    release of 252, 258
    royalties donated to VVAA 255
    writing of 246–8
Ingleburn Infantry Combat Training
    Centre 49–52

Jenkins, Harry 173
Johnson, Lyndon 10
Jones, Spike 51
Joye, Col 186, 270
Jumping Jack mines xxii, 121–2,
    132

Kapooka 31–41, 49, 52, 62, 130
Kelly, Lance Corporal Jim 60, 61,
    79, 99, 124, 135, 143, 161, 172,
    285
Kelly, Marie 218
Kelly, Mary 218